BLACK
MUSLIMS
IN BRITAIN

Copyright © 2009 Richard S. Reddie
This edition copyright © 2009 Lion Hudson

The author asserts the moral right
to be identified as the author of this work

A Lion Book
an imprint of
Lion Hudson plc
Wilkinson House, Jordan Hill Road,
Oxford, OX2 8DR, England
www.lionhudson.com

ISBN 978 0 7459 5320 5 (UK)

Distributed by:
Marston Book Services, PO Box 269, Abingdon, Oxon., OX14 4YN

First edition 2009
10 9 8 7 6 5 4 3 2 1 0

This book has been printed on paper and board independently certified
as having been produced from sustainable forests.
A catalogue record for this book is available
from the British Library.

Typeset in 10/13 Palatino

Printed and bound in Great Britain by CPI Cox & Wyman, Reading.

BLACK MUSLIMS IN BRITAIN

Richard S. Reddie

LION

To Noel and Lucille Reddie,
wonderful parents who have
always been an inspiration to me.

Contents

Introduction

Although the title of this book is *Black Muslims in Britain*, it is primarily about Black British Muslim converts, rather than all Black British people who are Muslims. Black conversion to Islam has been a growing phenomenon in Britain over the last two decades.

Black Muslims have been living in Britain for centuries; there is evidence of African Muslims in England as long ago as Tudor and Stuart times.[1] There was a significant Somali Muslim presence during the Victorian era, especially in the port cities of Liverpool and Cardiff, and also in London.[2] And inward migration from the New Commonwealth of decolonized countries after the Second World War also brought Black Muslims from West Africa to British shores.

But for all this rich history, very little has been written about Britain's Black Muslim presence *per se*. For instance, one cannot compare this history to those of Black Christians and the Black Majority Churches, which have been subject to a number of examinations over the last sixty years.[3] A good example of this disparity can be seen in the authoritative *Oxford Companion to Black British History*, which only carries a two-page entry on Black Muslims,[4] whereas the entry for Black Christian Faith comes in at a weighty six pages. *Black Muslims in Britain* takes a timely look at the growing Black Muslim convert presence, and seeks to inform and educate readers of all faiths, and none, about its increasing influence on British society.

The method deployed here has been to interview a cross-section of Black Muslim converts in as many parts of the country

7

as possible. The first people interviewed I had met during speaking engagements around the country between 2005 and 2008, both as part of my work to commemorate the bicentenary of the Abolition of the Slave Trade Act in 2007, and in the course of promoting my book *Abolition!* Those I encountered were subsequently interviewed, sometimes on several occasions. A number of these interviewees put me in contact with others who were prepared to participate. As a result, I conducted interviews with Black Muslim converts in Leeds, Manchester, Norwich, Birmingham, Walsall, Luton and London. In all these places and on all occasions I was careful to listen to the comments of those who gave opinions and faithful in recording their sentiments.

This book is not a comparative study of Christianity and Islam; rather it looks at the reasons why Muslim converts abandon their Christian backgrounds to embrace Islam. But in order to do this it must examine the role both of the Christian churches and of the Rastafari movement in the UK as well as taking an in-depth look at Islam. The former are important for a number of reasons – most obviously that a great many Muslim converts come from Christian backgrounds. The vast majority attended church during their formative years and have family members who still attend.

The focus on Rastafari is vital because it was the first counter-cultural religious force to capture the affiliations and imaginations of Black youth in Britain. A whole generation of Black youth, including some of my own relatives, became followers of Rastafari[5] in the 1970s and 1980s, having left the Christian church. There are clear resemblances between the subversive approach of the Rasta movement in Britain during its heyday and the current counter-cultural positioning of Islam.

I have also provided an analysis of the history and culture of Black people in Britain, to show the profound effect that this background has had on the religious choices of successive generations of Black Britons. If it is true that 'we are who we are because of what we believe' this makes it all the more important to understand the history surrounding our beliefs. Only when we look critically at the events and decisions of the past do the activities and choices of the present make any sense.

The writing of a book on Islam is never an easy undertaking, especially for a Christian. There is little doubt that the fact I am a Christian affected the tenor of the book – not from the standpoint of personal opinion, but from one of access. To write about Black Muslim converts in Britain requires access to such converts, many of whom are reluctant to talk. Whether or not we accept the theory that Islamophobia exists in Britain today, there is little doubt that the events of 9/11 and 7/7 have encouraged the media to peddle negative, pejorative stories about Muslims that link them to terrorism, extremism and hate.[6] And these associations are especially strong in the case of converts, who are portrayed as susceptible to the wiles of persuasive, fanatical preachers of hate. As a result, many were justifiably wary of my motives and took some persuading to participate in this project. I had to gain the trust of interviewees, convincing them of my sincerity and integrity in the way I intended to write about their faith. And in several cases those who agreed to take part subsequently withdrew, often at the last minute.

I took the decision to interview all those who defined or described themselves as 'Muslims', which meant including members of the Nation of Islam, an offshoot of the US Black Muslim movement, as well as Sunni or 'orthodox' Muslims, who form the majority of Britain's, and the world's, Muslim population. The Nation of Islam in the USA was initially established by Wallace D. Fard, also known as W. F. Muhammad and Master Fard Muhammad, and expanded by the 'Messenger', the Honourable Elijah Muhammad. Its current leader is the Honourable Louis Farrakhan.[7]

One of the first issues I had to grapple with when writing this book was whether one could even use the term 'Black' Muslim.[8]

There is a school of thought which argues that 'Black Muslim' is an oxymoron, and cannot exist within Islam for theological reasons. In theory, at least, Islam does not recognize 'race': consequently, people are simply Muslims or non-Muslims, and many of the 'Black' Muslims, especially those following Sunni Islam, interviewed for this book were keen to explain this. (The same argument can be made for Christianity.) However, if one believes in a God who made human beings in his own image, and created them as ethnically diverse, it can be argued that this diversity is important and needs to be recognized and affirmed. This diversity need not be seen as something that divides people, or grants a particular importance to one group over another. However, for a variety of reasons, we often do apply negative connotations to difference. And to ignore this reality is to ignore the truth that some face discrimination because of that difference.

It is common for most people to use the term 'convert' to describe someone who has either embraced a particular faith or exchanged one belief system for another. Many of the Black Muslims interviewed preferred the term 'revert' or 'reversion' to describe the process of their coming to faith. These terms suggest that they were always Muslims (Islam holds that it is the inherent belief system of human beings), but they had yet to acknowledge this truth. When they did embrace Islam it was regarded as coming back to the truth rather than finding it for the first time. As a result, I use the terms 'revert' and 'reversion' as well as 'convert' and 'conversion' almost interchangeably; in all instances, the sentiment is the same.

Out of deference to Muslims and the respect they have for the Prophet Muhammad – they always use the term 'Peace be upon him', sometimes abbreviated as PBUH – I use an asterisk (*) whenever the Prophet Muhammad* is mentioned to convey this respect.

It is my hope that this book will be the catalyst for more research into a phenomenon that could change the religious and

10

cultural landscape of Britain. Likewise, it should be a stimulus for churches to respond to the challenge presented by the growing Black Muslim presence, and to acknowledge the importance of engaging in dialogue with believers who are reaching out to a similar constituency with a myriad of needs, in a society that still remains unequal and reluctant to affirm difference. *Black Muslims in Britain* shows that Islam is providing a religious alternative for Black Britons seeking spiritual answers to life's eternal questions. This relatively new phenomenon takes its place alongside other aspects of the Black British experience, which continues to grapple with issues of identity and belonging in a society that remains indifferent at best, and hostile at worst.

The Black British experience, of education, race-relations, health, community and gender attitudes as well as religion, gives rise to a Black culture which has transformed Britain since the arrival of the SS *Empire Windrush*, with the first substantial group of West Indian migrants to Britain, in 1948.[9] Initially ignored, and then marginalized, Black culture is now embraced and has moved into the mainstream where it has been adapted and refined, but also diluted, to suit particular needs.

Black culture has undoubtedly been an agent of dynamic change, with the power to influence values, ideas and institutions within British society. Cultures and societies are never static, and are always open to new influences. It will be interesting to see how the Black Muslim presence plays its role in shaping both Black culture and the culture of Britain as a whole, and the degree to which it will adapt and change to the conditions surrounding it.

Chapter 1

Keeping the Faith: The Beliefs of Black British Muslim Converts

Any study of Black Muslims in Britain must begin with an analysis of their beliefs. Muslims the world over are adherents of Islam, the world's second largest, and arguably fastest growing, religion.[1] The term 'Islam' literally means 'submission to the will of God' – rather than, as is often claimed, 'religion of peace' – and every Muslim must recite the profession, 'There is no God but Allah, and Muhammad*[2] is the messenger of Allah', which is known as the *shahadah*. As Matthew S. Gordon explains, to 'submit to the divine will is therefore to bring about harmonious order to the universe. In this sense, Islam refers not simply to the act of submission but, more importantly, to its consequence – that is peace (salam).'[3]

Muhammad and the Origins of Islam

The Prophet Muhammad*, or Mohammed ibn Abdullah, was born in Mecca around AD 570, and is considered by Muslims as a *rasul*, or messenger, and a prophet of Allah.[4] He is regarded as the 'seal of the prophets', the last and greatest in a line of prophets going back to Adam. As well as possessing these religious attributes, Muhammad* was also renowned as a philosopher, reformer, general and diplomat.

12

Ironically, Mecca, which is now considered Islam's holiest city, home to the *Kaaba* shrine and the Grand Mosque, was a thriving trade centre known for its pagan religious practices at the time of Muhammad*'s birth. The Prophet was born into the Hashemite clan, who were part of the ruling Quraysh tribe. According to tradition his early life was marked by great sorrow because he was orphaned as a child; he was subsequently raised by his uncle.[5] Muhammad* became a merchant, initially for his uncle's prosperous caravan business. At the age of twenty-five he married a wealthy, prominent widow, Khadijah, who was fifteen years his senior. Together they had one surviving child, Fatima.[6]

Again, according to tradition, when he was about forty he received his first revelation from God, during the month of Ramadan. Muhammad* had retreated to a cave at Hira, near Mount Jabal Nur, for reflection and meditation when he received a visitation from the Archangel Gabriel, or Jibril.[7] The Prophet would recite the following revelation:

> Read in the name of your Lord Who created.
> He created man from a clot.
> Read and your Lord is most Honorable.
> Who taught (to write) with the pen.
> Taught man what he knew not.
> **Qur'an 96:1–5**[8]

For the remainder of his life he received other revelations, which were subsequently assembled as the Qur'an. According to tradition, a number of these revelations were written down, but the majority were memorized as the Prophet and some of his followers were uneducated.[9] Indeed, one interpretation of the name Qur'an is 'recitation'. The practice of memorizing and reciting the Qur'an has survived until today, with some believers, usually Islamic scholars, being described as *hafiz* (guardian) because they can recite the complete Qur'an from memory.

The Qur'an, often transliterated as the Koran or Al-Qur'an, is the sacred book of Islam, which Muslims believe provides heavenly assistance and guidance to human beings. As one commentator explains, 'the Qur'an does not consist of minutely detailed laws and regulations, but outlines the basic framework for each aspect of human activity – social life, commerce and economics, marriage and inheritance, penal laws and international conduct – by appealing to the mind and heart of each individual who reads it'.[10] The Qur'an contains 114 chapters, or *surahs*, which are 'unequal in length and ... not arranged in a way that reflects the order of the revelation'.[11] Each *surah* comprises numerous *ayat* or verses.

Islamic tradition also recounts how Muhammad* experienced an amazing night-time journey alongside the Archangel Gabriel from Mecca to Jerusalem, known as the *isra*, and another to heaven and hell where he spoke with the earlier prophets. In the eyes of his followers, this cemented his status as God's messenger.

On the basis of these revelations, Muhammad* began to preach monotheism, leading to a wider belief in the unity or *tawhid* of God: 'Allah is greater than anything else, or anything which can possibly be imagined.'[12] Along with the teaching that everyone should surrender to Allah and that Muhammad* was his messenger, his initial message either fell on deaf ears or caused offence among the pagan, polytheistic Meccans. Eventually offence won out over apathy and Muhammad* fled with his followers to Medina on a journey known as the *hijrah*, or withdrawal, in AD 622.

While in Medina, Muhammad* succeeded in bringing together the warring tribes and consolidating support to such an extent that he could amass a force of 10,000 to march on his native Mecca.[13] During what is known as the 'Conquest of Mecca', Muhammad*'s Quraysh tribe converted virtually *en masse* while he and his followers set about destroying the numerous idols and effigies within the *Kaaba* shrine as Muhammad* recited verses.[14] The *Kaaba* was rededicated for Islamic purposes and is, to this day, the site to which all able Muslims must make a pilgrimage. By the time of his death in AD 632 vast swathes of Arabia had converted to Islam and the faith which, only a few decades previously, had been largely shunned, was prevalent throughout the region.

Islamic Beliefs

Muslims worship Allah, the supreme and sole God, who they believe created everything and rules over all. In Islam, God or Allah is 'not so much a name as a description of a quality of Being'.[15] Allah is omnipotent (he can do anything that can be done), omniscient (he knows everything that can be known) and eternal (he has always existed and will always exist, beyond time and space) and has neither form nor shape. Allah is not only just and recompenses and reprimands fairly, Allah is also merciful (*rahim*) and is therefore worthy of all worship. The majority of Muslims follow a creed which states six articles of belief that include:

- belief in Allah;

- belief in all the messengers and prophets sent by Allah;

- belief in the angels;

- belief in the books sent by Allah such as the Qur'an;

- belief in the Day of Judgment;

- belief in destiny.

Muslims believe that Allah revealed the Qur'an to the Prophet Muhammad* through the Archangel Gabriel gradually from AD 610 to AD 632, when the Prophet died.[16] Muslims do not consider the Prophet Muhammad* as the originator of a new faith, but the re-establisher of the faith of Abraham (Ibrahim), Moses (Musa), Jesus (Isa) and other prophets such as David (Dawud), Noah (Nor), Enoch (Idris), Aaron (Haroon) and so on. As one commentator suggests, 'Islamic tradition holds that Jews and Christians distorted the revelations God gave to these prophets by either altering the text, introducing a false interpretation, or both.'[17]

Muslims attach no divine status to the Prophet Muhammad*, who is regarded as a messenger, albeit a very important one. Consequently, it is a gross error to use the term 'Muhammadan', like 'Christian', as Muslims are not followers of Muhammad*, but of Allah. Muslims regard the Qur'an as the literal word of Allah, a sacred manuscript whose recitation, alongside prayer, enables a believer to approach God. Prayer or *salat* forms one of the 'Five Pillars of Islam', commitments or obligations that every Muslim must fulfil in order to live a good and conscientious existence. The Five Pillars are:

- *Shahadah*: the Muslim declaration of faith, which summarizes core Muslim beliefs and must be uttered three times when somebody converts to Islam.

- *Salat*: the performance of ritual prayers in the proper way five times each day.

- *Zakah*: the payment of charity or alms tax to benefit the needy, which is seen as a form of worship and personal purification.

- *Sawm*: fasting during the month of Ramadan. The festival of *Id al-Fitr* marks the end of Ramadan, during which Muslims thank Allah for the strength to help them practise self-control.

- *Hajj*: the pilgrimage to Mecca, which all physically able Muslims must make once in a lifetime.

As one commentator has suggested, Islam is:

A complete way of life governing dress (especially in respect to women), economics, business ethics, rates of taxation, justice and punishment, weights and measures, politics, war and peace, marriage and inheritance, family and domestic life, the care of animals and livestock, sexual relations within marriage, education, diet, cookery, social behaviour, forms of greeting and rules of hospitality. Even the way in which a glass of water is to be drunk is governed by Islamic religious law.[18]

This law, or *fiqh*, is the legal system that seeks to interpret and apply *shariah*. It covers what is forbidden (*haram*), discouraged (*makruh*), neutral (*mubah*), recommended (*mustahabb*), and obligatory (*fard*). For instance, the Qur'an's meticulous dietary laws outlaw the consumption of pig meat, the flesh of carnivores, blood-based products and alcohol. It is only lawful to consume meat if the animal has been ritually slaughtered by a clean knife to the throat. Prior to any meal, Muslims traditionally say the word *Bismillah* ('in the name of God') as a word of thanks for their food.

Even those with only a basic knowledge of Islam are probably familiar with the terms *shariah*, *fatwa* and *jihad* – for a variety of mostly negative reasons. The first two are connected to aspects of Islamic law. In the West, *shariah* has become notorious for its perceived draconianism, when in reality it is simply the law which controls an Islamic way of life, private and public, both for those living under an Islamic legal system and for believers who do not. *Shariah* covers nearly all aspects of everyday life, including family, business, banking, politics and economics.[19] The term *fatwa*, which in fact means a legal or judicial opinion, is familiar from the furore surrounding Salman Rushdie's 1988 novel *The Satanic Verses*, whose contents some Muslims regarded as blasphemous. The *fatwa* pronounced against Rushdie by Ayatollah Khomeini, the then leader of Iran, called for his death.

The other Islamic term that has crept into common parlance is *jihad*, which, according to tabloid journalists, is a 'holy war' in whose name Muslims carry out extreme acts of violence and terror. Some fervent Muslims do indeed regard *jihad* as a 'sixth pillar of Islam', characterized by 'exerting one's utmost power, efforts, endeavors, or ability in contending with an object of disapprobation'.[20] The literal translation of *jihad* is 'striving' (to serve Allah),[21] which involves defending fellow Muslims when they are attacked for practising their faith.

Alongside the Qur'an, Muslims give special credence to the Hadith, collections of oral traditions about the Prophet Muhammad*'s words and deeds.[22] Hadith collections are regarded as important tools for determining the Muslim way of life by all traditional schools of jurisprudence.[23] According to one commentator, 'Pre-Islamic Arabs considered it a virtue to follow the example of one's forefathers. But in the Islamic period one could hardly follow the example of ancestors who were not Muslim, so a new tradition, or "Sunna" had to be found. This was the Sunna of Muhammad*. After Muhammad*'s death the learned began systematically to develop the doctrine of duties and beliefs in accordance with the new conditions.'[24]

Like early Christian traditions which avoided all visual representation of Jesus because of his divinity, Islam condemns depictions of Muhammad* and his family. And, as Nabil I. Matar writes:

It further discouraged the representation of living
creatures for such representation would lead to pagan
or polytheistic worship. As a result, Muslim artists did
not imitate the external world, but conveyed its inherent
meaning through the arabesque and geometric patterns.
Whenever they chose to draw living creatures, they
produced flat, two-dimensional illustrations that were
deliberately unrealistic, with no illusion of depth.[25]

Once an individual embraces Islam he or she becomes part of a family or community of believers known as the *ummah*. Fellow Muslims greet one another with the phrase *al-salaamu alaykumu* or 'peace be unto you', to which the traditional response is *wa-aleykum al-salaam* – 'and upon you be peace'. Islamic greetings are commonplace at a mosque or *masjid*, which serves as a place of worship as well as a location where Muslims can meet and study together. Mosques vary in size, but are invariably full for *salat-al-jumah* or Friday prayer, which is held just after midday and is usually led by an imam, a man who leads the mosque; Friday prayer can also include a sermon.

Like Christianity and Judaism, Islam is a monotheistic faith (it worships one God) that repudiates polytheism and paganism. Such beliefs are considered a form of *shirk* – denying the supremacy of Allah by sharing the true God's glory and power with others – and an unforgivable sin. Those who remain in such a state of 'hiding from God' or *kufr* face eternal damnation.[26] But Muslims see Christians and Jews as 'people of the Book', who recognize the God of Abraham or Ibrahim and share in God's revelation to mankind. In theory, this means they are afforded respect and treated with tolerance as they are considered *dhimmi* or protected persons.[27] History shows that in return for paying the Muslim *jizyah*, or religious tax, these non-Muslims were granted the protection of the state and assured freedom of worship, person and property. Having said that, they were still often regarded as second-class citizens and faced discomforts and inequalities. But in many Middle Eastern countries there were long histories of Jews, Christians and Muslims living side by side in relative peace, and, according to one source, 'Christian and Jewish communities thrived in almost all the Muslim conquests, in stark contrast to the failure of medieval Europe to incorporate permanently its subject communities of Muslims and Jews.'[28]

The Faith Divides

As with all faiths, there have been various schisms within Islam over interpretation and practices. The major theological divide is between the Sunni and Shii traditions. Statistics suggest that almost three-quarters of the world's Muslims describe themselves as Sunni, a term derived from the *Sunnah*, which is a collection of the six 'authentic' books of the Hadith; Sunnis are consequently described as 'people of the tradition and the community'.[29] Although both Sunnis and Shiis 'recognise the primacy of the Qur'an and the Sunnah', in deciding matters outside them the Sunnis depend on community consensus, whereas Shiis rely on the infallibility of the imams.[30] For Shiis, an imam signifies much more than the leader of a mosque. The title is applied to the divinely appointed successors of Muhammad*, who are regarded as infallible.

Sunnis recognize four legal traditions or schools, known as madhhab: *Hanafi, Maliki, Shafi'i* and *Hanbali*, named after their founders. The development of these schools was undoubtedly a response to the urgent need to find religious answers to society's problems.[31] Within Sunni theology the status of the *Mahdi* is extremely important. The *Mahdi* is the 'chosen one', a 'divinely guided political leader whom Allah will send to earth to unite all Muslims into a single political state shortly before the end of the world'.[32] Throughout the centuries there have been a number of *Mahdi*-related sects, led by charismatic teachers or mystical figures.

Many of the major Islamic dynasties and empires, such as the Mughal (Indian subcontinent) and the Ottoman (the Middle East and Eastern Europe), were Sunni, which has led to the dominance of this grouping over the centuries. Sunni Islam is still dominant throughout the Indian subcontinent, central Asia, the Arab world and from Africa to the periphery of Europe. By contrast, Shiis are concentrated in certain parts of the Middle East and Asia. To understand Shii beliefs one needs to investigate the development of Islam after the death of the Prophet Muhammad*.

Shiis maintain that the Prophet's family were the rightful leaders of the Islamic world,[33] and that the Prophet's son-in-law, Ali,[34] was the rightful *caliph* or leader of the Muslims after Muhammad*'s death in AD 632. In fact the Prophet's close friend Abu Bakr became *caliph* when he died. Ali, who in some traditions was also the Prophet's cousin, eventually became the fourth *caliph*, succeeding Uthman, who was murdered by rebels.[35] His accession was not without confrontation. Aisha, the Prophet Muhammad*'s wife, condemned his tardiness in catching Uthman's killers, leading to the battle of Camel or Jamal between their rival forces. A nephew of Uthman, Muawiyah Ummayad, also refused to recognize Ali's leadership until his uncle's killers were captured. This resulted in a second conflict, which ended in a truce that some of Ali's own men denounced as treachery. Tradition suggests that Ali was ultimately killed by his own supporters, whereupon Muawiyah became *caliph*. One of Ali's sons, Husayn, attempted to wrest back the caliphate, only to die a martyr's death at the battle of Karbala; this conflict is still marked today on the Day of Ashura, when a mass of pilgrims visit the Imam Hussein mosque in Karbala, Iraq.[36]

The lineage of the Prophet Muhammad* via Ali and Husayn continued until the twelfth Shii imam, the young Muhammad al-Mahdi, disappeared, apparently into seclusion. The Shiis refused to accept that he was dead, preferring to believe that he had been concealed from them and would return in the future. In his absence, religious authority was ceded to a council of scholars known as *ulama*, who elected a supreme imam. Forms of this practice still occur today, as with the election of Ayatollah Khomeini in Iran.

Shii theology is distinguished by its veneration of imams, who have a Pope-like status with regard to infallibility, virtue and power.[37] The Iranian Shiis consider their supreme imam or ayatollah as a spiritual guide who has inherited some of Muhammad*'s inspiration:[38] Ayatollah means 'Sign of Allah' and

Iran is one of the centres of Shii Islam and Shii adherents are also to be found in Iraq, Syria, Lebanon and Azerbaijan. There are three main branches of Shiism – the Ismailis (Seveners), the Ithna Asharis (Twelvers) and the Zaydis (Fivers) – each of which recognizes a different number of imams, but 'all of which are united by a common belief that the only legitimate leader of the Muslim community is a descendant of Ali and his wife Fatima, the daughter of the Prophet Muhammad*'.[39]

A powerful spiritual dimension of Islam can be found in Sufism, which some regard as Islamic mysticism. But Sufis are more accurately described as 'those who are interested in inner knowledge, those who are interested in finding a way or practice toward inner awakening and enlightenment'.[40] The enlightenment process involves the 'purification of the "heart" and safeguarding it from any affliction and that its end product is the correct and harmonious relationship between man and his Creator'.[41] Sufism is not a separate branch of Islam, as Sufi *tariqahs* or orders can be found within both Shii and Sunni groups and their influence, within and outside Islam, far outweighs their numbers. For instance, the legendary Islamic scholar, poet and mathematician Omar Khayyam is likely to have been a Sufi.

Growth, Conquest and Crusades

From its modest beginnings in the Arabian peninsula, Islam rapidly spread throughout the region and the world. Muslims often point out that Islam is more than a faith; it is also a socio-political and cultural force. The Islamic calendar takes AD 622, the year of the Prophet Muhammad*'s flight from Mecca to Medina, as year one.[42] The ten years between this date and the Prophet Muhammad*'s death saw the consolidation of his new teachings in Medina, from where they spread to Mecca.[43] The successors to the Prophet had to contend with internecine squabbles which complicated the task of maintaining unity. Certain local Arab tribes who had sworn allegiance to the Prophet Muhammad* were unsure about the credentials of his heirs and looked to revert to their former religious practices. However, rulers such as Umar ibn al-Khattab, who succeeded Abu Bakr to become the second *caliph*, consolidated a unified state and used the army to extend Islam in the Middle East in areas dominated by Christianity and Zoroastrianism, taking their justification from Qur'anic verses such as:

> So when the sacred months have passed away, then slay the idolaters wherever you find them, and take them captives and besiege them and lie in wait for them in every ambush,
> **Qur'an 9:5**

> Fight those who do not believe in Allah, nor in the latter day, nor do they prohibit what Allah and His Messenger have prohibited, nor follow the religion of truth, out of those who have been given the Book,
> **Qur'an 9:29**

Umar, for instance, waged war against the Byzantine empire, conquering Syria, Palestine and Lebanon. Muslim armies attacked the Sassanid empire in Iraq and Iran, and slowly overcame all opposition by about AD 650.[44] Umar's successor, Uthman, continued the conquests, taking parts of Egypt and Armenia. The caliphate of Abdul Malik (AD 685–705) saw the end of civil war between the Umayyad dynasty and the Shiis, and witnessed the capture of Carthage.[45] During the eighth century Islam spread further into Spain and central Asia, and under Cordoba's Emir, Abd al-Rahman II, Spain became a centre of Islamic learning. By 1082 Islam had spread as far as what is now Indonesia, via the growing trade links between the Middle East and the Far East.[46] However, all this activity had not gone unnoticed by Christendom, which began to consider how best to halt Islam's march. In 1095, the Pope launched a crusade to retake Jerusalem and reunite the Eastern and Western Christian empires.[47] Over the next few centuries, popes such as Urban II and Innocent III, kings such as Richard I of England and Louis IX of France, and the Holy Roman Emperors Frederick Barbarossa and Frederick II launched crusades to repel Islamic influence, confronting legendary Muslim figures such as Salah al-Din (Saladin).[48]

From the fourteenth century onwards the Ottoman empire witnessed the consolidation of Islam throughout the world from the centres of what is now Turkey and Asia during the Middle Ages.

The Forgotten History of African Muslims

In almost all books chronicling the rise of Islam, Africa barely gets a mention. If it is fortunate, it may appear in the final chapters, but usually writers explore the spread of Islam through Europe, central Asia and the Far East, placing Egypt firmly within the context of the Middle East rather than Africa.

Yet we know that Islam has had a profound impact on the African continent. One writer observes: 'for 700 years up to 1450 the Islamic world was virtually the only external influence on sub-Saharan Africa.'[49] Dr Ali Mazrui, a Kenyan-born academic and political writer on African and Islamic studies, has argued that Islamic culture was one of three traditions to influence the continent, along with traditional African culture and Western culture.[50] While other academics suggest that:

In the fourteen centuries since the introduction of
Islam, Muslims have played important roles in Africa's
development. Muslims were important in the process
of state-building, in creating commercial networks
between parts of the continent, in introducing literacy
(which saw Muslims become scribes in charge of state
records), as well as in exchanges of inter-state diplomacy
within Africa and beyond.[51]

24

According to Arab and African traditions, early Muslims fleeing persecution in the Arab peninsula took their faith with them to North Africa. One writer has argued that the Negus or king of Abyssinia protected Muslims seeking 'refuge from the Meccans, who abhorred Islam and the new Muslims. The Negus granted refuge to a people oppressed in their own land.'[52] Later, with the conquests of Amr ibn al-As during the seventh century, Islam spread throughout North Africa, confining the Christian influence to parts of Egypt and other pockets of territory. According to the African-American scholar Molefi Kete Asante, 'The Arabs had taken all of North Africa by the start of the eighth century, and, Kairouan as its capital, the whole of North Africa became a fruitful province of the fast expanding Islamic empire controlled by the caliphs in Damascus.'[53] However, Robin Walker suggests that the Arab invaders faced opposition from Africans: after an Arab invasion in AD 641 or 642, 'Nubians amassed a large army of 100,000 and struck back at the Arabs with such force that "the Muslims had never suffered a loss like the one they had in Nubia".'[54]

Tradition also suggests that Islam made inroads into the continent by way of the East African coast, where traders from the Persian Gulf made links with Africans. It is believed that the influence of these traders gave what are now Somalia, Eritrea, Tanzania and parts of Kenya their Islamic character.[55] However, Robin Walker argues that the 'first Muslims on the coast were Africans and not Arabs', and that the mosques in these countries were not founded by 'Arabs, Persians or other Islamised elements'. Islam was brought by African mariners using 'the monsoon winds… to sail to and from Asia'.[56]

Again, the traditional wisdom is that Islam was a 'modernising influence, imposing a consistent order among different societies, strengthening powers of government and breaking down ethnic loyalties'.[57] Yet to some this Islamic religious imperialism, like its Christian counterpart, was destructive, seeking to lay waste to traditional African religions in West Africa whose adherents 'believed in a Supreme Creator and numerous spirits who carried out the ordinary and daily tasks of making certain that humans remembered to do what they were supposed to do.'[58] Central to this belief system was the influence and authority of ancestors, who would be summoned to provide guidance on a range of questions.

Moreover Robert O. Collins has argued that the 'coming of the Arabs, the spread of Islam and the emergence of Muslim states increased the demand for African goods in return for those of the Mediterranean world, which could only be satisfied by the trans-Saharan slave trade'.[59] And historians such as Ronald Segal and Humphrey J. Fisher also argue that Arab Muslim traders 'were largely responsible for introducing the concept of slave trading on the African continent'.[60]

History shows that the great historical African kingdoms or empires that existed between the eighth and the fifteenth centuries, such as Mali and Songhay, were Islamic in character. This book is not the place to explore the wonders of African civilizations which built such cities as Timbuktu, Kumbi Saleh and Jenne, or discuss famous African leaders such as Mansa Kankan Musa, Sonni Ali Ber and Askia Muhammad Toure. But it is worth noting that many historians, especially those of African heritage, argue that these civilizations were equal to, if not in advance of, anything found in Europe at the time.

Africans were present at the very formation of Islam, as the life of Bilal ibn Rabah shows. Bilal was of Ethiopian origin, and Islamic tradition suggests that he was born in the late sixth century. He was freed from slavery by Abu Bakr, a companion of the Prophet Muhammad* and the first *caliph* following the Prophet's death. He also became a companion of the Prophet; some commentaries suggest that he was Muhammad*'s steward, which meant he accompanied Muhammad* on many of his campaigns. However, it was for his wonderful voice that Bilal was remembered, and he became the first official *muezzin* – the person who calls the faithful to prayer.

Out of Africa

Bilal is important for many Black Muslims because he clearly demonstrates the African dimension to Islam. In the United States, one of the largest African-American groups call themselves Bilalians, and once produced an internationally circulated paper entitled *Bilalian News*.[61] The name Bilal is particularly popular among Black converts to Islam in the USA and Europe. The fact that Bilal was freed from slavery also demonstrates Islam's anti-slavery credentials and commitment to racial equality, and makes the Prophet Muhammad* the first anti-racist pioneer in Islam.[62]

There is evidence that African Muslims arrived in the Americas centuries before Christopher Columbus 'discovered' the continent for Spain. The Guyanese-born academic Ivan van Sertima has made something of a career out of researching pre-Columbian African voyages across the Atlantic to the Americas. He argues that the 'Black Caribs', whom Columbus confronted on his first voyages to the Americas and whom many describe as indigenous people, displayed 'a number of qualities which associate them with the Islamic religion'. He goes on to suggest that 'Black Caribs possessed an Islamic name because they were, for the most part, Muslims, or at least their traditions say they were'.[63] Van Sertima is keen to point out that these African Muslims had travelled as free men and not slaves. Another expert, the Canadian Michael Bradley, has argued that Africans had also made the return journey from the Americas to Africa: he states that 'African [Muslims] knew that there were limits to the neighbouring sea and that another shore might be found to the west where... ships [had journeyed].'[64]

The academic C. Eric Lincoln argues that 'Islam first came to America with the Spanish adventurers, whose numerous expeditions were liberally sprinkled with "Blackamoors" or

Muslims from Black Africa who signed on as soldiers or sailors or for whatever tasks were called the "New World".[65]

But there is little doubt that historically the majority of Muslims who made the journey across the Atlantic did so as enslaved peoples, although very little is known about Islam during Atlantic chattel enslavement. The Franco-Senegalese historian Sylviane A. Diouf argues that, despite what tradition suggests, Islam was not rapidly subsumed into a new Christian setting, but flourished during slavery on a large scale. Diouf's research also highlights how African Muslims maintained their faith and spiritual lifestyle within an unreceptive environment. Although she does agree that an orthodox form of Islam did not survive in the Americas, it left its legacy in certain religious traditions and artistic creations of people of African descent. For instance, she argues that the military and literary aptitude of Muslims was pivotal in the Haitian Revolution and the early nineteenth-century revolts in the Brazilian state of Bahia.[66]

In Alex Haley's best-selling novel *Roots*, we see the Gambian-born enslaved African Kunta Kinte struggling, with some success, to hold on to his Islamic beliefs in a hostile environment. And Michael Muhammad Knight points out that 'some Muslims clung fiercely to their religion. Guinea-born Bilali Muhammad supervised up to 1,000 slaves and led an African Muslim community on Sapelo Island, Georgia [USA]. Preparing against a speculated British raid on the island, Bilali told his master, "I will answer for every Negro of the true faith, but not for these Christian dogs of yours."'[67] He adds that 'remnants of Islam are recognizable in the Ben Ishmaels of 18th century Kentucky', who practised polygamy and abstained from alcohol. But he adds that 'over time, syncretism and accommodation absorbed slaves' Islam into their masters' Christianity'.[68]

Notwithstanding what has been discussed above, most researchers looking at Black people and Islam or 'Black Muslims' focus on the USA and start their work in the late nineteenth century, a generation after slavery had been abolished. Islam in the USA is central to this book, as evidence suggests that many converts in Britain first took an interest in Islam as a result of developments and activities in the United States.

During the late nineteenth century, newly freed African-Americans embraced a range of religious beliefs which provided succour in the face of the vicious racism that still curtailed their freedoms and denied them basic human rights and any semblance of equality.[69] A number of 'race leaders' emerged from the confusion in the United States, committed to eliminating the state-sanctioned segregation of Jim Crow racism, lynching and the other nefarious activities of race-hate groups such as the Ku Klux Klan. What all these leaders had in common was that they were regarded as messianic figures among African-Americans, and it should come as no surprise that all were men of faith.

This leadership, however, can be divided into two distinct groups. Of the first John White writes, 'one of the anomalies of Afro-American history is that Blacks, as an ethnic group, have had only limited opportunities to select their own leaders.' As a result, brilliant leaders such as Booker T. Washington and W. E. B. Dubois relied in part on White approval: Washington 'owed his elevation as much to... influential white patrons... as to his own remarkable abilities'. And W. E. B. Dubois came to prominence 'only with the approval and financial support of upper-class white reformers of the Progressive era'.[70]

The Moorish Temple

Other Black leaders such as Noble Drew Ali, Marcus Garvey and W. D. Fard shared the grass-roots support of African-Americans with those mentioned above, but were less fêted by the White power-structure because of their reluctance to compromise on race matters. Marcus Garvey was arguably one of the most influential men of African heritage who ever lived, and his legacy can be seen in the Pan-Africanist movement as well as in Rastafari and various Islamic organizations.[71] He established the Universal Negro Improvement Association (UNIA), an international self-help organization committed to the advancement of Black people across the globe.[72] During the 1920s the UNIA could boast a membership of millions, and its various subsidiary entities included businesses such as the Black Star steamship line, as well as bodies dedicated to education and social improvement. Although a combination of politically inspired interference, racism and general mismanagement brought about the downfall of UNIA[73] and of Garvey, his ideas continued to have an influence on religious movements. Garvey himself was a deeply religious man who flirted with Ethiopian Orthodox Christianity, but who is described as having a 'peculiar conception of God... from which he obtained his notion of self-reliance, self-determination and the responsibility for individuals and groups'.[74]

It has been argued that Garvey's religious and socio-economic influence can be seen in the growth of one of the first 'Black Muslim' organizations in the USA: Drew Ali's Moorish Science Temple. According to one writer, many of Drew Ali's followers were former Garveyites, and Drew Ali himself said:

> In these modern days there came a forerunner, who was divinely prepared by the great God-Allah and his name is Marcus Garvey, who did teach and warn the nations of the earth to prepare to meet the coming Prophet; who was to bring the true and divine Creed of Islam, and his name is Noble Drew Ali: who was prepared and sent to this earth by Allah, to teach him the old time religion and the everlasting gospel of the sons of men.[75]

Timothy Drew, who later styled himself Noble Drew Ali, was born in North Carolina, and established his first Temple in 1913 in New Jersey. According to the US academic C. Eric Lincoln, Drew Ali was particularly impressed with the lack of race consciousness in Oriental religious thought and saw in it a possible answer to the black's plight in a colour-conscious America. If blacks could somehow establish an identity with the oriental peoples, whose religious philosophies either knew nothing of the 'curse of Canaan' or else found it irrelevant, they might be less susceptible to the every day hazards of being 'everyday negroes' in America.[76]

According to Drew Ali, Black people were Asiatics or 'Moors' who were God's chosen people, and Islam was the religion of God's people. As a result, membership of the Temple was exclusive to 'Asiatics' and adherents followed, 'not classical Islam', but beliefs which mixed 'Islam expressions of Ismailiyya, Ahmadiyya, and Sufism with Freemasonry, the gnosticism of Eliphas Levis, and Black nationalism'.[77] The vital tenets of Drew Ali's version of Islam were contained in his *Holy Koran of the Moorish Holy Temple of Science*, a fifty-page publication in which White people or Caucasians were seen as devils and the enemies of the Asiatics.[78] The chosen people were instructed to avoid meat, alcohol and tobacco; men were prohibited from shaving, and women had to abstain from using cosmetics and hair straighteners.[79]

Drew Ali's idiosyncratic message of Black solidarity and self-sufficiency appealed to African-Americans suffering the consequences of America's failure to address the social, political and economic issues affecting them. But eventually internal power struggles related to Temple finances led to a series of brutal murders connected to the movement. Drew Ali was arrested for one of the murders, then released; but it was the death of the 'Prophet' himself which still continues to cause controversy.

Some have suggested that his death was a result of a police beating,[80] or a 'subsequent beating administered by rivals within the movement seeking power'.[81] Like all religious movements dominated by charismatic leadership, the Moorish Science

Temple became susceptible to fissures and factionalism once its leader had gone, and fell into a marked decline. Although the group still survives, arguably its greatest legacy is the use of the 'Islamic' salutation 'salaam' or 'peace'. This has penetrated far into the American mainstream owing to its use by rappers influenced by the Temple and related movements.

The Nation of Islam

A more controversial legacy concerns the degree to which Drew Ali's Moorish Temple has influenced the Nation of Islam (NOI) which, from the early 1930s to the 1970s, was the face of American Islam. The NOI originated with the mysterious and enigmatic figure of Wallace D. Fard (or Farad), who was later known as W. F. Muhammad and Master Fard Muhammad. According to the late Honourable Elijah Muhammad, who led the NOI from 1933 to 1975 as Fard's successor, Fard was born in the Holy Islamic city of Mecca[82] on 26 February 1877.[83] (This date is now known as Saviour's Day, a holy day for Muslims in the NOI.) Both Fard's birthdate and birthplace are open to question,[84] as is his ethnicity, since all existing photographs of the Nation's founder show an olive-skinned man with 'delicate' features. Elijah Muhammad observed that he was 'part of each side (black and white), half and half. Therefore, being born or made from both people, He is able to go among both black and white without being discovered or recognized.'[85]

Fard's ambiguous ethnicity was important because he began to preach a message of 'Black' solidarity, which some would argue was Black supremacy,[86] among the 'lost and found' Black people of the United States. Fard began his work in 1930 in the guise of a trader; but his *entrée* into the homes of African-Americans in Detroit to peddle silk was little more than a ruse to outline his teachings, which covered everything from theology to diet and physical well-being.

Context is paramount when discussing the milieu from which Fard's ideas sprang. By 1930 the Great Depression had begun to bite in the US, with African-Americans at the sharp end of the economic downturn. In many towns and cities in the northern United States, Black families were forced to live in ghastly, dilapidated tenements paying exorbitant rents. Work and adequate healthcare provision were nonexistent, and the education system was rudimentary, failing practically all who passed through it. An entrenched racism at best denied African-Americans their basic human rights, and at worst treated them as subhuman.[87]

Fard was well aware of these conditions, and liberally used both the Qur'an and the Bible to demonstrate Black virtue and innocence, and highlight White perfidy. Islam was the 'natural religion of Black people', and Christianity, which had been foisted on them by their one-time slave-masters, was there to brainwash them. The Asiatics had to 'give back to the White man his religion (Christianity), his church and his names. These three are chains of slavery that hold us in bondage to them. We are free when we give up the above three.'[88]

Fard reversed biblical tradition and centuries of symbolism, which invariably treat what is dark or black as malevolent, by identifying white, and Whites, with evil.[89] For Fard the 'white race' was created 6,000 years ago by a scientist named Yakub (also spelt Yacub), by a process of grafting which lasted 600 years.[90] Fard believed that everything black was good and everything white was evil, and this led him to teach that Allah is Black. And if God or Allah was Black, Jesus (whom Fard, unlike orthodox Muslims, regarded as the son of Allah) could not be White. Here Fard tapped into ideas that had already been propagated by the Garveyites – and many others since – who attacked the notion of a 'White' Jesus.[91] The Western tradition has invariably represented the figure of Christ as a Caucasian or European. The British National Gallery's exhibition *Seeing Salvation: The Image of Christ*, which ran in early 2000, included paintings, sculptures, coins and engravings examining 'different aspects of the visual identity of Christ and the different pictorial questions that artists have confronted as they made his image'.[92] But all these visual representations depicted Jesus (who was a Palestinian Jew born in the Middle East) as a White European.

Fard suggested that Whites had used what he called 'tricknology', including Christianity, to convince Asiatics of the lie that they were inferior to Caucasians and should therefore be subject to them.[93] Islam was the only way Black people could free themselves from this trap, and the one to free them was Fard. According to the Honourable Elijah Muhammad, Fard was the 'Mahdi' – the Messiah or Chosen One. The Honourable Elijah Muhammad questioned Fard about his divine status: 'I asked him, "Who are you, and what is your real name?" He [Fard] said, "I am that one the world has been expecting for the past 2,000 years." I said to him again, "What is your name?" He said, "My name is Mahdi; I am God, I came to guide you into the right path that you may be successful and see the hereafter."'[94]

Although Fard believed that African-Americans were the 'Lost Nation of Islam in North America', they were also from the tribe of Shabazz, the original people who were 'first to discover the best part of our planet to live on'.[95] The original people had to return to their original names and Fard, like Drew Ali, instructed his followers to discard their 'slave names' in favour of Islamic ones. Elijah Muhammad was born Elijah Poole; and among famous converts Cassius Clay would become Muhammad Ali, and Malcolm Little would come to be known as Malcolm X.[96]

As well as changing their names, new converts were required to live according to new rules or laws. In his autobiography, Malcolm X describes a typical day in a 'Black Muslim' household: the 'father, the family protector and provider' would rise first to prepare the way, and would then perform morning ablutions. Wives and children would do likewise in that order. The right hand, and then the left would be washed and the teeth would be brushed. The mouth would be rinsed three times; and a shower completed the 'whole body's purification' in readiness for prayer. Prayers were said barefoot 'in robes, lined up facing East... stand[ing] on a prayer rug'.[97] Prayers were followed by a breakfast of juice and coffee – no solid food was allowed. Other dietary stipulations included eating only once a day and abstinence from 'poisonous food' such as catfish, corn bread and pork. New converts were also instructed to avoid alcohol, cigarettes and drugs.[98]

Fard's Muslims were encouraged to dress neatly but modestly, and to keep their homes spotless. Marriage was heartily promoted and divorce was frowned upon. But interracial relationships were (and still are) disapproved of and could lead to expulsion, as the Honourable Elijah Muhammad would later 'define miscegenation as a type of "mongolisation" which would culminate in the genetic and social destruction of the Black race'.[99]

Fard established a 'University of Islam', an elementary and secondary school that was designed to de-programme Muslim pupils from 'tricknology' and inculcate a knowledge of the self through mathematics, general knowledge and astronomy.[100] Fard's teaching was not palatable to everyone and, aware of this, he also established the Fruit of Islam (FOI), a paramilitary unit whose job it was to protect the faithful from possible attack and persecution.

However, the FOI was powerless to intervene in the internal tensions and jealousies within the Nation, especially after Fard designated the Honourable Elijah Muhammad his Supreme Minister and successor. Like Drew Ali's Moorish Temple, the Nation became embroiled in the murder of an acolyte and Fard was arrested. After the police encouraged Fard to leave Detroit, the leader decamped to Chicago and left the organization to Elijah Muhammad.[101] Fard subsequently disappeared, leading some followers to suggest that he had returned to Mecca.

With Fard gone, Elijah Muhammad had to struggle to hold the Nation together, but then his life had been replete with struggle since his birth in 1897 in Georgia. Elijah's parents were sharecroppers, and a young Elijah only learned 'the rudiments of reading, writing, and arithmetic before he had to go to the fields to help his family earn a living'.[102] Elijah's father, William, was a Baptist preacher and Elijah grew up in a Christian home, where the Bible was always read. Although he states that he never became a practising Christian, he was keenly interested in theology and was captivated by religious debates. As a young boy, he experienced the horrors of the racism of the Deep South, including witnessing a number of lynchings at the hands of Klansmen. Like many other African-Americans, he travelled to the industrialized north in the 1920s to escape Jim Crow racism and take advantage of what he hoped would be a better life in Detroit. At this point, Elijah was married with a growing family, but he found the relocation difficult. In an attempt to improve his life, he followed the example of many before him and joined both Marcus Garvey's UNIA and, in 1924, the Prince Hall Masonic Lodge, which was 'Freemasonry for Black people'.[103]

Neither Garveyism nor Freemasonry filled Elijah's spiritual vacuum, and it was an encounter in 1931 with W. D. Fard, who also lived in Detroit, that was to change his life for ever. After a few meetings, the then Elijah Poole became convinced that Fard was the saviour and began his forty-four-year association with the NOI. The US academic Anthony Pinn has argued that the development and growth of the NOI was related to the Great Migration of African-Americans from the south to the north, of which Elijah Poole was part. He argues that many, like Poole, did not 'find opportunity and prosperity in big cities but discrimination, poor conditions and poverty… the Nation's growth resulted primarily from the inclusion of those angered by their existential condition'.[104] Pinn appears to suggest that many early conversions to the NOI had more to do with a rational decision than a spiritual experience or encounter with God. He argues that the letters potential converts had to draft during the early years are evidence of this:

> Dear Savior Allah, Our Deliverer:
>
> I have attended the teachings of Islam, two or three
> times, as taught by one of your ministers, I believe in it.
> I bear witness that there is no God but Thee. And that
> the Muhammad is Thy Servant and Apostle. I desire to
> reclaim My Own. Please give me my Original name. My
> slave name is as follows.[105]

During the Honourable Elijah Muhammad's tenure as leader the NOI grew inexorably. Relying heavily on his Garveyite grounding, the Messenger, as he was known, unveiled an 'Economic Blueprint' consisting of five simple propositions which championed Black economic empowerment and encouraged industriousness. African-Americans should work for themselves, buy Black and pool their resources like other ethnic communities.[106] Under Muhammad's leadership the NOI established a number of enterprises, such as clothing and grocery stores, barbers and restaurants in cities where temples were found. (During the early years, NOI places of worship were known as temples rather than mosques.)

As numbers began to grow, Muhammad continued to encourage Black Muslims to live frugally, dress modestly, eat healthily and act with self-discipline. His Garveyite roots prompted him to emphasize the great contributions of Black people to America and the world. He regarded White America as racist and dangerous, and called for separate states in the USA for African-Americans. He did not see this as a form of 'self-segregation'; as Malcolm X later wrote, 'Segregat[ion] means to control. Segregation is that which is forced upon inferiors by superiors. But separation is that which is done voluntarily, by two equals – for the good of both.'[107] Accordingly the Honourable Elijah Muhammad and his supporters wanted half a dozen states in the south-west of the USA for Black settlement.[108]

The Nation of Islam and Wider Society

Under the Honourable Elijah Muhammad's leadership, the NOI gained a reputation as being able to 'clean up' or rehabilitate 'the Black man', and it carried out what even its detractors acknowledged sterling work in prisons. Institutional racism in the US criminal justice system ensured that African-American men were disproportionately incarcerated – as they still are.[109] Malcolm X, who became one of the leading figures within the NOI, became a Muslim while in prison. And Eldridge Cleaver, a leading figure in the Black Panthers in the 1960s, observed that his first initial contact with the Muslims occurred in prison. He wrote:

> During the early 1960s Elijah Muhammad gained a
> substantial nationwide following [in prison]… Elijah was
> building self-esteem into the lives of the lowest Blacks. To
> those locked up, he gave dignity, belonging, and a cause…
> and became the most singularly powerful group in the
> California prisons… The drug free life for many prisoners
> began inside the slammer. And it was a powerful witness
> to the Muslim faith.[110]

The writer C. Eric Lincoln has observed: 'When prisoners are released, they are not often wanted by the Christian churches, but a ready-made fellowship awaits them at the Muslim Temple.'[111] Those with drug or alcohol problems went to the NOI to induct themselves into rehabilitation programmes. But although the NOI had a thriving prison ministry, it also sought to attract Black people from all social strata. According to Malcolm X, 'Mr Muhammad's version of Islam now had been getting in some other types of black people. We began now getting those with some education, both academic, and vocations and trades, and even some with "positions" in the white world…'[112]

One such person was Sam Cooke, the legendary African-American gospel turned soul singer. Cooke was a close friend of the boxer Muhammad Ali – he even recorded a song with Ali – and according to his biographer, Daniel Wolff, 'Sam had been reading up not just on the religion [Islam] but on black history in general and was fascinated.'[113] The Nation was robbed of a potential high-profile recruit when Cooke was shot dead in a Hollywood motel in December 1964, a few months before Malcolm X's assassination. Cooke's brand new cherry-red Ferrari, which was parked in the motel's car park, had a copy of the NOI newspaper *Muhammad Speaks* on the back seat.[114]

It is impossible to quantify the psychological or emotional power that the Honourable Elijah Muhammad's teaching had on Black people during the 1940s and 1950s in particular. If one strips away the religious rhetoric, what remains are ideas and attitudes reminiscent of those of Marcus Garvey and other Black Nationalist leaders who asserted the 'somebodyness', the human dignity, of downtrodden Black people who were a few generations out of chattel enslavement but still living on the slave-master's plantation. Unlike the Jamaican-born Marcus Garvey, the Honourable Elijah Muhammad could not be deported for expressing views which he believed would enable Black people to 'stand tall' and look White folks 'clearly in the eye'. It must be remembered that this was an era when African-Americans could be lynched for talking back to Whites, and looking Whites in the eye or using their first names was considered 'uppity' or disrespectful. To hear or read about a man who stood up to White racists, and who resisted a system that was used to getting rid of Black dissent by any means, came as a tonic to Black people. Even if they did not share the Messenger's esoteric beliefs, many felt a real sense of pride that he appeared to be standing up for them without compromise.

However, not everyone appreciated the work of the NOI, or the Black Muslims' approach to gaining converts. During the Honourable Elijah Muhammad's time his supporters would often congregate outside churches on Sunday morning encouraging

African-American worshippers to 'hear the real message' at their temple or mosque. For some in the churches, this was not only disrespectful but 'fishing in our pool'. The Honourable Elijah Muhammad's column in the once-struggling *Pittsburgh Courier* rescued the newspaper, but it also drew heavy criticism. Many people disliked the idea of the Messenger using one of America's most widely circulated Black newspapers to peddle his theories on religion and race.

African-American leaders and politicians were divided about Muhammad's movement and how to deal with him. Politicians, with one eye on the potential of Black Muslims as voters (although Muslims at this time eschewed the political process), met with the Messenger and his cohorts. Conversely, Black leaders from the church and secular institutions such as Dr Martin Luther King, Thurgood Marshall, James Farmer, A. Philip Randolph, Adam Clayton Powell and Roy Wilkins were reluctant to attend NOI-sponsored debates.[115] (Dr King met both the Honourable Elijah Muhammad and Malcolm X – he famously encountered the latter in 1964 and they spent just enough time together to be photographed!)

The US authorities were in no doubt that the NOI, like Marcus Garvey's UNIA, presented a threat to the American way of life. They used all necessary means to undermine the organization's work and its appeal to African-Americans. In 1942, for example, Elijah Muhammad was sentenced to five years in prison for draft-dodging, even though he was too old to serve during the Second World War. (The NOI's Muslims were forbidden to serve in the military.)[116] By 1956 the infamous head of the FBI, J. Edgar Hoover, established the Counter Intelligence Program, or COINTELPRO, which carried out covert and often illegal operations against what it deemed subversive groups or activities taking place in the USA. The Nation appeared on the COINTELPRO radar after the 1959 television programme *The Hate that Hate Produced*, in which the presenter Mike Wallace used Malcolm X's life to examine the NOI. It was a broadcast which generated interest and fear in equal measure among White Americans.[117]

Malcolm X states that after this, 'Black agents were sent to infiltrate us. But… some of them, after joining us, and hearing, seeing and feeling the truth for every black man, revealed their roles to us.'[118] The writer Mattias Gardell has uncovered numerous FBI efforts to stir up trouble within the Nation through the dissemination of misinformation in the press and media as COINTELPRO activities.[119] At the time it was generally believed that some so-called Black leaders were colluding with the White authorities to undermine the work of the NOI. The NOI counter-attacked by denouncing their White critics as racists and their Black ones, especially Black clergy, as agents of the White man in his work to brainwash and subjugate the Black masses. Prior to his break with the NOI, Malcolm X appears to have had little time for Dr Martin Luther King, whom he called 'Reverend Chicken Wing'[120] and a 'dreamer' who ought to face up to the nightmare confronting his Black brothers and sisters.[121]

The Nation of Islam and Traditional Islam

Not all critiques of the NOI's belief systems, or criticisms of the Honourable Elijah Muhammad's leadership, could be dismissed as theological ignorance, Uncle Tom collusion or petty jealousy. The 'Islamic' tenets of the NOI, or 'Fardian' Islam, are out of step with both Sunni and Shii Islam, especially the acclamation of W. D. Fard as the Messiah or living God. The historical figure of Yacub and his role in creating the White race, and the belief in a Black divinity, are not present in the Qur'an or Hadith.[122] In his autobiography, Malcolm X points out how completing the *hajj* or pilgrimage to Mecca first made him aware of the major theological discrepancies in liturgical practice between the NOI and Sunni Islam. For instance, he points out that the physical position in which Black Muslims prayed bore no resemblance to what he saw in Mecca or elsewhere on his travels. NOI adherents

41

invariably ignored the *jumah* or Friday prayers in favour of Sunday 'services' similar to those of a Christian church.

The Honourable Elijah Muhammad's detractors accuse him of everything from deifying W. D. Fard[123] to muddled theology; Eldridge Cleaver argued that 'his teachings boiled in and out of the Bible, [and] were a mishmash of Islam, incense and nonsense'.[124] The African-American writer Stanley Crouch testifies, 'When charged with distorting Islam, [the Honourable Elijah Muhammad] explained that this was a special medicine for a special case, a people who had "no knowledge of self".'[125] Critics would argue that Islam is for all humankind and cannot be adapted to special circumstances or limited to the Asiatic or Black 'race', by pointing to verses from the Qur'an such as:

And mankind is naught but a single nation.
Qur'an 2:213

O you men! surely We have created you of a male and a female, and made you tribes and families that you may know each other; surely the most honorable of you with Allah is the one among you most careful (of his duty).
Qur'an 49:13

Others have asserted that under the Honourable Elijah Muhammad's leadership the NOI was failing the very people it was there to serve by refusing to engage in 'acts of civil disobedience or social protest' for Black human rights. According to the African-American academic Michael Eric Dyson, there was a 'glaring disparity between the Nation's aggressive rhetoric and its refusal to become politically engaged'.[126]

The Messenger's dalliance with the leader of the American Nazi Party, the White Supremacist George Lincoln Rockwell, raised eyebrows in many circles; records reveal that on 25 February 1962, Elijah Muhammad 'spoke publicly on Saviour's Day at the

Chicago International Amphitheatre, before an audience which included Rockwell and other Nazi party members'.[127] It has been pointed out that the two shared a belief in racial separation,[128] yet an association with such a well-known racist was not only a union of strange bedfellows, but cast doubt on the Messenger's judgment and credibility.

Others were critical of the Messenger's moral behaviour, and it has been alleged that he had numerous extra-marital affairs, which resulted in offspring.[129] It can be argued that Malcolm X's unseemly departure from the NOI was hastened by his rather public comments about the sexual impropriety of the Honourable Elijah Muhammad with the young women who worked as his secretaries.[130]

Malcolm X

Before his rather public falling-out with the Messenger, Malcolm X was arguably the face and voice of American Islam, and largely responsible for its growing numbers and notoriety in the USA. Malcolm X, born Malcolm Little in Omaha, Nebraska, in 1925, is, according to one writer, 'a member of the pantheon of twentieth-century black saints'.[131] His bold, brave and uncompromising approach instilled a sense of pride and renewal in many African-Americans. Malcolm was well over six feet, light-skinned (but saw no virtue in this) and was bespectacled as a result of his hunger to read while incarcerated in a dimly lit prison cell. (His characteristic spectacles are now known as 'Malcolm X glasses' by many Black people.) He said many of the things that Black people only thought about 'White' America, and held it to account for its hypocrisy and duplicity with regard to Black civil rights, equality and freedom. Most White Americans did not know how to react to him; for those who thought Dr King was a troublemaker,[132] Malcolm X must have been totally off the scale.[133] He possessed a razor-sharp mind and spell-binding oratorical skills that naturally drew people to him and resulted in new converts for the NOI after any speaking engagement.

43

Malcolm's break with the Honourable Elijah Muhammad has some poignancy when one considers that their relationship was virtually one of father and son. In his autobiography, Malcolm was not slow to praise Elijah Muhammad, who 'found me here in America in the muck and mire of the filthiest civilisation and society on this earth, and pulled me out, cleaned me up, and stood me on my feet, and made me the man I am today'.[134] The Messenger believed in him when no one else did and, after Malcolm completed a prison term for larceny, placed him in positions of responsibility within several of the NOI's temples. Malcolm, for his part, was totally devoted to the Messenger, and once said that he would lay down his life for him.[135]

Malcolm X had little time for 'Uncle Tom Negro preachers', and his vehemence against Christianity belied the fact that his father, Earl Little, was a Baptist preacher. Earl Little was also a Garveyite and a believer in Black self-determination. However, Malcolm's upbringing was dysfunctional: his father was killed by White racists while he was still a boy, leaving his mother, Louise, struggling to look after a houseful of young children. Eventually Mrs Little would succumb to mental illness and the family would be taken into foster care by the state authorities, which were rife with racism. Reflecting on this experience later, Malcolm spoke bitterly of how the authorities destroyed his family. Having been told that 'a lawyer was no profession for a nigger' by a teacher during a school lesson, a precocious but wayward young Malcolm lost interest in education and took to a life of 'hustling' on the streets, which resulted in stretches in Michigan and Massachusetts prisons from 1945.

It was while he was in prison that 'Detroit Red', as he was known during his hustling days, first heard the message of Islam, and he was attracted to its spiritual and social message like a moth to a flame.[136] From his release in 1952 to his eventual departure from the NOI in March 1964, he followed a 'Fardian' version of Islam, until, on his pilgrimage to Mecca in April 1964,

44

he encountered the universal brotherhood of Sunni Islam, which he found to contradict the religious tenets and practices of the NOI.[137] He assumed the name El Hajj Malik Shabazz, having completed the *hajj*, and embraced orthodox Islam, which treats everyone as equal, leaving behind belief in Yacub and the UFO theories of Ezekiel's Wheel and the Mother Plane.[138]

Malcolm X's linear account of his religious transformation in the *Autobiography* is persuasive, but it has come in for much scrutiny from those who have studied his life. Records show that Malcolm X first went to Mecca in 1959,[139] so the experiences dated in his autobiography to 1964 must have taken place five years earlier. The tensions he experienced within the NOI in the early 1960s need to be placed within this context.[140] If one adds jealousy to the mix, it is obvious that the outcome would be explosive.

By the early 1960s the Messenger's health had taken a turn for the worse and his bronchial condition reduced both public appearances and speaking engagements, resulting in increased deputizing duties for Malcolm X. Not everyone within the NOI was happy with this situation, and some argued that Malcolm was becoming 'uppity' and using the NOI to promote himself rather than the movement or the Honourable Elijah Muhammad. Certainly there is evidence of Malcolm omitting to make important references to the Honourable Elijah Muhammad in speeches and interviews.[141] Malcolm X was aware of disapproval within the NOI and noted that his name did not appear in *Muhammad Speaks*, a newspaper he claimed to have established, for practically the whole of 1963.[142]

The situation came to a head in late 1963, when Malcolm made his infamous 'chickens coming home to roost' retort to the news of President John F. Kennedy's assassination. The NOI were caught up in the country's sombre mood after the assassination and publicly censured Malcolm X for his comments. It is still unclear whether Malcolm X's suspension reflected fears of a White backlash, or whether the issue was no more than a pretext to constrain him, but commentators note the irony of a religious organization that spent its time denouncing 'blue-eyed devils' suddenly becoming concerned about what these 'devils' thought of it.[143] Whatever the real reasons, the upshot was a ninety-day ban from public speaking which spelt the end for Malcolm X inside the NOI. By March 1964, after the ban had expired, Malcolm officially severed all ties with the NOI, citing theological differences, and established two new organizations: Muslim Mosque, Inc., a religious grouping, and the secular Organization of Afro-American Unity, which enabled him to pursue the political agenda denied to him within the non-political Nation.[144] This realignment gave Malcolm X a greater opportunity to express his own thoughts on the situation facing African-Americans in the USA and Africans in the diaspora. Malcolm X's thinking was maturing during this time and his ideas embraced Black nationalism, socialism and an internationalist outlook.[145] He also travelled extensively throughout Africa and Europe, and addressed the Oxford Union a few weeks before his death.

Malcolm X became very vocal in his criticism of the Honourable Elijah Muhammad and the NOI, using speeches and interviews to lambaste his former mentor.[146] During the last few months of his life, he experienced numerous death-threats which he claimed were connected to the NOI, including the bombing of his house.[147] These threats became a reality when he was shot dead during a talk at the Audubon Ballroom in Manhattan, New York on 21 February 1965 by several assailants who were linked to the NOI.[148] Others have connected his killing to federal agents of the FBI or CIA.[149] Malcolm's legacy has been debated and reassessed by books, films and plays: today he remains an icon and an inspiration to Black people the world over.

The Successor
The man who benefited most from Malcolm X's departure from the NOI was Louis E. Walcott, who was born in Massachusetts

of Caribbean extraction. The young Louis was baptized as a Christian and attended an Episcopalian church with his mother. Walcott displayed a precocious musical talent and, but for the lack of funds, his aptitude for the violin would have led to the prestigious Julliard School of Music. Instead, Walcott attended a teacher-training college, but was forced to drop out as a result of family problems. By 1955 he was using his musical skills to pursue a career as a calypso singer under the name 'The Charmer'.[150] Like many a young man at the time, he found himself attending the NOI's Saviour's Day celebration and was captivated by Elijah Muhammad's charisma. Although he did not immediately join up, a subsequent meeting with Malcolm X convinced him of the NOI's merits, and he was renamed Louis X. He soon became Minister of the Boston Temple and displayed great leadership ability; Malcolm X described him as 'an outstanding Minister'.[151] Drawing on his musical talents he wrote the song 'White Man's Heaven is a Black Man's Hell', and also authored the NOI's first play, *Orgena* ('a negro' spelt backwards).

Louis X was regarded as Malcolm X's protégé, displaying his mentor's panache and dynamism to great effect in his growing Boston Temple.[152] Louis X would later take the surname Farrakhan, and his time within the NOI would be characterized by an unswerving devotion to the Honourable Elijah Muhammad. Indeed, he proved more theologically loyal to the Messenger than Elijah Muhammad's own son, Wallace Deen Muhammad, who would ultimately succeed his father, but whose involvement in the NOI during his father's leadership was characterized by suspensions and controversy. While Louis Farrakhan sided with the Honourable Elijah Muhammad over Malcolm X's sexual allegations against him, Wallace questioned his father's moral integrity, theology and leadership of the NOI, leading to a decade of tension.

Farrakhan worked with the Honourable Elijah Muhammad to expand the NOI in terms of numbers, so successfully that by the end of the 1960s the *Readers' Digest* were calling the Messenger 'the most powerful Blackman [sic] in America'. The NOI's finances also flourished, resulting in mosques or temples being built in virtually every US city with a sizeable Black population. Moreover, this era saw further purchases of real estate, businesses such as farms, supermarkets and restaurants, and other financial investments. According to the writer Claude Andrew Clegg III, 'By 1971 the NOI's farm in Michigan had roughly one hundred cows... and 20,000 chickens were producing enough eggs to keep Chicago retail operations well supplied. The Temple Farms holding in Georgia consisted of a large dairy, a cannery, 700 head of cattle and almost 1,000 acres of corn, soybeans and peanuts.'[153] And by 1974, African-Americans in forty-six cities were sending their children to the Nation's elementary and secondary schools.[154]

The only downside to this success was the Messenger's health, which continued to fail with the advance of age, and led to the obvious discussions about who would succeed him. By the 1970s Honourable Elijah Muhammad was spending his winters in Phoenix, Arizona, on doctor's orders because the air was good for his bronchial condition.[155] But the NOI still continued to attract new followers, increasingly from middle-income families who gave the organization further credibility and financial stability, and a gravitas to the Black community within White society at large. As always, it was impossible to gauge the number of the NOI's adherents, which has always been kept secret. Suffice it to say, membership was large enough for politicians and decision-makers to take the Honourable Elijah Muhammad seriously.

The year 1975 proved a pivotal one for the NOI: the Honourable Elijah Muhammad passed away and, to the surprise of many, his son, Wallace Deen, became the leader. Wallace, who had often been critical of his father's leadership and sceptical of the NOI's theology, wasted no time in 'reforming' the movement. Wallace had been jailed in 1961 for draft-dodging and spent his three years in prison studying Islam. It was during this time that he discovered the variances between his father's Islam and the Islam followed by Sunni or Shii Muslims.[156]

As the new leader he dropped the title 'Supreme Minister' and became Imam Warith Deen Mohammed. He set about unravelling the work of his father in order to bring the NOI in line with traditional Islamic beliefs. Like Deen himself, the NOI was given a new name, the 'World Community of Islam in the West', adopting Sunni Islam in the process. A result of this theological change was the acceptance of Whites, and the renunciation of beliefs in 'blue-eyed devils', Yacub, Ezekiel's Wheel, and, most importantly, W. D. Fard being God. He encouraged believers to study Islam and make the *hajj* to Mecca. Imam Warith Deen Mohammed also suggested that the Nation's finances were far from healthy and set about offloading land, businesses and financial ventures, including the national newspapers.[157] He established the *Bilalian News* and subsequently changed the organization's name once again from 'World Community of Islam in the West' to the 'American Muslim Mission'. He also loosened the rigid gender roles that applied under his father's leadership of the NOI, and under his charge women had greater importance.

The End of the Nation of Islam

A couple of years after Warith Deen Mohammed assumed the leadership, the NOI effectively no longer existed, and any memory of its founders had been totally expunged. These developments were greatly welcomed by long-standing critics such as the one-time Black Panther Minister of Information, Eldridge Cleaver, who described Imam Warith Deen Mohammed's actions as a 'master stroke, which cut the ground from under the feet of people like Farrakhan'. He added that Imam Warith Deen Mohammed 'has completely outmanoeuvered his rivals and has made a major breakthrough and advance in healing the theological and spiritual divisions plaguing black Americans... and renews the challenge which the Black Muslims originally laid at the door of Christianity'.[158]

Louis Farrakhan

For others within the former NOI, however, Imam Warith Deen Mohammed's theological changes were toxic. Chief among his detractors was, naturally, Louis Farrakhan, who had initially kept his counsel out of respect for the new leader – he was after all the son of the Messenger. Farrakhan even kept his poise when Imam Warith Deen Mohammed moved him from his prosperous New York setting to a less successful one in Chicago, a transfer, it was said, that was designed to help Mohammed keep a closer watch on his potential rival. Farrakhan's patience was, no doubt, further tested when the new leader instructed him to take on the name Abdul Haleem Farrakhan. For some commentators, Farrakhan's treatment was designed to humiliate him and force his hand to leave. For Farrakhan, this behaviour was a 'trial' that was there to teach him greater humility and to fortify him for the struggles to come.

The situation came to a head in 1978, when Farrakhan felt he could no longer stand by and allow the 'true teachings of the NOI' to be corrupted and the legacy of the Honourable Elijah Muhammad to be squandered. Farrakhan reconstituted the defunct NOI and began to revive the teachings of both W. D. Fard and the Honourable Elijah Muhammad in newly established mosques.[159] Part of this work involved the production of a new national newspaper, the *Final Call*, which Black Muslim brothers would sell on street corners; their 'sales totals [would] directly affect their standing'.[160] Farrakhan used his considerable charisma and oratorical and organizational skills to build up the NOI to its former standing; he was and is still one of the best public speakers in the world.

By October 1985 he could fill venues such as Madison Square Gardens in New York, something the controversial African-American cultural critic Stanley Crouch has argued that even Malcolm X could never have done. According to Crouch, while some African-Americans went to hear Farrakhan speak out of curiosity, most attended because they had 'never been to a rally to hear a speaker who didn't appear to care what White people thought of him, a man who seemed to think their ears were more important than those of Caucasians'.[161] It was these traits that enabled him to draw a crowd of around a million African-Americans a decade later for the so-called 'Million Man March' on Washington.[162] It has been suggested that the march also increased Black male participation in political organizations and encouraged Black men to vote.[163] Buoyed by this success, Farrakhan embarked on a presidential-style tour of the Middle East and Africa, where he met with heads of state and had audiences with dignitaries. During the 1984 US presidential campaign of the Revd Jesse Jackson, a former colleague of Dr Martin Luther King, Farrakhan provided him with security. (The Fruit of Islam performed a similar function almost two decades later for the singer Michael Jackson when he was on trial for child abuse.)

A 1994 poll carried out by *Time*/CNN among African-Americans showed that:

> 73% of those surveyed were familiar with him [Farrakhan]
> – more than with any other Black political figure except
> Jesse Jackson and Supreme Court Justice Clarence Thomas
> – and two thirds of those familiar with Farrakhan viewed
> him favourably. Some 62% who are familiar with him said
> he was good for the Black community; 63% said he speaks
> the truth and 67% said he is an effective leader.[164]

Under Farrakhan's leadership there has been nuanced change in the NOI's theology, which now regards White supremacy as demonic, rather than White people *per se*. A greater emphasis has been placed on the 'Qur'an as the basis of knowledge for both orthodox Muslims and those in the NOI, leading to a Qur'anic study program', and there has been a 'gradual embrace of more

51

orthodox worship activities and patterns'.[165] There was also some *rapprochement* with Warith Deen Mohammed prior to his death in September 2008. In February 2002, the US journalist Daniel B. Wood reported a meeting between the two men at *jumah*, or Friday prayers, at the Los Angeles Convention Center. This encounter was important not only because of their personal history, but also because it involved a religious practice associated with the 'orthodox' Islam practised by Warith Deen Mohammed. The meeting was said to show a softening of Farrakhan's attitude in the light of a protracted, but successful, battle against cancer and of the events of 11 September 2001.[166]

Farrakhan has continued the Nation's predilection for 'cleaning up the Black man', carrying out work among victims of the upsurge in crack-cocaine addiction in the 1980s. The Reagan era was particularly unkind to those members of the working class in the US, including many African-Americans, who failed to benefit from so-called 'trickle down' economics. Under Reagan the rich got richer and the poor were left behind. African-American neighbourhoods were flooded with drugs and taken over by gangs. In the housing projects in Chicago's South Side the NOI's Fruit of Islam opposed the activities of drug dealers and petty criminals, winning both respect and converts in the process. A *Time* magazine feature on Louis Farrakhan included an interview with the chairman of Chicago Housing Authority, who argued, 'I've seen what Black Muslims have done with hardened criminals – they go into the penal system and work with these young men, so when they come out they are no longer on drugs and respect their women and neighbors.'[167]

Farrakhan's NOI combined such familiar social-action programmes with a new interest in mainstream American politics. The writer Anthony Pinn has argued that Honourable Louis Farrakhan's book *A Torchlight for America* marked his entry into mainstream political discourse, critiquing contemporary America's socio-economic and political system from his unique religious perspective.[168] Farrakhan has also engaged with popular culture through his interest in the 'hip-hop' phenomenon, which he believes can play a key role in transforming African-American society – there will be more about this in Chapter 9. According to African-American academic Manning Marable all this is part of the Honourable Louis Farrakhan's attempt to 'repackage' himself as a mainstream leader of the African-American community.[169] It can be argued that Spike Lee's seminal cinematic biography of Malcolm X, as well as the re-emergence of Afrocentrism and Black nationalism in the early 1990s, has helped to generate greater interest in the NOI.

Like Elijah Muhammad, the Honourable Louis Farrakhan has attracted both praise and censure for his work. The most common criticism has been that of anti-Semitism, a serious charge which both he and the Nation vehemently deny, but one which has nevertheless been very damaging. Chief among his critics is the Anti-Defamation League (ADL), which was founded in 1913 'to stop the defamation of the Jewish people and to secure justice and fair treatment to all'. The League has amassed quotations from Farrakhan's writings and speeches which it denounces as anti-Semitic, and its 1998 Annual Report describes 'aggressive stands against the hate-filled rhetoric of NOI leader Louis Farrakhan'.[170] Farrakhan and his associates in the NOI have vigorously defended themselves against these accusations and claim to have been misquoted. Indeed, Minister Farrakhan has threatened to sue the Anti-Defamation League in the USA.

Other allegations against the Honourable Louis Farrakhan include associating with extremist figures who have espoused racist and anti-Semitic views. Farrakhan had ties to the maverick politician and conspiracy theorist Lyndon LaRouche in the 1990s, who in turn has connections to Nazism, White supremacy and the Ku Klux Klan.[171] A decade earlier, Farrakhan's 'activities and speeches' had allegedly come to the attention of British fascists, who quickly embraced his programme of racial separation. According to one writer, the far-right National Front praised Farrakhan as 'God sent' and subsequently distributed leaflets defending the NOI's positions.[172] Yet further accusations levelled against the Nation's leader are that he has promoted a conservative fundamentalist agenda that excludes women (the 'Million *Man* March') and is latently homophobic.[173]

A long-standing British government ban, dating back to 1986, has meant that Minister Farrakhan cannot visit Britain because his presence might alledgedly spark public disorder. Some argue that this ban undermines freedom of speech and expression within a liberal democracy, especially since other controversial figures such as the French far-right politician Jean-Marie Le Pen, who has expressed racist and anti-Semitic views, have been allowed into Britain. For some Muslims, this suggests hypocrisy and double standards; it is possible anyway to circumvent the ban by listening to Minister Farrakhan's speeches via satellite or the internet.

Now in his seventy-sixth year, neither illness nor criticism has slowed down the Honourable Louis Farrakhan. During his tenure the Nation has become an international movement with branches in the Americas and Europe,[174] leading many to believe that he and the NOI are the voice of Islam in America. This is despite the fact that the 'vast majority of African-American Muslims (over 2.5 million) follow [Sunni Islam], while Farrakhan's adherents are in six figures'.[175] The late Warith Deen Mohammed became the 'first imam to lead prayers on the floor of the US Senate in 1993 and was the Muslim representative at the inaugural interfaith breakfast organised by President Bill Clinton'.[176] He also met the Pope in 1996, and later addressed a gathering of 100,000 at the Vatican in 1999. He has taken part in high-level inter-faith meetings with Catholics and Jews.[177] At the time of his retirement in 2001 he was seen as the leader of America's Muslims, but as the writer Monique Parsons suggests, he was 'the most important Muslim you've never heard of' and his death in the USA on 9 September 2008 was overshadowed by plans to mark the seventh anniversary of the 9/11 outrages.

The NOI and Imam Warith Deen Mohammed's American Muslim Mission are just two of the many US Islamic groups that vie for the attention of African-American believers. Long before the son of the Messenger took the NOI down the road of orthodoxy, the Black Hanafi Muslims under Ernest McGhee had broken away from the Honourable Elijah Muhammad to embrace Sunni Islam. McGhee, who subsequently became Hamaas Abdul Khaalis, maintained a confrontational attitude toward the Nation which led to an outbreak of violence between the two groups after he publicly denounced the Honourable Elijah Muhammad.[178] Other splinter groups include the Five Percenters, who were formed by a former NOI adherent, Clarence 13X, in the early 1960s. The Five Percenters remain a small group, whose beliefs are remote from orthodox Islam, but their influence has been massive on the growth and development of hip hop in the USA. Many of the best known and biggest selling artists are involved with this movement (see Chapter 9).

Migration to the US from Middle Eastern and North African countries has also added a new dimension to Islam in the USA, especially with the arrival of Ahmadi Muslim communities fleeing persecution in Pakistan. The arrival of large numbers of Black Muslims from Africa, including Nigerian Ahmadis, has also increased the diversity of US Islam. Growing migration to the USA and birth rate trends have made Muslims an increasingly important force in America. As the American Muslim academic Eboo Patel writes: 'with the total population of Muslims in America at six million, about the same as the number of Jews and almost triple the number of Episcopalians [...] What notes will Islam contribute to the American song?'[179]

Chapter 2

Windrush: The Rise of Britain's Black Community

In order to determine why Black Britons are converting to Islam it is vital to be aware of the milieu from which they typically come, and which often informs their decision. The majority of converts are of African-Caribbean origin and have Christian backgrounds; they can often trace their connection to Britain to the immigration that began with the arrival of the SS *Empire Windrush* steamship in 1948.

The *Empire Windrush* and Caribbean Emigration

The African-Caribbean men and women who arrived on the *Empire Windrush* brought with them a rich culture which they sought to reproduce in an alien and often hostile environment. In time, this transformed Britain and has become crucial to mainstream popular culture. However, it is important to recognize that the *Empire Windrush* is not the starting point for this development, because Black people have lived in Britain for hundreds of years. One only has to look at the histories of Liverpool,[1] Cardiff and the East End of London to 'recognise practices, values, ideas and beliefs that lived side by side with those of the majority (White) community'. Nonetheless, the arrival of large numbers of African-Caribbean people after the Second World War and the disintegration of the British empire provided a critical space for the examination of race, migration, identity and nation in this country.[2]

There is little doubt that the sixtieth anniversary, on 22 June 2008, of the SS *Empire Windrush*'s arrival from the Caribbean island of Jamaica went largely unnoticed. Although there were muted celebrations in towns and cities with a sizeable African-Caribbean population, as one would expect, there was little coverage in the local or national media. By overlooking this anniversary, both the media and Britain as a whole were failing to recognize the roots of modern-day, multi-ethnic Britain.[3] Prior to 1948, Britain was overwhelmingly a White society, and most UK-bound migrants came from Europe. Between 1945 and 1951, anything from 70,000 to 100,000 Irish people entered Britain, while it has been estimated that Britain had a Polish population of 127,900 people in 1949.[4] What made the *Empire Windrush*'s arrival real news was the fact that nearly all its passengers were Black, and this generated curiosity and consternation in equal measure among White Britons at the time.

Even before the ship docked at Tilbury, the arrival of these Black travellers began to generate column-inches in the press and debate in Parliament.[5] Such was the uproar in the House of Commons that the then Prime Minister, Clement Attlee, was forced to make a statement to calm MP's fears.[6] Not for the first time, or the last, right-wing MPs used race and immigration as ways to bolster support by playing on the fears of indigenous White Britons. It was argued that Britain was not prepared to cope with unchecked Black migration and that Black faces would overrun the country within the space of a decade. History has a way of embarrassing politicians who make wild projections about the growth of minority ethnic populations. Statistics in fact reveal that 'between 1948 and 1953 Caribbean migration never exceeded 2,300 in any one year',[7] with the census figures for 1951 showing that London had around 15,000 Caribbean-born residents.[8] Interestingly, not all sections of the media shared the early concerns of British politicians about African-Caribbean migration, and some were downright sympathetic. For instance, the *Daily Mail*, which has a reputation for being conservative, was initially welcoming of the *Windrush* passengers and pointed out to its readers that '52 of the Jamaicans will volunteer for the RAF.'[9]

There is little doubt that the 492 passengers were unaware of the arguments raging in Parliament over their arrival when their newly polished shoes stepped on to the docks at Tilbury. The monochrome footage and photographs of these Black men and women disembarking from the *Windrush* are some of the most iconic images of post-war Britain.[10] Pathé film shows men in fedoras cocked at a rakish angle, and wearing generously cut suits that belied the frugality of the times. Black women wore flamboyant headwear that was more at home in a Caribbean church than on a converted troopship like *Windrush*. As the writer and cultural critic Ekow Eshun has observed, 'Black people have placed an emphasis on dress since they first settled here in numbers after the Second World War.'[11]

This Caribbean style was in stark contrast to the sobriety of the times in Britain, where food, furniture and clothing continued to be rationed, in some cases until 1954.[12] According to one Caribbean settler at the time: 'There was rationing, wasn't there? Clothes rationing, food rationing. They had to get used to the life in this country which at that time was hard, very hard, especially if you've been used to, say, going up and buying a bag of sugar if you wanted it, or some fruit if you wanted. They had none of that over here. Just nothing. Just your bare necessities rationing wise.'[13] As Peter Hennessy writes: 'In the first few years after the war, everybody, from the highest to the lowest in the land, shared the same fixation. "Food, clothes and fuel are the main topics of conversation with us all," the King wrote to his brother the Duke of Gloucester.'[14]

No Irish, Blacks or Dogs: The Struggle for Accommodation

One topic of conversation not mentioned by His Majesty, for obvious reasons, but which was of real concern to Caribbean settlers, was accommodation. Many of the first Caribbean pioneers struggled to find suitable lodgings as a result of the post-war privations and a 'colour bar'. Overt forms of racism became worse as the numbers of Black settlers increased, so that by the mid 1950s 'more than eight out of ten London landladies said they would refuse to house students who were "very dark Africans or West Indians", while a survey in Birmingham found just 15 landladies out of a thousand who would let rooms to non-white families'.[15] As a result, many Caribbean settlers were forced to rent dilapidated, cramped lodgings at exorbitant rates, and it was not unknown for several Caribbean families to share a small house or even a single room. This practice became known as 'Rachmanism' (after the infamous slum landlord Peter Rachman): cynical, self-seeking landlords taking advantage of Britain's racism and Black people's desperate housing needs to line their pockets. One pioneer of the time, May Cambridge, reminisced that:

> Rooms were offered at the princely sum of £2 4 shillings with six or seven people sharing the facilities. You'd have to queue in the kitchen with your pot to cook and then you were lucky to have a roof over your head... The 'no Irish, Blacks or dogs' signs are no myth – sometimes you would knock on the door with a vacant sign in the window, some would say the room had just gone, others would just slam the door in your face while [the] less forthright would not bother opening the door but you could see the curtains twitching.[16]

If the Caribbean settlers faced a struggle to find suitable

accommodation, their search for work was equally challenging. Although Britain was in need of labour to rebuild its economy, it was still choosy about its workforce,[17] and a personal account by one Caribbean settler describes how 'The Labour Exchange sent you to vacancies but employers would say the job was filled or somebody was due to start. But the following day the Labour staff would inform you the vacancy was still open.'[18] Caribbean settlers were seen as cheap labour carrying out activities that British workers were unwilling to do. Although many were qualified, or studying to become qualified, they often found themselves in entry-level jobs as cleaners, porters, canteen workers, maids and general labourers.

The arrival of the Caribbean settlers in 1948 coincided with the formation of the National Health Service (NHS) in Britain, which soon became a Godsend for many Black people. This free health service was one of the central planks of the Labour government's commitment to a welfare state with 'cradle to grave' provision for Britons.[19] But it was also a career opportunity for Caribbean workers, women in particular, who found work as state registered and auxiliary nurses. Such was its fondness for Caribbean female labour that the NHS began to recruit directly in the early 1950s. Indeed, the authors Beverley Bryan, Stella Dadzie and Suzanne Scafe argue that 'the NHS has got – and is getting still – a huge captive, low-waged Black women's labour force'.[20] Another mass employer was London Transport, which began recruiting employees in Barbados in the 1950s to work on its buses and the Underground.

The arrival of the *Windrush* generation and the emergence of the welfare state were two of the many socio-economic and political changes that occurred in post-war Britain. It is said that Britain went into the Second World War as a major performer on the world stage, but came out a 'bit-part player'. By 1948 the euphoria of defeating Germany and its allies had given way to the stark reality that victory had come at a great cost, resulting in the disruption of industry and social structures and the undermining of Britain's self-esteem.[21] According to one historian, '[Winston] Churchill had been obliged by the need for American support to accept the Atlantic Charter which, among other things, encompassed the break-up of empire. Concession did, in fact, begin to come thick and fast in several parts of the Empire during the war. Jamaica achieved adult suffrage [1944].'[22]

By the time SS *Empire Windrush* docked at Tilbury, Britain had lost its Indian colonies (1947), and a new generation of African leaders such as Hastings Banda (later President of Malawi), Kwame Nkrumah (later President of Ghana), Obafemi Awolowo (later Premier of the South West Region of Nigeria) and Jomo Kenyatta (later President of Kenya) had met in Manchester for the fifth Pan-African Congress (1945) to discuss, among other matters, African self-determination.

While some of the *Windrush* passengers would return to the Caribbean to be political leaders, the vast majority of the 492 remained in Britain to face a welcome that was as warm as the winter weather.[23] Any student of migration is familiar with the inherent contradictions of the way so-called enlightened societies respond to the arrival of newcomers. In theory, most countries accentuate the positives of cultural enrichment, greater diversity and a bolstering of the labour force. In practice in Britain there was 'intense debate within government departments, and in the public circles, about the impact of black immigration on housing, the welfare state, crime and other social problems'.[24] Politicians and anti-immigrant groups argued that the new Black presence would also undermine social cohesion and a sense of 'Britishness'. This was despite the fact that most of these men and women came from Anglophone Caribbean colonies which were very familiar with British customs and culture. Yet it was still asserted that their values had the potential to corrupt and pervert, resulting in many indigenous Britons adopting a 'lock up your daughters' mentality in the late 1940s and early 1950s, especially after being

61

told that the majority of Caribbean migrants were single men.[25]

Historians agree that it was in the decade after the arrival of the *Windrush* generation that many Caribbean folk decided to put down permanent roots and settle in Britain. For those who were keen to purchase a property rather than rent, the 'Pardner' system proved the ideal solution to meeting a mortgage deposit. The 'Pardner' is an informal banking system involving the pooling of monies by a number of people on a weekly or fortnightly basis. The recipient of a week's pot of money would use what could often be a considerable sum of cash to meet the costs of anything from a deposit on a house to a down-payment on a car. (Initially, these monies were used to pay off loans accrued for passages from the Caribbean to the UK or to make necessary purchases such as furniture and household goods for new accommodation.) It needs to be remembered that during this era, far too many financial institutions were unwilling to loan Black people money, so an alternative means had to be found. The 'Pardner' system went into decline when banks and financial institutions became more enlightened in their lending practices.

Such was Britain's lack of preparedness for the *Windrush* passengers that over 200 were forced to stay in the Clapham South air-raid shelter in south London. In order to find work they would travel from this grim accommodation to the nearby labour exchange in Brixton. In time, many naturally gravitated toward this area of south London, especially as African and Caribbean landlords became established who were more inclined to rent accommodation to new arrivals. As a result, Brixton became the first real 'home from home' for Black settlers.[26] One commentator points out: 'from the 1950s Brixton had been regarded as a prime destination of Caribbean migrants, and streets such as Somerlayton, Railton, Mayall, Shakespeare and other roads had become familiar to many Caribbean people, particularly Jamaicans'.[27] Other enclaves in west London (Notting Hill) and north London (Finsbury Park and Tottenham) also attracted

Caribbean settlers in significant numbers. Outside the capital, African-Caribbean settlement took place in former industrial cities such as Birmingham and northern areas where work could be found in mills and factories.[28]

It was in these areas that African-Caribbean people began to reproduce or adapt aspects of their culture in their new environment. Many of these Black people lived cheek by jowl with White working-class indigenous communities, and with immigrant communities that had arrived in previous decades. It was among the latter that there was the greatest interaction in the realms of passion, friction and hope. One writer has argued that there was a unique and curious empathy between the Black and Irish communities which saw 'considerable *esprit de corps*... between these two sets of often-despised arrivals – employment adverts frequently featured the words "no blacks or Irish" while accommodation notices would routinely expand this slogan to read "No dogs, blacks or Irish"'.[29]

Lord Kitchener and Calypso

The SS *Empire Windrush* provided Britons with a taste of Caribbean culture. One of its passengers was Aldwyn Roberts, a Trinidadian who was better known on his native island as 'Lord Kitchener'. Kitchener, or Dr Kitch, was a nightclub performer who kept his fellow passengers entertained with his off-the-cuff compositions during the Atlantic passage. One of his ocean ditties was the now iconic 'London is the Place for Me', in which Dr Kitch lauded the splendours of London life.[30] Once the ship landed, Dr Kitch headed straight for the capital's night spots, where he introduced whole new audiences to Trinidad's leading form of popular music, the calypso. Like so many cultural forms in the Caribbean, the calypso has its roots in Africa and is arguably a derivative of the West African *kaiso*, brought to the island by Africans during enslavement. Calypsos usually fuse political commentary, social satire, double-entendre and a dash of tomfoolery; it is a throwback to the days of slavery where enslaved Africans used songs to ridicule the slave masters.[31]

In Britain, calypsonians continued this trend; only the subject matter changed with the environment. Their songs focused on the problems of securing decent accommodation, the (cold) weather, the difficulty in obtaining news from 'back home' and more joyful matters such as a wedding or the arrival of a friend or loved one. It is said that calypso became 'the official sound-track of Black Britain' in the 1950s and early 1960s. The respected writer and academic Professor Stuart Hall writes:

> Calypso was the first popular music transported directly from the West Indies and, in the early days, migrants from the southern Caribbean would meet to listen nostalgically to the recording of that year's winning calypso or their favourite calypsonian, and relive memories of the street marching, the costume floats and steel pan music that dominate Port of Spain in the four-day saturnalia leading up to the beginning of Lent.[32]

Like subsequent Caribbean musical forms, calypso was first played on a front-room gramophone, but could soon be heard in a few pubs and night spots in south and west London which had gained a largely Black clientele.[33] It was here that singers like Kitchener plied their trade to an eager, ever-growing audience who travelled from all over London to hear home-grown sounds.

What proved the real catalyst for the dissemination of Caribbean culture among indigenous Britons was the famous West Indian test cricket victory against England at Lords in 1950. The test victory was the first time a West Indian team had beaten the old colonial master at cricket in England, and what made the victory even sweeter was that it occurred at Lords, the British headquarters of the game.[34]

Even more symbolic was the fact that a small but vocal West Indian crowd was there to witness the occasion. Before, test matches between the two nations were bereft of a Black presence, but courtesy of *Windrush*, the 'Windies' could count on local support to cheer them on. Lord Kitchener was on hand to coordinate celebrations, which began in St John's Wood and ended up by the statue of Eros at Piccadilly Circus, central London. According to Kitchener, 'People stared at this extraordinary sight out of windows – I think it was the first time they'd ever seen such a thing in England... And we're dancing Trinidad-style, like mas, and dance right down Piccadilly and... around Eros.'[35] Stuart Hall comments: 'The Caribbean ethos and style of celebration was the most commented upon aspect of the game and marks the moment when a distinctively new Caribbean spirit and rhythm first announced itself as an emergent element in the rapidly changing national culture.'[36]

The so-called Caribbean rhythm also played a role in bringing ethnicities together on the dance-floor as Black and White embraced, dancing to the latest sounds from Port of Spain or New York. A real absence of Black women led many Black men straight into the arms of White females, to the chagrin of some in Britain. But despite some racist reactions, interracial relationships, largely between Black men and White women, moved from the dance-floor or the workplace to the registry office or church aisle. This development would be one of the primary means of cultural transference between African-Caribbean and indigenous populations in Britain.

The Struggle with Racism

Any history of race relations in post-war Britain must include the Notting Hill and Nottingham riots in 1958 and the racist killing of Kelso Cochrane the following year.[37] Both were watershed moments which questioned Britain's supposed tolerance and sense of fair play for all. The Notting Hill riots took place in

August 1958 against the backdrop of rising community tensions. According to some accounts, 'Teddy Boys' (a White sub-culture) took umbrage at a relationship between a Black man and a Swedish woman and attacked the lady as she was returning home.[38] The mob later attacked a house occupied by Black people who were having a party, claiming they were 'nigger hunting'. What followed was four nights of violence, during which the local Black community 'gave as good as it got', in sporadic, but almost daily, racial attacks. The situation was made worse by the intervention of opportunist far-right supporters and some excitable coverage in the media.[39] The other key incident involved the killing of the thirty-two-year-old Antiguan carpenter Kelso Cochrane by a group of White youths at Notting Hill Gate. The Cochrane killing was treated as a robbery 'gone wrong' rather than a racial attack, and no one was ever convicted. However, many historians regard his murder as Britain's first recorded racial killing. Once again the rising racial tension in Notting Hill, exacerbated by the presence of the far-right group the National Labour Party, provided the backdrop for violence. The Notting Hill race riots and the killing of Kelso Cochrane coincided with a 'concerted campaign within Parliament, the media and political parties to "curb the dangers of unrestricted immigration"'.[40] This led to the introduction of the Commonwealth Immigration Bill in 1961, 'about the formulation of legislation which could exclude black labour from entry and settlement'.[41] The Commonwealth Immigrant Act, introduced by the Conservative government in 1962, forced Commonwealth citizens to obtain three types of employment vouchers to work legally in Britain. What the Act did not curtail was the possibility of dependants joining their families in Britain from the Caribbean. This phenomenon increased as African-Caribbean people put down roots in Britain in the late 1950s and early 1960s. Moreover, during this period West Africans took advantage of the 'dependants' clause' to swell their numbers to around 10,000 by the early 1960s.[42]

In certain Westminster corridors and Fleet Street offices it was acknowledged that the 1962 Commonwealth Immigrant Act had singularly failed to curtail the numbers of Black foreigners coming to Britain. In the minds of some in Britain, large-scale immigration was bad for race relations because it complicated the 'integration of large numbers of immigrants into the host community'. Some historians have argued that the 1962 Act reinforced the notion that Britain had a 'race problem' and it gave licence to certain politicians to 'play the race card'.[43] And it has been argued that 'the practice of racism by the state in keeping out black people has only served to legitimise racism in society as a whole',[44] leading to scenarios like the one in which a Conservative candidate unseated the sitting Labour MP for Smethwick in the 1964 General Elections by using the slogan 'If you want a nigger for a neighbour vote Labour'.[45]

Interestingly, even the replacement of a faltering Conservative government by a dynamic Labour one led by Harold Wilson in 1964 did not result in the repeal of the 1962 Act. According to one writer, the Labour Party 'was notoriously ambiguous about immigration, leading some immigrants and liberals to believe that they intended to repeal the 1962 Act'.[46] But despite criticism of this Labour government for its reluctance to fight racism, it did pass the Race Relations Act of 1965 to combat discrimination. It also established the Race Relations Board to 'promote racial harmony, fight against racial prejudice and handle complaints'. A follow-up Act was passed in 1968 which strengthened the powers of the Race Relations Board, allowing it to carry out its own investigations into discrimination in housing and employment.[47] As always, these Acts were only passed with the help of sterling contributions from Black protest groups and trades unions who persistently lobbied Parliament for change.

Not for the first time, the United States proved a source of inspiration for Britain's Black communities. The USA had even greater entrenched racial problems, after centuries of slavery and decades of 'Jim Crow' segregation laws, which separated the races and reduced African-Americans to the level of non-people in the country of their birth. In response to this perennial discrimination, a number of Black freedom fighters such as the Baptist minister Revd Dr Martin Luther King and the Muslim activist Malcolm X (Malcolm X's influence will be explored in Chapter 3) fought for the civil rights of African-Americans. By the early 1960s, both of these US civil rights activists had made sojourns in Britain to juxtapose the racial situations in the USA and UK, and to encourage Black Britons in their struggle. Dr King visited the UK en route to Oslo to receive the Nobel Peace Prize in 1964, and met with the Lord Chancellor and members of the British Parliament to discuss race matters. He also participated with Black and Asian people in London in the 'organisation of a movement to bring together coloured people'.[48]

King's visit provided the catalyst for immigrant support organizations to mobilize and form the umbrella group Campaign Against Racial Discrimination (CARD), which was established in 1965 to oppose racial prejudice and call for laws to fight discrimination.[49] CARD's potential to tackle racism, however, was always marred by internal division and strife because its affiliated organizations were united solely by their opposition to racism. It singularly failed to make a significant impact with the Black community at a grass-roots level and remained an alien entity for all but a few.

In truth, organic Black struggle against racism began in earnest in 1958/59 with the emergence of the 'West Indian Standing Conference' which aimed to 'represent Caribbean people living in UK, to make recommendations as considered necessary to government and institutions inside and outside UK, to address racial issues'.[50] Other important interventions included that of the Jamaican politician and People's National Party founder Norman Washington Manley, who made a visit to riot-torn Notting Hill in 1959 to offer his support to fellow Jamaicans. That same year the legendary Trinidadian-born activist Claudia Jones established the campaigning newspaper *The West Indian World*.[51] Jones's lasting legacy was to establish the Caribbean carnival in Britain. This first took place in St Pancras Town Hall in north London in 1959, as a response to the racial tensions in west London.[52] By the mid 1960s the carnival had moved from an indoor venue in Camden to an outdoor one in Notting Hill. The initial soundtrack of the carnival was the ubiquitous calypso, and its first staging featured the legendary calypsonian the Mighty Sparrow. Since that time, calypso has had to share the stage with Jamaican music as the event has grown to become 'the most powerful contemporary symbol of the right to mass assembly and celebration'.[53]

As we have seen, calypso music was the first and initially the most prominent manifestation of Black culture in post-war Britain. The difficulty of defining 'Black culture', like 'culture' itself, does not deter the regular use of the phrase. The critic Dick Hebdige describes culture as a 'notoriously ambiguous concept… refracted through centuries of usage, the word has acquired a number of quite different, often contradictory, meanings'.[54] And Raymond Williams calls the term 'one of the two or three most complicated words in the English language'.[55] Any serious examination of culture invariably draws the reader into the territory of ideology, a move which is seen by some academics as 'crucial to a real understanding of the nature of culture',[56] and which demands a range of theoretical and philosophical borrowings, from structuralism, semiotics, Freudian psychoanalysis, feminist theory and Marxism. This book does not have the space to explore the intricacies of culture or the ideological and theoretical terrains associated with it, fascinating though they are. For the purposes of this study it is useful to adopt one of the definitions from the *Oxford English Dictionary*: 'the customs, institutions, and achievements of a particular nation, people or group'. In the case of Black culture, music has a particularly important place alongside religion, poetry and prose, language or dialect, sport, and fashion and style. Music remains unique and pre-eminent because of its immediate, direct impact.

According to the writer Dick Hebdige, Caribbean culture had its greatest influence on working-class sub-cultures in the early 1960s, rather than in the 1940s and 1950s when the Caribbean community was in a fledgling state of development.[57] During the early 1960s Jamaican ska (often known as Blue Beat in the UK after the record label) became the dominant form of Caribbean popular music. Ska was born in the tenement yards of Kingston, Jamaica in the late 1950s, created by a combination of frustrated, classically trained musicians and disaffected young singers.[58] It soon became Jamaica's first 'national sound' and naturally found a home in Britain among the Jamaican community.[59] Official census statistics for the early 1960s reveal that over 60 per cent of Caribbean people in Britain were from Jamaica or of a Jamaican background,[60] so it comes as no surprise that ska replaced calypso as the music of choice for Caribbean folk in Britain.

In time a whole sub-culture connected to ska evolved within a British context with sound systems (mobile discotheques), DJs or soundmen and dances. A lawn or garden on a humid Kingston night would be replaced by a hall or a cellar on a colder English one – a different location but a similar experience.[61] And while a Jamaican dance was largely an all Black affair, the English version always also attracted a White clientele. Many of them came from the same neighbourhoods as the Black patrons and were attracted by the excitement and sense of danger that has always been associated with such spontaneous parties. Many White youths regarded African-Caribbeans as 'cool', setting trends in style, fashion and language.[62]

In 1960s London, sound system dances run by the likes of Duke Vin, Count Suckle, Sir Neville and Count Shelley played to packed audiences willing to travel many miles to hear the latest sounds from Jamaica. In time, the more progressive music establishments such as Brixton's Ram Jam, Lewisham's El

Partido and Soho's Flamingo and Roaring Twenties clubs played the latest Prince Buster or Derrick Morgan ska tunes, which were often spun by Jamaican DJs who had graduated from the local house party and 'shebeen' scene to take up residence in London night spots.

Such was the popularity of Jamaican ska music in Britain that Emile Shallit, a Jewish entrepreneur, established the record label Blue Beat in 1961 to cater for this growing market.[63] Shallit signed deals with Jamaican record producers to distribute their products in the UK. Being an astute businessman, he realized that this music had crossover appeal and aimed his records at young White teenagers, especially the 'Modernists' or mods, who wanted something more 'hep' than the Mersey-beat music which dominated British pop charts in the early 1960s. As a result, when Jamaican singers such as Prince Buster toured Britain, promoters would ensure that concerts took place in largely White towns and cities for patrons who were desperate to see their favourite artists perform live.[64] According to one commentator, 'Jamaican music found an even larger and more avid audience than in its country of origin, with sales of records frequently exceeding those in Jamaica itself during the 1960s. Britain rapidly became one of the Jamaican recording industry's largest and most lucrative markets... '[65]

By the late 1960s skinheads had replaced mods as the latest youth sub-culture to fixate on Black culture. The mods were hooked on ska and idolized Prince Buster, but the skinheads were gripped by reggae and found a hero in the Jamaican singer Desmond Dekker.[66] According to one writer 'White reggae fans began mixing with the Black Rudies sub-culture and copying their style'. Black rudies or rude boys were regarded as cool and tough, and skinheads copied their penchant for Crombie overcoats, tapered half-mast trousers and big boots.[67] Such was the affinity between skinheads and reggae music that Jamaican artists began writing songs with the word 'skinhead' in the title as a homage to

71

their aficionados, and reggae itself was labelled 'skinhead music' by sections of the press. In later years skinheads would gain a reputation for racial violence and football hooliganism; but the first skinheads were keener on collecting reggae records than on antagonising ethnic minorities or rioting on football terraces.

The rise of the Black consciousness movement in the USA in the 1960s had a knock-on effect in the Caribbean, with writers, musicians and artists falling under the influence of their African-American counterparts. Jamaica's relatively close proximity to the United States meant that the island was a natural port of call. At the same time, Black people in the UK, who had always taken an interest in African-American music and culture, were also influenced by these developments. It can be argued that the reggae that emerged in the late 1960s was influenced both by events taking place in the USA and by socio-religious developments in Jamaica, particularly the emergence of the Rastafari faith. Rastafaris believe that the late Emperor Haile Selassie of Ethiopia is the 'King of Kings' and the 'Black Redeemer'. Rasta culture involves wearing dreadlocks, the use of marijuana (ganja) as a spiritual practice, and reggae music (especially that of Bob Marley).

Rastafari would influence Jamaican music in the 1970s to such an extent that the relationship would become almost symbiotic, with the majority of Jamaica's leading singers embracing Rasta beliefs and laying down its central tenets on their records.[68] In many respects the emergence of Rastafari as a socio-religious force in the late 1960s and early 1970s was in keeping with an era that championed Black pride, self-help and self-determination. It was very much seen as a religion offering solace to the poor or the 'sufferers', Jamaica's Black population.[69]

The gospel of Rastafari was spread by reggae, and in Britain it found disciples among disaffected Black youths who were struggling with issues of race and identity. Although many of these youths were born in Britain they were still seen as foreigners because of their skin colour, and they struggled for acceptance and recognition. They also struggled to identify with an oppressive country whose racism had thwarted their parents' dreams of a better life. Some youths decided to engage with their African-Caribbean heritage, but, since many had never visited the Caribbean, it was difficult for them to embrace this identity with integrity and authenticity. This crisis of identity and culture led some to embrace Rastafari, which posited Africa as their real homeland and a Black man, Haile Selassie, as their saviour.[70]

Rasta beliefs are counter-cultural in that they despise Western values as oppressive and racist, and call on Black people either to leave or to destroy 'Babylon' (Western society) in order to return to Zion (Africa).[71] During the 1970s Black youths in Britain were attracted to this rebellious, anti-establishment message. Unlike their humble, acquiescent parents who 'were thought of as a law-abiding group', but wound up 'identified as a problem',[72] these youths would take the advice of Bob Marley and the Wailers and 'stand up for their rights'.

The Rasta movement was also part of the Black consciousness movement or Afro-centricism, and reggae music played its part, with tunes such as 'It's a Black Man's Time', 'Message to a Black Man', 'Arise Blackman' and so on, which gave Black British youths a sense of pride and dignity about being Black. During this era, Black people were referred to as 'coloured' in polite circles, and in worse terms elsewhere.

White youths were also drawn to the defiance and counter-cultural attitude of Rastafari and 'roots' reggae music. The punk movement exploded in Britain during 1976/77, typified by the music of the Sex Pistols, the Clash, the Damned and the Buzzcocks. It had links to a number of 'roots' reggae artists and groups such as Burning Spear, Linton Kwesi Johnson, Aswad, Culture, Steel Pulse and Misty (in Roots). By contrast with the mod and skinhead sub-cultures, the musical inspiration was as much Jamaican as it was Black British. But it gave Black British artists the opportunity to sing, or, in the case of dub poets, speak, about their own experiences of being Black and British in 'Babylon'. According to one writer:

> Although punk was fast and guitar-based and reggae slow and bass-heavy, the punk look (spiky hair, leather jackets and combat trousers) wasn't much different to Rastafarian chic (dreadlocks, leather jackets and combat gear). Visually and otherwise, punk and reggae audiences were seen as outcasts.

> 'The bond was very simple,' explains Peter Harris, a British reggae guitarist who played on 'Punky Reggae Party'. 'Blacks were getting marginalised.' British Irish kids – like [Johnny] Rotten – and Black youths were forced together because of signs on pub doorways that read "No Irish, No Blacks, No Dogs", which became the title of Rotten's autobiography. 'The punks were the same. They were seen as dregs of society. We were all anti-establishment, so there was a natural synergy between us.'[73]

In a show of militancy British Rastas often favoured combat jackets and other military clothing, which was often copied by fashion-conscious punks. Like the homage paid to the skinheads by the reggae group Symarip ('Skinhead Moon Stomp'), the great Bob Marley cut the record 'Punky-Reggae Party' in recognition of the alliance between the two disparate groups. Although the association was largely welcomed, not everyone was happy with Marley's intervention, which one writer described as 'trite and vapid'.[74] This was also the era of the Rock Against Racism, a campaign which brought together a range of musicians to promote friendship between Black and White in the face of increasing racism.[75]

It can be argued that this Black and White alliance heralded the rise of two-tone, a hybrid musical form which fused 1960s Jamaican ska and punk to produce music which addressed the plight of multiracial Britain in the late 1970s and early 1980s.[76] 'Two-Tone' was also the name of the record label established by the ska band The Specials,[77] which, alongside The Selector and The Beat, united Black and White musicians and exemplified the 'Black and White, unite and fight' message popular with anti-racist groups of the time.

The 1980s proved a pivotal decade in the history of the Black community in Britain. For many, this period is associated with the worst excesses of Thatcherism, the rise of the Yuppie and conspicuous consumption. But it can be argued that Black people became truly British during this era, finding their voice and asserting a new self-assurance in many socio-economic and political aspects of life. Depressingly, the decade began with disturbances in English towns and cities with large Black populations. In April 1981 the streets of Brixton were the scene of several nights of disorder as Black youths vented their frustration at heavy-handed policing and mass unemployment; 400 people were injured.[78] Many of those who took part in these disturbances were either born in Britain or had grown up in this country, and were unwilling to tolerate the worst excesses of racism. Unlike their parents' generation, who had always regarded the Caribbean as 'home', this generation had no such direct connection. And while many were still uncomfortable calling Britain 'home', a generation nurtured on militant reggae which argued that Black people should 'get up, stand up' for their rights, was prepared to take direct action to bring about change.

It was during this era that Black British soul acts began to produce music that explored and expressed the views of Black people living in Margaret Thatcher's Britain. Groups such as the Real Thing, Hot Chocolate, Galaxy, Lynx, Imagination and Loose Ends, and individual artists such as Junior Giscombe and Billy

Ocean, grew in originality and popularity as they capitalized on the struggles of their predecessors. Although this music still borrowed heavily from US soul and jazz funk, it included a vibe and feel that was truly British and did not involve Black Britons imitating their American counterparts.

However, Black British music truly came of age in 1988 with the emergence of Soul II Soul, a group that first formed in the early 1980s and was also forged in the fires of Thatcher's Britain. Having built up a solid fan base playing club nights at the Africa Centre in Covent Garden, Soul II Soul signed a record deal with Virgin in the UK which enabled them to reproduce their club sound on record. The group's debut outing, 'Fairplay', was released in 1988 and helped to redefine Black music. Jazzy B, the group's founder, drew on reggae sound-system influences and fused them with soul and R&B to produce tunes that still sound fresh today. He was assisted by star vocalist Caron Wheeler, who put the 'soul' into Soul II Soul's music. The group's follow-up tunes, 'Keep on Moving' and 'Back to Life' continued in a similar vein and can be found on the group's debut album, *Club Classics Vol. I.*

Black British culture, a hybrid of US, Caribbean and African influences forged in the dynamism of British towns and cities, has increasingly become the default culture for White teenagers, irrespective of where they live in the country. According to a report by the TRBI marketing agency, 'The days when popular culture was controlled by White artists and pushed by cultural organisations have faded. Black youth have a disproportionate influence on mainstream culture.'[79] Black culture has always been regarded as subversive, counter-cultural and cool, and today's young people are only doing what the mods, skinheads and punks did a few decades before. The primary difference between then and now is the fact that it is not one subset of British White youth that chooses to copy Black style, but the majority. The same report on youth culture suggests that White teenagers believe that the coolest people in school are those who dress and talk Black.[80]

The forces behind this influence are hip hop and R&B derived musical genres, in which British acts such as Dizzee Rascal, Wiley, Ironik, Sway, Taio Cruz, Roots Manuva and Estelle are currently the prime movers. And although Black people make up just 2 per cent of the population, Black or 'urban' music, as it as known in some circles, accounts for almost a fifth of UK records sales.[81] Equally, by 2004 at least half of the best-selling albums and singles in the Top 40 charts belonged to Black artists, and several of the singers won Music of Black Origin (MOBO) awards that year.[82]

Fashions linked to this music have also become *de rigueur* among teenagers: baggy jeans worn well below the waist to reveal designer underwear, and outsized T-shirts under 'hoodie' tops. The so-called 'hoodie', a sweatshirt with a hood, has become a notorious symbol of all that is considered negative about street culture and associated with crime. The former Prime Minister Tony Blair even called for a ban on 'hoodies'.[83]

There is, however, more to Black style than street fashions, which was demonstrated by the Victoria and Albert Museum's exhibition 'Black British Style', which ran between October 2004 and January 2005. It covered half a century of fashion, from the elegance of the Caribbean and African diaspora to hip-hop street wear. According to one of the exhibitors, Walé Adeyemi, 'It was more than about clothes. It was about lifestyle. It has always been about showing what you have got and making the best of what you have. Style and fashion is a big way of expression for the community. Some of the glamorous women's outfits hung up here could be straight out of my mother's wardrobe. Seeing the outfits similar to what my parents would wear made me realise how glamorous they were…'[84]

The V&A show has been seen as a sign that Black British style has come of age. It now influences celebrities from the football superstar David Beckham to the singer Lily Allen.[85] Indeed Beckham, who has been crudely described as a Black man in a White man's skin,[86] was the subject of the Channel 4 television documentary *Black Like Beckham*. This controversial programme 'set out to prove that Beckham is Britain's most famous Black man' and argued that 'he may really be White but he has borrowed and begged so much from Black culture that he should be considered Black'.[87]

Another aspect of cultural influence is the emergence of 'Blinglish', an argot fusing Jamaican dialect, African-American slang and English street language. In many English inner cities it is difficult to differentiate ethnicity on the basis of the way young people speak, since most pepper their sentences with this vernacular. White youths who choose to adopt Black style and sensibilities are no longer ridiculed as wannabe Black people or 'wiggas' – a pejorative term which is becoming as unacceptable as its antecedent.[88]

Not everyone is comfortable with a situation in which Black 'street culture' or 'urban' fashion is increasingly seen as the sum total of Black culture. This, it is argued, is reductive and fails to recognize the full range of Black cultural expression in Britain. 'Street culture' is also attacked for being materialistic and too closely associated with the ostentatious 'bling-bling' lifestyle of US rappers. Some critics, especially opportunistic politicians, see the association between hip hop and 'bling' as an incentive toward anti-social behaviour and gun crime.[89] More thoughtful commentators have appreciated that this is simplistic, but it is nevertheless important to examine the way in which the marketing men have pushed expensive items and a champagne lifestyle to people who cannot afford this kind of luxury.

This notion of Black culture is also blamed for encouraging misogyny and a form of hyper-masculinity 'that constructs Black men as both sources of pleasure and sources of danger to White listeners and spectators'.[90] One persistent critic of this appropriation of Black youth culture is Dr Tony Sewell, whose regular columns in the *The Voice* newspaper, a weekly publication aimed at Britain's Black population, constantly lambaste this phenomenon. Dr Sewell, an educationist, has argued that the media and society's fixation with Black culture have affected the way Black youths are perceived, and perceive themselves, and encourage stereotyping.[91]

Despite these criticisms it remains true that the style, music, vernacular and even behaviours once specifically associated with Black Britons are now mainstream and normative within popular culture. It is possible to hear broadcasters on Radio 4, surely the bastion of British tradition, use terms such as 'biggin' up' to describe the promotion or endorsement of an individual or activity. And the Radio 1 music presenter Tim Westwood, who is regarded as the epitome of the 'Black Beckham syndrome', treats his listeners to a 'Jamaica meets Harlem' lingo while spinning the latest hip-hop, R&B and soul tunes.

This process of acculturation continues at a rapid pace and has even entered into the area of religion. In his excellent book *Jesus is Dread*, Dr Robert Beckford has shown how a leading Christian singer-songwriter, Graham Kendrick, appropriates 'distinctive rhythms and styles of the Black church' and uses Black musicians and producers'.[92] And the Rastafari movement, once the preserve of Black people, now has as many White adherents as Black ones. There is little doubt that reggae music, as well as the apparently rebellious attitude of Rastas, is an attraction of the faith.[93] Dreadlocks, often the most obvious outward manifestation of a person's adherence to Rastafari, are now a common hairstyle among White people.

The obvious question here is whether the form of Islam embraced by growing numbers of Black people is equally attractive to those in the wider culture who are searching for a more spiritual significance to life. Where Rastafari had reggae music as a means to disseminate its message, Islam in Britain (and in the USA) is using the incredible cultural force of hip hop to promote the tenets of what is arguably the world's fastest growing faith.[94]

In his book *Black Culture, White Youth*, Simon Jones argues: 'One of the most profound cultural changes that has occurred in British society over the last 25 years has been the impact of Jamaican popular music on the young white population.'[95] Jones's comments were correct at the time of writing (1988), but appear out of touch with musical developments and taste today. Although Black culture still continues to hold a disproportionate influence over British society, the dominant Black musical style comes, not from Jamaica, but from the USA and the UK. The sounds that are shaking up the town are not reggae but hip hop, in both US and UK forms. This music has been in the ascendant for the last decade and it does not appear as though it will lose its crown in the near future.

Chapter 3

Faith Matters

Incurably Religious

In his book *Faith, Stories and the Experience of Black Elders*, the writer and academic Dr Anthony Reddie suggests, 'Black people are incurably religious.' He goes on to argue: 'A belief in powers higher than the temporal, mortal realm of humankind, lies at the very heart of our understanding and relationship to the created world order. The struggles of our ancestors in Africa and the Caribbean were forged in relationship with a belief in the benevolent power of the Creator.'[1] It would be wrong to suggest that all Black people are hardwired with a kind of 'spirituality chip' that makes them disposed to religion, regardless of how it is packaged, because atheists and agnostics exist within the Black community. There are some who regard religion as a negative force, especially in Black people's history, pointing to the way in which it was used to justify the enslavement of Africans and to make them acquiescent in their servitude.[2] Others regard religion as irrelevant, with no bearing on their lives, and only come into contact with it at church services for births, deaths and marriages. Then there are those for whom the inexorable march of science, philosophical rationalism and common sense renders anything of a religious nature pure foolishness. These men and women regard following any religion as a sign of a reluctance to come to terms with human progress.

Since the 1920s, a number of prominent Black intellectuals have become communists, and have adopted materialist ideas which regard religion as, in Karl Marx's expression, an 'opiate'. Caribbean intellectuals and writers such as Claude McKay, C. L. R. James and George Padmore were some of the earliest exponents of these beliefs. The Black Power movement in the US in the 1960s was primarily secular, with many adherents such as Stokely Carmichael, Huey P. Newton, Bobby Seale, Angela Y. Davis and Kathleen Cleaver preferring progress through direct action to more passive Christian attitudes.[3] And those who joined revolutionary organizations in the UK such as the former MP Bernie Grant,[4] Bernard Coard and Darcus Howe were not religiously minded, often considering faith to be an obstacle to revolutionary change.

However, Anthony Reddie's association between Black people and faith remains true and is almost a default position. In many societies Christianity is the faith of choice; in Britain it is estimated that as many as eight out of ten Black people describe themselves as Christian.[5] While it would be wrong to suggest that all these men and women are 'born again' Christians, church attendance is particularly high within Britain's Black community.

Walking Away from Church

Anecdotal evidence suggests that many Black people who convert or revert to Islam have previously had some association with the churches. Some of them were regular attenders at Anglican, Roman Catholic or Pentecostal churches and may have been regarded as the next generation of stewards, choir members, deacons and, in some cases, pastors. For others, their connection to the church was through parents or other relatives who were churchmen and women, sometimes pastors or leaders within their churches who, no doubt, had dreams of their children following them.

For a number of reasons that will be explained in this chapter, many members of this younger generation stopped attending church during their teens or early twenties. My research suggests that they still maintained their religious beliefs, but their ceasing of church attendance was a first and obvious sign that they were unhappy with their spiritual lives. When converts to Islam are questioned about their former Christianity they often appear more critical of the church than of the actual tenets of the Christian faith. It is therefore important to look at the churches to find out why an increasing number of Black people are turning their backs on them. It is also vitally important to examine the Rastafari movement, which, a generation or two ago, was providing the same kind of counter-cultural religious alternative that Islam is providing today.

A great many Black converts to Islam are of an African-Caribbean heritage and hence hail from a region where the church has been entrenched since Caribbean enslavement. The 'Black church' in Britain is generally regarded as one of the real Black 'success stories' and arguably the 'most cohesive representation of the Black British community'[6]. Figures produced by the Christian statistic-gathering organization Christian Research suggest that Black churches have the fastest-growing congregations in Britain – a fact which led one Church of England bishop to suggest that 'had it not been for the Black Majority Churches... the Christian cause in many of our cities would have looked a lost one'.[7] For the purposes of this book I will be using the term Black Majority Church or BMC because of its inclusiveness – it embraces both Black people in historic denominations and those in denominations that emerged after 1948 and are invariably Pentecostal.

Academics such as Tony Sewell link the birth of the Black church to the arrival of the SS *Empire Windrush* in 1948.[8] BMCs certainly celebrated the sixtieth anniversary of the *Windrush* in June 2008 with services and other events. However, as Mark Sturge points out in *Look What the Lord Has Done*, Britain's Black

Christian heritage did not begin in 1948, but is hundreds of years old, and was particularly strong during the eighteenth and nineteenth centuries, when Atlantic slavery was still in existence. He argues: 'The Black Christian presence within the British church was not a passive one... Black Christians were actively occupied not only as evangelists and missionaries, but also as important agents seeking to bring about transformation within the church and society.'[9] Many of those working to effect change were particularly involved in the campaign to end the transatlantic slave trade and the enslavement of Black people in the Americas. In his excellent book, *Voices from Slavery*, the Nigerian-born Anglican priest Chigor Chike highlights the contributions of figures such as Ignatius Sancho, Ukawsaw Gronniosaw, Olaudah Equiano and Ottobah Cugoano, alongside their White counterparts, to agitate for abolition in Britain.[10]

Black British Churches

Although Britain was a prime mover in the slave trade, during the eighteenth century many runaway enslaved Africans were under the impression that once they arrived on these shores and were baptized they would be free.[11] As a result, scores of Africans were baptized at St Margaret's Church in Westminster, swelling the size of the congregation. The academic David Killingray has produced some excellent work looking at Black Christians in Georgian, Victorian and Edwardian Britain, exploring the lives of Mary Prince, Phyllis Wheatley, Thomas Birch Freeman, Joseph Jackson Fuller, Samuel Barber, Peter Standord, Celestine Edwards and Dr Harold Moody.[12] These men and women can be considered early pioneers of BMCs in that they sought to incorporate aspects of their religious and cultural heritage into the places where they worshipped – with varying degrees of success.

Black people living in the British colonies in Africa and the Caribbean continued to travel to Britain and London out of a sense of wanderlust, to obtain an education and skills, or to escape the grinding poverty that existed in their homelands. The great Jamaican Marcus Garvey, who travelled to Britain in the spring of 1912, was one of many Black people of faith who came in search of an education (and, in Garvey's case, a mission in life). A few months after his arrival, Garvey's sister, Indiana, joined him in London. Indiana was a fellow believer and her church experiences would mirror those of later generations of Black Britons. We are told that on one occasion, when 'sitting alone amongst a sea of white faces in the local church, she suffered quietly in her discomfort; after the service, she attracted the unsubtle attention of the congregation who were delighted with the opportunity she presented to test their pseudo-scientific racial theories. At the end of one service, "the minister's daughter asked where she had hidden her tail!".'[13]

Other Black people came to Britain around this time to enlist as soldiers to defend king and country during the First World War. The British West Indies regiment, 'whose rank and file were almost entirely Black',[14] recruited 14,000 men who saw active service in France, Italy and the Middle East;[15] they 'lost 1,250 men and were awarded over sixty medals'.[16] Many servicemen decided to stay in Britain after the war.

Notwithstanding this history, the arrival of the SS *Empire Windrush* and the migration that followed were unparalleled in Britain. A fair proportion of the Black people who travelled to Britain during this time were regular churchgoers and were keen to continue their devotions in British churches. Church should have been the one 'known among a multitude of unknowns'.[17] Much has been written about the churches' response to these Black Christian arrivals, which swung between British reserve and outright racism. The experiences of Io Smith, who was one of Britain's foremost Black Christian leaders, typify this: 'The first place I visited was a church, but nobody said, "Welcome". Everybody stared at me as if I was some strange person from

Mars or something. When the service was finished I didn't get a handshake. Nobody came out to me and said, "Come again".'[18] Many others faced greetings that were far from Christian. In his book *Cold Arrival: Life in a Second Homeland*, Steve Stephenson writes: 'I recalled in the early days turning up at places and being told we are not letting any of you in tonight. I had similar experiences in the church. On the first and second Sunday we were made welcome. On the third Sunday we were met at the door and told to make our visits less frequent. We got the message and did not return.'[19]

The churches should have been a safe haven from the racism and ignorance faced by Black people when they first came to this country; lamentably, many were not. It would be wrong to suggest that the churches wholly failed Black people during this era because there were good examples of excellent practice in London and Birmingham. Likewise, the former British Council of Churches (BCC) was one of the most progressive institutions in considering how to ensure that church and society met the myriad needs of Black migrants. But ideas were one thing, and the reality was another. Many Black people were forced to establish their own places of worship. As the former Evangelical Alliance General Director Joel Edwards points out, racism was not the only reason for the birth of Black churches. He argues that, 'Black churches came into being to fulfil spiritual, social and cultural needs which would otherwise have gone unmet – and the African and Caribbean church in the UK is an indication of God's ability to meet a people's need through their own ministry to themselves.'[20]

However, it is important to note that for every Black person who left the historic churches to join a newly formed 'Black' one, two stayed to fight for change within the existing church. Academics such as Dr Anthony Reddie have written widely about these developments and the emergence of the racial justice movement and Black theology as a response to racism in church – and society.[21] Those Black people who went on to establish their own places of worship first met 'for prayer and fellowship in a home, sometimes moving from house to house... After a while the home would become too small, and a community school or church hall would be booked. The next step was to purchase a building of their own as numbers grew...'[22] Some of the first Pentecostal churches established by Black Christians in Britain were transplanted from the Caribbean, such as the Church of God in Christ (COGIC) and the New Testament Church of God (NTCOG), which were established in Britain in the late 1940s and early 1950s respectively, providing believers with some of the spirit and soul they had experienced in the Caribbean.

There is evidence that these churches really began to develop in the early 1960s with the growth of the Black population. It was around this time that 'race' became a major issue in mainstream politics. According to one author, '[Black] churchgoers perceived in the attitudes of White Christians the same attitudes which were evident in some politicians. The mainstream denominations lost [Black] membership and adherents and the Black church gained in almost proportionate numbers.'[23] The mainstream churches, through the auspices of the BCC, responded to perceived racism with a number of initiatives – usually the commissioning of reports which were filed in someone's drawer after publication. However, it was during this era that both Black and White church activists, such as the Revd Wilfred Wood, the former Bishop of Croydon, Gus John, the Revd Tony Holden and the Revd David Haslam came to the fore in the struggle for racial justice. Bishop Wood was one of the founders of the Committee for Black Anglican Concerns and was a pioneer in the Black Supplementary School sector and the Black Housing Association movement.[24] And progressive White Christians established the Community and Race Relations Unit (CRRU) in 1971 to champion the issue of racial justice in church and society. The CRRU examined structures within the historic denominations and argued for greater inclusion of Black and Asian faces within leadership as well as campaigning against the government's policy on immigration and asylum.[25]

Leadership

The pastor or 'man of God' has always been a seminal figure within the Black community. In Britain, many of the first pastors combined their clerical duties with full-time jobs owing to the straitened circumstances of many churches. These men – initially they were all male – combined their spiritual role as preacher with those of resident social worker, psychologist and general confidants to parishioners and those in the community. For many Pentecostal leaders emphasis was placed on an indwelling of the Holy Spirit rather than intellectual knowledge, and it is still the situation that pastors in Pentecostal churches are often not as theologically knowledgeable as those in the historic denominations. Having said that, because they come from the communities they serve, such pastors have few problems identifying with congregations and their needs. And pastors in these BMCs are usually Black – whereas the historic churches still struggle to achieve Black leadership commensurate with congregational numbers.[26] Such churches are also important because they have provided one of the few opportunities for Black people to exercise power in some capacity and have a degree of autonomy over their lives.[27]

According to Mark Sturge, in the 1970s 'the greatest challenge facing the BMCs was the new generation of young people who needed nurturing'.[28] Children born in the Caribbean, but who came to Britain to join their parents during this time, found it very difficult to settle in a new environment and engage with the peculiarities of British culture. Like their peers who were born in Britain, they grappled with the prevalent racism evident from the police on the street and hostile teachers in the classroom. For Black youths, the church was more the problem than the solution; the historic denominations were reluctant to acknowledge the topic of race, and continued to frustrate Black potential within their structures. The newly formed Pentecostal churches, which were by nature socially conservative, were more likely to blame youth themselves rather than societal ills for the problems faced by young people.

The Challenge of Rastafari

It was in this confused situation that Rastafari started to take root in Britain. According to the academic Anthony Reddie, 'Rastafari as a movement of cultural and political protest became a potent symbol for the alienated mass of disaffected and marginalized Black youth in 1970s Britain. It made Black youth feel they had a legitimate place in society, and gave them the confidence to reject the status quo and the biased self-serving thoughts of mainstream society.'[29] In the previous chapter we looked briefly at the role of Rastafari, but it is worth exploring the beliefs and ideology of this movement in more detail, as they have been instrumental in advancing notions of resistance and anti-establishment attitudes within religious movements.

History shows that Rastafari not only gave British youth in the 1970s a sense of belonging, it inverted the prevalent negative connotations of what it meant to be Black and African.[30] Rastafari told Black youths they were exiles from 'Zion' or Africa, and that they should be proud of their African roots. This was in stark contrast to the perceptions of their parents' generation, who appeared more comfortable with using the terms 'West Indian' and 'coloured',[31] and felt uncomfortable with using 'Black' and 'African'.

According to Tony Sewell, the Rastafari movement was part of a wider Afrocentric and Black consciousness that began in the USA in the 1960s and had spread through Britain in the following decade.[32] Working through reggae music and its great exponent, the Jamaican-born Bob Marley, Rasta championed the 'sufferahs' and 'downpressed' (the poor and oppressed) in 'Babylon' (any Western country where Black people suffered).[33]

Such Rasta language became the argot of Black youth, much to the displeasure of their parents for whom Rastas were ungodly, lawless people.

Although parents may not have liked it, their offspring embraced Rasta in great numbers in Britain. These young people were followers of a monotheistic faith which emerged in Jamaica in the early 1930s following the coronation of Ras Tafari, who became Emperor Haile Selassie I of Ethiopia.[34] Rastafari has no formal creed and there are significant differences between different groups, which may reflect the fact that Rastafari has very few theologians and social theorists to codify and systematize its beliefs.[35] What we do know is that some people in Jamaica juxtaposed the events of 1930 with biblical texts which 'gave concrete proof' to believers that Selassie I was indeed the reincarnated Christ, the returned or new messiah, the Black Redeemer come to release the children of Israel out of Egypt.[36] It can be argued that the roots of Rastafari are traceable to George Liele's Ethiopian Baptist Church that was formed in Jamaica in the 1780s to meet the spiritual needs of enslaved Africans. Liele's church proved the catalyst for other syncretic denominations which fused aspects of Christianity with traditional African beliefs. These churches also identified positively with Africa or 'Ethiopia', as the whole continent was often known, with some holding the belief that believers would either return to Africa, like the biblical Hebrews returning to Zion after exile in Babylon (the West), or that Africa would 'raise up a modern-day Moses to lead them out of the wilderness'.[37]

The emergence of Marcus Garvey in the early part of the twentieth century witnessed the appearance of a mass movement (UNIA) dedicated to instilling pride and dignity into Black people and championing the cause of 'Ethiopianism' – 'the generic term for the promotion of a Negro ethical ideal and African autonomy'.[38] As a student of African history, Garvey was acutely aware of the situation in Ethiopia, and peppered his speeches in the USA and Jamaica with the phrase 'Princes shall come out of Egypt' – a reference which some connected to the eventual coronation of Ras Tafari in 1930.[39] It was said that Selassie was a direct descendant of the union between King Solomon and the Queen of Sheba and that he was crowned as 'King of Kings, Lord of Lords, the Conquering Lion of the Tribe of Judah'.[40]

Rastafari Leaders

There is little doubt that Haile Selassie's coronation generated great excitement among Jamaica's Bible-reading urban and rural poor, for whom it was the fulfilment of biblical prophecy signifying the end of their exile and misery. One result of the news headlines in the *Jamaica Gleaner* newspaper was the emergence of a number of preachers who espoused their versions of what is now known as Rastafari. Preachers such as Leonard Howell, H. Archibald Dunkley, Robert Hinds and Joseph Nathaniel fused aspects of African-Christian syncretism such as Myal and Pukumina with Freemasonry, esoteric Eastern mysticism and even occultism in their initial message of Rastafari.[41] They used the term 'Jah' for God, frequently with reference to Selassie, and believed in the redemption of Black people by a Black saviour. These preachers gathered around them a number of acolytes, who were usually described as 'brethren' or 'brothermen', and who studied their pronouncements in newly established 'Rasta' communes.

Italy's invasion of Ethiopia in 1935 enraged Rasta sympathizers, who regarded it as the intrusion of corrupt Rome into the Ethiopian Zion. The invasion helped to galvanize support for the Rasta cause by encouraging hesitant supporters to become fully fledged believers in the struggle to rid the fatherland from an imperial power.[42] Some Rastas were even prepared to sail to Africa to fight for their brethren.

The movement began to grow in post-war Jamaica, where hurricanes, diseases and poor harvests decimated the sugar-cane and banana industries. The failure of these cash crops forced ·

many to abandon rural life and head for the capital, Kingston, where they swelled the numbers of those living in the run-down areas of 'downtown' and Western Kingston.[43] Many of these urban poor were attracted to the message of Rastafari, which often preached 'redemption' and freedom to the descendants of enslaved Africans if they returned to Africa.

This doctrine was a rehash of ideas promulgated by Marcus Garvey, whose slogan, 'Africa for the Africans', was a clarion call for Blacks in the West to return to their ancestral home to recolonize and redevelop the continent.[44] In Jamaica preachers such as Claudius Henry encouraged followers to gather at Kingston harbour and wait for ships that would take them back to Africa.[45] Although these ships never docked, the movement was not discredited as a result of such outlandish prophecies. In fact, it continued to grow, and in 1960 a government-backed research project carried out by academics from the University of the West Indies was launched to investigate the beliefs and ideas of Jamaica's Rasta community. These academics identified the central teachings as being the divinity of Haile Selassie (Rastafari), the crucial importance of Africa as motherland of all Black people, and Black redemption via repatriation to Africa.[46]

What really transformed the Rasta movement was the visit of Haile Selassie to Jamaica in April 1966. Expectant Rasta brethren went to the airport to welcome His Imperial Majesty and, according to one account:

> There was utter pandemonium when the Emperor's jet broke through the cloud cover and descended to the runway. From nowhere a flock of snow-white doves materialised and flew over the impatient throng. When assembled Rastafarians beheld the imperial lion on the plane's fuselage, thousands rampaged through police lines and swarmed all over the plane even as the engines were being shut down... The air was full of singing

and chanting and the recitation of psalms. Hundreds
prostrated themselves on the tarmac and waited for the
Emperor to come out.[47]

Staring from his window, Selassie appeared so taken aback by this
welcome that he was reluctant to disembark from the plane. It took
the intervention of the Rastafari elder Mortimer Planno to coax
His Imperial Majesty from his jet. A tearful Selassie eventually
disembarked with Planno, and when he began waving to the
crowd some believers claimed they saw stigmata on his palms –
the marks of the crucifixion indicating that he was the Christ.[48]

In what became a coup for the Rasta movement, Planno
subsequently accompanied the Emperor on many of his official
engagements in Jamaica, much to the chagrin of the Jamaican
establishment, who considered Rastafari *persona non grata*. Until
that point Rastas had been a persecuted minority who were
shunned by society – especially those who wore dreadlocks and
smoked ganja or marijuana. The Jamaican police were encouraged
to keep Rastas from public view and would often arrest them
on sight if they were seen on the streets of Kingston. The police
used old vagrancy laws and obsolete public order offences as
pretexts for their heavy-handed actions. Once locked up, a Rasta
was often 'trimmed' – shorn of his locks – and fed a diet of pork
and other 'non-ital' (taboo) foods. The intention was to use every
opportunity to belittle and undermine a movement that was seen
as a threat to an insecure post-Independence Jamaica.

It is difficult to ascertain what the Emperor truly made of
his visit to Jamaica and the veneration of the Rastafari. We do
know that Haile Selassie was associated with the Ethiopian
Coptic Church, which is part of the Orthodox tradition and is
considered one of the oldest Christian presences in Africa.[49] As
such, he held Trinitarian Christian beliefs which meant he would
reject any suggestion of his own divinity. It is suggested that his
reluctance to disembark from his plane was due to the deification

he was being afforded by Rastas. The academic William D. Spencer has suggested that he was so appalled by the Rastas' misinterpretation of biblical prophecy and his own divinity that he sent his own Orthodox priest to Jamaica to teach them the scriptures.[50]

Rastafari was undoubtedly benefited by the visit of Haile Selassie to Jamaica, but it was also assisted by the emergence of reggae music in the late 1960s and the rise of the Black consciousness movement. Reggae songs espousing Black solidarity and a pride in all things African also encouraged a resurgence of the ideas espoused by Marcus Garvey, and those of a new figure, the dynamic Guyanese lecturer Dr Walter Rodney. In the mid 1960s Rodney had moved to Jamaica to take up a teaching post at the University of the West Indies, but his extra-curricular activities involved discussions with Jamaica's urban poor and dispossessed, in particular the Rastas whose cause he appeared to champion in lectures and writings. Rodney's brilliance was to connect the conditions of poor Black Jamaicans to the White imperialism that dominated the island. He also championed both formal and informal education among Kingston's urban masses as a means of liberation.[51]

Although Rodney was not a Rasta himself he gave the movement academic gravitas and his ideas also attracted middle-class students and dissident intellectuals.[52] Such was the concern over Rodney's interest in Rastafari and Black consciousness that the Jamaican government, led at the time by a Black Prime Minister, Hugh Lawson Shearer, refused to allow him to re-enter the island after he attended a conference in Canada in October 1968. Rastafari, reggae artists and Rodney supporters reacted to this affront to civil liberties by organizing demonstrations in Kingston.[53] And leading Jamaican singers, some of whom were Rastas, cut records in support of Dr Rodney which were subsequently banned by the state-owned radio station.

By the 1970s Rasta and reggae had become such a potent socio-cultural force in Jamaica that politicians began to embrace it and use it as a campaigning tool. In the 1972 Jamaican General Election, the People's National Party leader, Michael Manley, swept to power on the back of Rasta singer Delroy Wilson's catchy song 'Better Must Come'.[54] On the campaign trail he was often accompanied by the leading reggae singer, producer and political activist Clancy Eccles, who organized concerts and lined up singers to show their support for Manley.[55]

The rise of Bob Marley to superstardom catapulted the Rastafari movement to international fame. Marley was an adherent of the Twelve Tribes of Israel movement, one of several religious associations that had emerged with their own interpretation of Rastafari spiritual and social tenets. His 1970s output with the group the Wailers on Chris Blackwell's Island Records label helped to redefine reggae and bring the Jamaican sound to every part of the globe, making Marley the 'King of Reggae' in the process.[56] His music made him the leading advocate of Rastafari and placed him alongside Marcus Garvey as an icon of the faith. Marley's role was particularly important after the official passing of Haile Selassie in 1975, when the singer contended in his songs and numerous interviews that, far from being dead, 'Jah Lives' in another form and dispensation. This not only reassured the brethren but also brought new adherents to the faith. A failed assassination attempt in 1976 saw the reggae star decamp to London for almost two years to avoid the rising political violence that was overtaking the island and into which he was increasingly drawn.[57] Although Marley professed political neutrality, politicians from the two Jamaican parties were keen either to secure his endorsement or to make sure the other party did not obtain it.

Natty Dread in Brixton

Marley's sojourn in London undoubtedly influenced the music and religious ideas of Black British artists such as Aswad, Steel Pulse, the Cimarrons, Delroy Washington, Misty (in Roots) and Matumbi. According to the academic Dick Hebdige (writing in 1987):

> Most of the British reggae groups are Rasta-influenced at the moment. And many of the songs reflect the familiar themes of Jamaican reggae – Haile Selassie, Ethiopia, Back to Africa and so on. But at the same time, the lyrics often refer quite directly to the conditions facing Black people in Britain. For instance, songs by Aswad like 'Three Babylon' and 'Can't Walk the Streets' deal with the problems of police harassment and the notorious 'sus' law (the Suspected Persons Act, whereby the police can arrest anyone suspected of planning to commit a crime without any evidence).[58]

Many Black British youths could identify with the social message of these British reggae groups because they were singing about their own experiences. The more conscious Rasta singers and groups would not only highlight problems facing Black youth but sing about how Jah or God would provide succour and provision for the oppressed, righteous youth. It should come as no surprise that Black youth were attracted to this message in huge numbers because no one else at that time, either within or outside the Black community, had any answers to the predicament facing them.[59] This was an era lacking any government policy to deal humanely with youths who felt they had been tossed on the scrap heap and a generation of Black British youth, left to its own devices, naturally turned toward a faith that was the preserve of the marginalized in Jamaica.

During the 1970s and 1980s BMCs simply ignored both the issues facing Black youth and the challenge of Rastafari. Evidence of this myopia can be seen in the numbers of reflections, histories and reports written for the churches which fail to mention Rastafari or analyse its impact on Black youth. The academic Dr

Robert Beckford, a Black British Pentecostal Christian, suggests that many of his parents' generation considered Rasta politics 'anti-Christian' and 'rebellious', and Rastas themselves 'dirty'.[60] Beckford has accused some BMCs of 'chasing after the aspiring Black middle class, adopting prosperity doctrines to justify their status and augment conservative behaviour while breaking its connection with the Black masses'.[61] In another of his books, *Dread and Pentecostal*, Beckford argues that Rastafari has much to teach the BMCs with regard to speaking prophetically about social and political life in Britain.[62]

In the 1970s some Black Christians singularly failed to engage with politics, preferring to adopt a lofty spiritual elevation over the 'things of this earth'. These included issues directly affecting their communities such as immigration control, the 'sus' laws, racial attacks and racism *per se*. They still felt comfortable with images of a White Saviour being displayed in a church full of Black worshippers, and the reading of biblical commentaries and the singing of hymns which depreciated anything dark or black. Consequently the churches had very little credibility for many Black youths at that time.

Some churches were more concerned with a person's appearance than their reasons for attending in the first place. In 1991 I had the misfortune to witness a disagreement between church stewards and a young man wearing a 'Tam O'Shanter' hat at a Baptist church in Tulse Hill, south London. The young man walked out after ten minutes of heated argument over his refusal to remove the hat. He was not a Rasta, and one can imagine his reception if he had been.

African Christianity

The last few decades have seen the emergence of churches transplanted from Africa as increasing numbers of West Africans arrive in Britain as students, settlers, asylum seekers and so on.[63] Over 80 per cent of this African community live in London,[64] and there are now huge numbers of African Pentecostal churches in the capital. The Redeemed Christian Church of God (RCCOG), which has its roots in Nigeria, is arguably the largest African BMC in Britain, with membership in its tens of thousands. Many places of worship have grown up to meet the spiritual needs of newly arrived African brethren, but some combine this activity with missionary work that aims to reverse the trend toward secularism in Britain and 'bring back the gospel' to the country which first brought the 'Good News' to parts of Africa and the Caribbean centuries ago.[65]

The African churches have had a tremendous impact on the spiritual climate of this country and the real exponential growth within Britain's BMCs is among these African brethren rather than among Caribbean-derived churches.[66] When HRH Prince Charles and his wife, Camilla, the Duchess of Cornwall, chose to celebrate the prince's fifty-ninth birthday at Jesus House Church in Brent Cross, London, it was a sign that these churches had come of age. (Jesus House, which is part of the RCCOG, is a large multi-ministry mega-church which attracts worshippers in their thousands. [67])

It can be argued that although they are important spiritually, the African churches have yet to make a real socio-cultural impact in this country through robust initiatives to tackle issues facing Black people in the UK. If anything, these churches tend to be even more socially conservative than their Caribbean-derived counterparts and prefer to eschew all talk of 'Blackness' and racism.[68] Certain larger 'Black' denominations prefer to steer clear of the BMC label and call themselves 'International churches'. This supposedly symbolizes the universalism of the gospel and the diverse nationalities of their worshippers – an array of national flags is sometimes on display inside the church building. But on closer inspection the 'internationalism' in these churches is largely limited to various African countries. Although Christians should embrace diversity and inclusiveness, they should not use this as a way of denying their own identities. Churches that are grappling with their identity in this way will undoubtedly struggle to develop a strategic and cogent response to the issues facing their Black youth.

Faith and Political Engagement

Academics such as Robert Beckford and Ronald Nathan are correct in calling for greater political engagement from BMCs, because they are the backbone of the Black community and everyone looks to the church – rightly or wrongly – to find answers to the problems facing the community. Where one may disagree with Beckford, in particular, is in the choice of 'Dread theology' as the appropriate muse to influence BMCs in this country.

The death of Bob Marley in 1981 robbed Rasta of its most influential champion, and the movement went into decline among its original adherents after that date. While it retains a global presence, Rasta is no longer the socio-cultural and political force among Black youth that it once was. Although it would be wrong to suggest that the Rastafari movement is no longer rebellious or counter-cultural, aspects of Rasta symbolism and culture such as the red, green and gold colours, the 'Lion of Judah', dreadlock hairstyles and Bob Marley's music have become part of the mainstream and have lost some of their cultural power. Reggae morphed into raggamuffin and dance hall music after Marley's death, which appear more interested in materialism, misogyny and murder than roots and culture and Black people.

Today it is Islam which has the potential to provide a counter-cultural, social force among Black Britons. Like Rastafari before it, it appeals to the zeitgeist with regard to the socio-economic and political situation of Black Britons, especially the young.[69] The following chapters will explore why so many young people are embracing this faith.

Chapter 4

Taking a Stand: Responses to Black Community Issues

Community Matters

Although the *Windrush* generation worked valiantly to establish solid foundations in Britain, the subsequent generations have struggled, for a number of reasons, to build on those foundations. A major factor in this struggle has been the racism, both systematic and unwitting, which continues to blight Black lives in Britain.

For instance, a recent education report argued that 'Black Caribbean pupils are being subjected to institutional racism in English schools which can dramatically undermine their chances of academic success'. The research 'uncovered evidence that teachers are routinely under-estimating the abilities of some black pupils', and its findings 'add weight to the theory that low achievement among some black students is made worse because teachers don't expect them to succeed'.[1]

A disproportionate number of Black youngsters (three times the national average) are excluded from school before they have a chance to make the educational grade. Figures produced by the Office for Standards in Education reveal that 'nearly 70 per cent of school-age children sentenced for criminal offences have either been excluded from school or have persistently failed to attend school.'[2] Black communities are also on the sharp end of health policies which see 'Black groups up to 44 per cent more likely to be detained under the Mental Health Act compared to the average'.[3] Other health inequalities include a lack of provision for illnesses which disproportionately affect the Black community such as sickle-cell anaemia, age-related onset diabetes, high blood pressure and prostate cancer.

Moreover, even during the economic boom unemployment rates within Britain's Black community were considerably higher than the national average, which has made the struggle to break out of poverty all the more difficult.[4] This poverty and a lack of statutory provision have been cited as factors in the increase of 'gun and gang crime in deprived black communities'.[5]

Education

Black pupils are perennially failed by an education system that excludes them disproportionately and sees far too many leaving school without adequate qualifications. Although recent GCSE exam results reveal an improvement in the attainment of Black pupils, with 49.1 per cent of students having obtained five good grades in 2007 compared with 44.4 per cent in 2006, the figure for White children remains significantly higher at 59.5 per cent.[6] Moreover, every year 1,000 Black pupils are permanently excluded from school while nearly 30,000 receive a fixed-period exclusion.[7]

In 2000 alarming statistics of this kind forced the African and Caribbean Evangelical Alliance (ACEA) to admit that the 'church must enter the education debate' and do more to reverse the educational failure of Black pupils.[8] The ACEA's former General Director, Mark Sturge, has commented, 'We need to help children in great need whose lives are in danger of being bankrupted because of the failures of the education system.' He went on to suggest that: 'Black majority churches know they can make a difference. They can initiate and deliver change for the better. They are no longer prepared to delegate that fundamental responsibility to local authorities, national government or any other agency.'[9] In practice, however, it has been government and other agencies that have taken the lead in addressing the problems of Black education.

The ACEA's concerns were borne of a perceived lack of government action over a number of years. In 1985 the then Conservative government under Margaret Thatcher chose to shelve the findings of the Swann Report which, among other issues, looked at the education of Black pupils.[10] The report reinforced the views of Bernard Coard, a Grenadian-born, UK-based teacher, who in 1971 published a seminal pamphlet entitled: *How the West Indian Child is Made Educationally Subnormal in the British School System*. This work chastized government education policy and the way it was continuing to fail Black pupils. Coard's work has been followed by contributions from academics such as Professor Gus John, David Gilborn, Maude Blair, Jill Bourne, Tony Sewell, Heidi Mirza, Richard Majors and Robin Richardson, to name only a few.

Much of this research has now been adopted by what used to be the Department for Education and Skills and is currently the Department for Children, Schools and Families. The government-related Education Minority Achievement Service and the Aiming High: African Caribbean Achievement programme have their roots in the research and agitation of such academics. And the annual London Schools and Black Child conferences, established by the Labour MP for Hackney Diane Abbott as a response to the educational failure of Black pupils in her parliamentary constituency, have become a hub for discussion among those interested in raising the educational achievement of Black pupils.

There have also been sterling contributions from social policy think-tanks such as Race On The Agenda, whose *Inclusive Schools, Inclusive Society* blazed a trail in calling for 'holistic' responses to raising the attainment levels of Black pupils.[11] A number of British

Pan-African groups have established supplementary schools and other education projects based on Afrocentric models of parenting and rites of passage as responses to educational failure. Other education responses included the late Len Garrison's African and Caribbean Educational Resource (Acer), which was supported by the Inner London Education Authority. 'Acer also spawned a series of schemes for older children and young adults, the best known of which was the Young Penmanship awards for creative writing.'[12]

Mark Sturge's comments were prophetic and radical, and were calling on BMCs to recover their radical educational heritage: Black clergy established some of the first supplementary schools for Black pupils in Britain in the 1960s.[13] They have, however, largely gone unheeded. Although under his aegis ACEA established Making the Grade, an education conference for those working with Black pupils,[14] educational intervention by BMCs has been the exception rather than the rule. Apart from the National Black Boys Can Association initiative established by the Church of God of Prophecy, action has been largely limited to dissident voices on the margins of the churches calling for BMCs to establish 'Black church schools'. This suggestion would always be regarded as separatist and divisive and so such a proposal would never in practice go forward. Current BMC educational interventions are largely church-based and focus solely on young people connected to the congregation who are nurtured and prepared to take their GCSEs and A-levels at the local Church of England school.[15]

The National Black Boys Can Association (NBBCA) initiative, however, is an imaginative and progressive BMC response to a recognized need. NBBCA is 'a proactive, action-oriented initiative that aims to provide black boys with educational opportunity, valuable life-skills, and the self-esteem, confidence and determination to succeed'.[16] It has a franchise structure which has seen projects established around England, invariably in towns and cities with a sizeable Black population. Its work has seen a marked improvement in the attainment levels of Black pupils wherever an association is established and, according to service users, 'the concept is very well conceived, which actually links the aspirations of children and parents as well as their thinking'.[17]

Many older Black people grew up with the dictum 'Silver and gold will vanish away, but a good education will never decay!' What was true when they were young is still true today. Education is the bedrock for life and, while the work of BMCs in this area has been patchy, there is evidence that Black Muslims are increasingly making headway in both mainstream and supplementary schools. At one time the Nation of Islam (UK) ran two schools in the capital, one in west London, the other in south London. Muslim supplementary school education for children and adults, which includes copious amounts of Black history, is regarded as a tool to liberate Black minds.

Abdul Hashim teaches at a supplementary school just off the Old Kent Road in south-east London. He is critical of the church's involvement in efforts to raise attainment levels of Black pupils. He says:

> What I can't understand is that these churches own a whole heap of buildings around this part of London but they never use them for supplementary education. When we were looking to set up our school we really struggled to find suitable premises. We approached about five churches to use their facilities but none were interested. I wasn't sure whether they refused because they could see I was a Muslim [the school is not Muslim but non-religious] or that they didn't value what we were trying to do. Some said they needed the building for church work, but I know for a fact that nothing happens at that time and their doors are locked up.

Black Muslims are aware that children who are failed by the education system are more likely to fall into a life of crime and subsequently need the help of further projects to turn their lives around.

Church Responses to Social Issues

The churches have been slow to respond to the needs of those who have already dropped out of the education system, but, where they have, some initiatives have carried out excellent work. One example is the Street Pastors project, an inter-denominational church response to urban problems engaging with people on the streets to care, listen and dialogue.[18] The instigator of the project is the Revd Les Isaac, a former Rasta whose conversion to Christianity gave the BMCs some much-needed inspiration, relevance and credibility.[19] Isaac, who heads the charity the Ascension Trust, first began working as a Street Pastor in 2003, in some of the most challenging areas of Britain's inner cities. The results were amazing: 'In Southwark, South London, a nine-month police evaluation recorded up to a 95 per cent reduction in calls relating to public disorder whenever the Pastors were deployed.'[20] The Conservative Party leader David Cameron has said, 'It's absolutely fantastic the job the Street Pastors are doing… What we need is more people out in the community supporting the police, who can't do the job of beating antisocial behaviour on their own.'[21] Like the NBBCA, the Street Pastors initiative is a franchise-like project that is now found in many parts of the country, including in areas with few, if any, Black people.

Another church-inspired crime-reducing initiative that now operates at the national level is the Peace Alliance, which was started by the Revd Nims Obunge in the London borough of Haringey in 2001 and is dedicated to reducing violence and hate crime. The Peace Alliance led to the concept of London Peace Week, an annual week of high-profile events, initiatives and action to promote greater community cohesion, safety and peace across the capital. It is supported by the Metropolitan Police, the Mayor of London and virtually all the London boroughs.

The Bringing Hope project is a Christian charitable organization with similar ambitions to the Street Pastors initiative, 'working to transform and reform lives and communities influenced and impacted by the evils of anti-social behaviour resulting in negative lifestyles and outcomes'.[22]

Across the city, the PEERS project (Policing, Education, Employment, Rights and Self-esteem) provides guidance to young people between the ages of eleven and twenty-five with a practical toolkit of resources to help them develop their roles as active citizens in their local communities. PEERS was established several years ago by the Churches Commission for Racial Justice (now the Churches Racial Justice Network), following discussions with Neville Lawrence, the father of murdered teenager Stephen Lawrence. Although PEERS is not regarded as a Black project, many of its clients are Black.

The work of mentoring and inspiring young men to achieve their full potential is at the heart of the work of the Men's Room, which has its roots in the Church of God of Prophecy, and was established by Clive Lewis. The Men's Room works to 'help men discover their role in society, and to develop better men, husbands, lovers and fathers'.[23] Its day-to-day work involves providing an environment for intellectual and emotional challenge and fostering an atmosphere in which differences are seen as an opportunity for mature dialogue and debate.

Another African-Caribbean man named Lewis, this time Ray Lewis, was responsible for Eastside Young Leaders Academy (EYLA), which exists to nurture and develop the leadership potential of young African and Caribbean males, empowering them to become the next generation of successful leaders. It provides educational and emotional support for boys aged eight to eighteen, particularly those identified as being at risk of social exclusion.[24]

In 2008, African and Caribbean church leaders publicly launched the African Development Forum (ADF) to encourage Britain's African and Caribbean Christian community to become more actively involved in the issue of poverty in Africa. The ADF seeks to contribute to economic and social progress in Africa through education and advocacy activities.[25]

Central to many of these church-based initiatives is the Church of God of Prophecy, which, under the imaginative leadership of Bishop Wilton Powell, has become involved in a number of efficacious projects in the UK and abroad.[26] Its latest endeavour is the Renewal, Advancement, Financial Autonomy international development agency, which operates in the developing world, primarily in Africa, on particular regeneration projects including water and food security, micro enterprises, ICT, primary and secondary schooling, and support for people with HIV and AIDS.

The projects mentioned here address a range of socio-cultural issues within the Black community, and for every one mentioned, anecdotal evidence reveals that there are five or six more at a local or community level carrying out vital work with varying degrees of success.[27] However, if one considers the scale and the depth of the problems affecting the Black community in the areas of healthcare, employment, education, training and skills, housing, the criminal justice system, immigration and asylum, and civic engagement, it becomes apparent that there are not enough BMCs involved in real social action. It has been difficult to gauge the number of BMCs in Britain because one opens every week. The first edition of the *Black UK Christian Directory* suggests that it contains 'over 4,000 black-majority and black-led churches nationwide, plus thousands of organisations and individuals providing Christian services to the thriving BME [Black and Minority Ethnic] Christian community'.[28] Yet there is little doubt that hundreds, if not thousands, of BMCs of all sizes are not included in this publication. This underlines how few

BMCs are involved in social engagement, and calls into question the authority of church leaders to take on the role of community leaders and spokespeople.

Gun and Knife Crime

In July 2008 the ecumenical church bodies Churches Together in England and Churches Together in Britain and Ireland produced the groundbreaking report *Who Is My Neighbour? A Church Response to Social Disorder Linked to Gangs, Drugs, Guns and Knives*, a response to the recent upsurge in violent crime involving young people, gangs and weapons.[29] The report was spearheaded by Bishop Dr Joe Aldred, a stalwart of the Black-dominated Church of God of Prophecy, and primarily showcased the response of BMCs to problems affecting Britain's Black community, especially its youth. The report seeks to show how BMCs are willing to engage in social action and have ceased to ignore social problems.[30]

BMCs have responded to the upsurge in the numbers of youths killed by guns or knives between 2006 and 2008 with a new vigour. But *Who Is My Neighbour?* came a full decade after the Metropolitan Police established Operation Trident to investigate crimes linked to drugs and the activities of Jamaican 'Yardie' gangs.[31] It can be argued that the report should have appeared a decade earlier, when 'lateral violence' (a more useful term than the media expression 'Black on Black violence') was a low-level, if troubling, criminal activity within sections of the Black community.[32] What has changed during the decade of Operation Trident is that most of its work is now investigating the killing of Black teenagers by other Black teenagers.

Although many of the killings are gang-related, there have also been 'innocent' victims of gun and knife crime such as the Birmingham teenagers Charlene Ellis and Letisha Shakespeare, who were killed in a drive-by shooting on 2 January 2003.[33] These killings shocked the nation, and showed people that gun crime and gang violence could easily spill out of the enclaves where they had previously been contained into places where passers-by could be caught in the crossfire.

It can be argued that the age and innocence of these youngsters stunned the BMCs into action after years of apparent inactivity.[34] Many BMCs, like other socially conservative institutions, had fallen into the notion that all those caught up in criminal activities were somehow criminals, or known to criminals. And although both Charlene Ellis and Letisha Shakespeare had links to Pentecostal churches,[35] some Christians were still keen to point out that 'good church girls' should not have been roaming the streets late at night. And some were also less concerned because one of the girls had familial links to gang members.[36]

This kind of thinking has led to groups such as the Pan-African human rights organization Ligali to suggest that the BMCs'

> ... sanctimonious preaching or collective silence on issues such as education, deaths in custody, stop and search, gun crime, mental health, immigration, human rights abuses, capitalisation on African enslavement, the systematic failure of development programmes in Africa... has spoken volumes of the African churches' long term failure in providing substantive physical and economic resources to our community and authoritative, moral and spiritual leadership to African Christians.[37]

Although groups such as Ligali are no friends of BMCs, they do speak for a good many non-church people who see a long-standing reluctance among the BMCs to play a more strategic role in relation to the Black community's myriad socio-economic problems.

BMCs are often at the heart of the community geographically, but not emotionally or socially. Much of the initial wave of gun and knife crime took place in Black-owned or Black-run nightspots in towns and cities with large Black populations. These venues, which often date back decades, sprang up at a time when Black people were establishing their own entertainment places to compensate for the racist atmosphere and lack of cultural appeal of mainstream night-time entertainment. Like the Black churches, Black bars and clubs provided a cathartic release for those facing daily racism and other pressures. And unlike the churches they did not judge a person's suitability; as long as they had the entrance fee, they were free to patronize the establishment until 'rooster time'.

The recently released documentary film *Legacy in the Dust: The Four Aces Story*, directed by Winston Whitter, provides a snapshot of such Black nightclubs. The Four Aces was located in Dalston, east London, and was regarded as a premier attraction for Black revellers between the 1960s and 1990s.[38] However, the nightspot experienced a fair number of scuffles and incidents, some involving the police. Close by were several Pentecostal, Apostolic Pentecostal, Methodist, Baptist and Church of England churches.[39] For those attending Pentecostal churches or churches rooted in the 'Holiness' tradition one could not be a Saturday night sinner and a Sunday morning saint.[40] The two worlds were completely separate. Pastors would often remind their flocks that it is better to 'be a doorkeeper in the house of my God than dwell in the tents of wickedness', and that self-denial and sacrifice were at the heart of the Christian gospel.

If a person had frequented pubs and clubs prior to becoming a Christian, they were expected to renounce such activities on becoming a believer or being accepted into church membership. Saturday nights would now be spent in prayer or in preparation for Sunday service. Many churches began to offer their own brand of wholesome Saturday night entertainment, as a diversion for the frustrated, and an enticement for would-be believers. Of course, all such activity ended at a reasonable hour, enabling congregants to get a good night's sleep before morning service, where they would hear pastors respond to any trouble there might have been the previous night with advice-driven sympathy such as, 'It's a shame, but the young man would still be alive had he spent the evening praying.'[41]

It is important not to fall back on clichés or stereotypes when looking at BMCs and social action and political engagement. BMCs, like the Black community itself, are not homogenous groupings who think and act as if they had a single will. While BMCs invariably use scripture as the starting point for all spiritual and social engagement, those that also consider culture, tradition and context display a variety of responses to the world about them. However, some socially conservative BMCs still practise an almost complete withdrawal from everything taking place in the world. When the pastors of such churches turn their attention to earthly matters affecting their community, any attempt to resolve socio-economic and political problems is likely to be solely on the basis of prayer, and their overall tone is often judgmental, displaying little of Christ's compassion for the last, the least and the lost.

Prisons

One area that has come in for much scrutiny and criticism is prison ministry among incarcerated Black people. The more progressive BMCs carry out some form of outreach work with prisoners – the content and efficacy of such work has not been examined, but the programmes do exist. However, given that 'Black prisoners account for the largest number of minority ethnic prisoners and their numbers are rising',[42] and given that there is a biblical mandate (Matthew 25) to visit those who are in gaol, one would expect more to have carried out this function.

The *Black UK Christian Directory* 2008 provides an insight into the mindset and preoccupations of the BMCs. Styled as the essential guide to Britain's thriving BMCs and Christian community, it not only lists the most prominent BMCs, but also offers a comprehensive register of organizations and businesses offering services to them – everything from jewellers, IT, catering, clothing and fashion to choirs, pilgrimages and church suppliers.[43] The only entry under 'prisons' lists the Prison Fellowship of England, a mainstream evangelical grouping which carries out the lion's share of prison ministry. Evidence suggests that Prison Fellowship of England is doing a good job in this area, but there is undoubtedly a need for an organization catering to the particular socio-cultural and spiritual needs of Black people – given both the scale of Black incarceration and the increasing numbers of Black prisoners with mental health problems. Yet, at a meeting in Brixton, south London, in May 2005 dealing with gun crime, one pastor rose to his feet and, pointing angrily in the direction of the prison, asserted, 'Britain's prisons were not built with Black people in mind, so no right-minded Black man should find himself there.'

This unrealistic and inhumane attitude is in stark contrast to that of Muslim groups in Britain, who see prison almost as a recruiting ground. Many prisons in London not only have Muslim chaplains, they also receive regular visits from groups and individuals who offer support to those whose mistakes have left them behind bars. Moreover, these Muslim programmes are clearly successful since they often employ former prisoners – men who can empathize with prisoners and help them both survive the soul-destroying experience of prison and stay out after release. As Muslims, they naturally point to Islam as the source of inspiration and strength which has enabled them to overcome these trials. However, it can be argued that it is more often the support network at their mosque that makes the real difference. These places offer outreach workers, counselling for dependency problems and strong peer-to-peer mentoring for new converts. Although this system is not as well recognized, or well funded, as that of the United States, it performs serious remedial work that treats the mind, body and soul.

Criticism of the Black Majority Churches

The previous chapter discussed the phenomenal growth of African-derived BMCs and the way they have transformed Britain spiritually. However, it is debatable whether these churches have had a similar impact on the cultural and political environment, especially with regard to Black communities. Statistics for London reveal that continental Africans living in Britain are in socio-economic situations similar to, if not worse than, those of their brothers and sisters from the Caribbean.[44] Yet very few are involved in efforts to ensure that those working in entry-level occupations in the service sector, such as cleaning and security work, get a fair day's wage.

Ibrahim Hassan is a Muslim convert from Tower Hamlets, east London, who has been involved in the London Citizens initiative, which campaigns for a living wage for London's low-paid workers. He says:

> I was tasked to work with churches in the London borough of Newham and Tower Hamlets because our research showed a lot of their worshippers were doing low-paid jobs. I couldn't believe the number who said it wasn't important to them. I really couldn't believe it. In the end, what I had to do was change tack. My parents go to one of those churches where people throw a tenth of their cash into the plate, I think they call it a tithe or something like that. I used to tell these churches that if they supported our campaign their worshippers would have more cash to throw in the collection plate. I must admit that I got a better response after that.

Another Muslim with a criticism of these churches is Yasmin Mohammed, a British-born Muslim convert living in Enfield. She says:

113

My sister Chantelle went to one of those 'clap hand churches' [African Pentecostal] and she met this guy from Nigeria. They got really close, but the problem was that he was an asylum seeker or illegal immigrant, either way he didn't have the right to stay here. He was getting all this hassle from the government. They used to arrest him and stuff. Anyway, while this was happening his church wouldn't do nothing. They wouldn't help him at all with his lawyers or MP. In the end they sent him back home. My sister was devastated. She left the church. The worst thing was that they had a whole heap of them like this in that church. If the police ever visited there they'd have a field day.

This criticism may appear a little harsh, since the church in question could not necessarily have responded to this man's needs. But evidence suggests that a good number of African-born Christians have been affected by the tightening of Britain's immigration and asylum laws. Despite this, the BMCs show little interest in these issues, although there is no shortage of African Christians engaged in the legal profession who might be asked to help in this vital work.

It has been argued that BMCs are the most coherent, dynamic and successful representatives of the Black community as a whole.[45] Many church leaders in cities such as London, Birmingham and Manchester have congregations in the hundreds, and sometimes in the thousands.[46] Very few non-church Black community leaders can claim to speak for such large constituencies. Consequently BMC pastors are often the first people to whom government, local authorities, the police and schools turn as default representatives or spokespeople for the Black community. This is analogous to the situation in the United States where, over the last fifty years, the Black church has provided a key leadership role within the huge African-American community.[47]

However, unlike the USA, Britain has never produced leaders like Martin Luther King or Jesse Jackson – though there has always been a clamour for Black British leaders of this stature. It can be argued that no other minority ethnic community in Britain is as fixated on having 'community leaders' as the Black community, and it has consequently allowed unqualified individuals to fill the void, beginning with the Muslim convert Michael de Freitas or Michael X in the 1960s – see Chapter 5.[48]

It should come as no surprise that those in decision-making positions approach Black pastors to speak on behalf of the Black community: they are accessible and usually available (except on Sundays). Most full-time pastors can move dates in their diaries for meetings with politicians or interviews with the press. Some community leaders have an innate distrust of the police and politicians and are reluctant to meet with them, but pastors are more inclined to do so because of the reconciliatory nature of their work. Indeed the question arises as to whether, when they are called to meetings with key decision-makers, they may become too conciliatory and fail to convey the passion, hurt or fear of those they claim to represent. A more fundamental question posed by pastors fulfilling this role, however, is whether being a representative of a church qualifies them to speak for the community.

According to the theologian Ronald A. Nathan, 'Black youth's involvement in African spirituality, Rastafarianism and the Nation of Islam does not point to laziness or a lack of spiritual discipline but a choice based on relevance.'[49] One person who believes that the churches are no longer relevant is the educator and entertainer Leo Muhammad, who found national fame in the BBC's popular television sketch show *The Real McCoy*.[50] Muhammad, who joined the Nation of Islam in the early 1990s, says:

> As a small child in Jamaica I always knew there was
> something not quite right about Christianity... I

remember smelling the strong scent of whiskey on the Caucasian vicar's breath. Which perhaps had something to do with it. I got into martial arts and dabbled in Taoism… I was a Rastafarian for a while. Being a Rastafarian was a religion for me but when I realized that it was simply a fashion statement to others I became disillusioned.[51]

Slavery

Other Muslims interviewed for this book have juxtaposed the historic churches' role in slavery with the racism faced by their parents to condemn those churches' failure to address questions of social justice. Abdul Wasim Aziz, a forty-something Muslim currently living in Streatham, states:

In 2007 the church had a chance to say something serious about what it did during slavery and talk about racism in church against Black people. What did they do? Well, they put on this service in the [Westminster] Abbey with the Queen and politicians and a whole heap of hypocrites. All they did was praise Wilberforce and his White friends for ending something they started. No wonder brother Toyin [Agbetu] did his thing. It was typical of the church. It is full of hypocrites.[52]

Another Muslim convert, Dixon Yusuf Ali, comments:

My mother has attended this Methodist church in north-west London since she arrived in Britain. Every five years they change the minister but not once in all that time have they got a Black minister. In fact, she told me she can count the times a Black person has preached at the church on the fingers of one hand. She said they only talk about racism on Racial [Justice] Sunday and one year they had some man talking about the persecution of White people in Zimbabwe and how racism affects White people as well. She told me that another preacher did this service on John Newton and he said that Africans were selling each other into slavery before Christians set them free. It's pure foolishness. I don't know why she goes. I keep telling her, they are a bunch of jokers and she shouldn't waste her time with them.

Tariq Iqbal, a twenty-five-year-old Jamaican convert living in Tottenham, argues:

As a boy in Jamaica they tried to keep all of this [slavery and Marcus Garvey] from us. I went to a City Mission church in Spanish Town and all they had was pictures of a White Jesus on the walls. It was when I came to this country that I first read about our true history. About ten years ago some Muslim brothers in Dalston [east London] gave me a book and a tape that spoke about Black people and their culture and history. After reading and listening to the tape, and speaking to some other Muslim brothers, I couldn't go back to church. The few times I went to the Baptist church in Tottenham, I did not hear the pastor say anything about Black people, even in Black history month.

Faith and African Enslavement

The subjects of African chattel enslavement and the racism that sprang from it have proved a litmus test for churches and how far they are willing to acknowledge their own past. The historic churches at times used verses from the Bible to justify African enslavement, and Christians participated in this atrocity. At the same time, Christians were also some of the first people to oppose African enslavement and were responsible for the major White

117

opposition to it.[53] The bicentenary of the slave trade's abolition in Britain gave churches an opportunity to examine this history and as a result, in late 2004, the ecumenical body Churches Together in England (CTE) established what would become the Set All Free project. This project was tasked to 'remember, reflect and respond' to old and new forms of slavery and to draw upon the lessons of the past to resolve present day problems.[54]

Set All Free is particularly interested in BMCs because they include the descendants of enslaved Africans, for whom this subject is particularly resonant; and from the outset they were approached for their support.[55] However, with the exception of a handful of churches in London and a constructive response from Birmingham, most Black Christians were reluctant to get involved in the bicentenary. They were either not interested in their history or believed it would stir up too many emotions that should remain buried.

Some who did seek to engage with the subject matter were as guilty of distorting Scripture as slavery's former White apologists. Several Black pastors attempted to place a theological spin on African slavery, deciding that it was part of 'God's divine, redemptive plan for the "Black race"'. Such arguments lack a proper appreciation of a history which saw tens of millions of Africans suffer and die over four centuries during the largest forced mass migration the world has ever witnessed.[56]

Either way, it was largely left to White people to tell the story of slavery and abolition, sometimes in ways that suggested White virtue and agency and Black inertia and complicity. It also became apparent to the Set All Free project that many Black Christians had only a very basic knowledge of their history and were susceptible to believing half-truths and downright lies about the roles of Black and White in Atlantic slavery.[57] This collective apathy about the bicentenary flew in the face of government, media and community responses which involved a flurry of activity during 2007. Britain adopted a slavery memorial day,[58] and the government announced that from September 2008 the history of the slave trade would become a compulsory subject in English schools, to ensure that pupils learnt about the history and impact of slavery so that future generations would be less ignorant about the role of Britain in slavery and abolition.

Whereas many in the churches demonstrated ignorance about this aspect of their history, the same could not be said of the Black Muslim brethren who were often critical of the church's role in slavery. During numerous conferences, seminars, talks and meetings hosted by the Cross Community Forum,[59] Set All Free and other groups between 2005 and 2007, I heard Black Christians accused of everything from following the 'slave master's religion' to being 'House Negroes'.[60] Many struggled to respond to these accusations.[61]

The bicentenary should have been an opportunity for Christians to offer apologies with apologetics – that is to say, to admit to the failings of the churches during this terrible era, but also to highlight the way Christianity and the churches fought against African enslavement, and their continuing role in all Black struggles for equal rights and justice. Sadly this was not what happened.

The Way Ahead
There is little doubt that BMCs have come a long way during the sixty years of their existence. Mark Sturge's *Look What the Lord Has Done!* chronicles their growth and development and the way in which they have gained real confidence and verve to engage with government, local authorities and other official bodies. However, while BMCs continue to talk up their role in society and their growing numbers, there has been a failure to observe the growth of Islam among the very people who are the churches' natural constituency. And without a doubt, Muslims have tackled more of the issues affecting Black people, and Black youth in particular, in the post-9/11 and 7/7 environment.

Chapter 5

The X Factor: Michael Abdul Malik and the Birth of British Political Islamic Activism

Dread and Pentecostal

In his fascinating but arguably flawed book *Dread and Pentecostal*, the academic and cultural commentator Robert Beckford argued for a new model of Black political engagement which incorporates Rastafari, Black Pentecostalism and liberation theology. Dr Beckford's book was aimed at a church constituency with a known dislike for anything connected to Rastafari, and even his persuasive arguments have failed to change the thinking of church leaders who associate it only with ganja smoking and the colours red, green and gold. On a more profound level, his book failed to connect because it arrived fifteen years too late. As we approached the millennium it was evident that Rasta no longer captured the hearts and minds of Britain's Black youth and that the creative, cultural muse of the movement, 'roots reggae', had been usurped by the less socially conscious dance hall or ragga music.

What is more important here is a casual yet telling reference to Islam: '...before the emergence of Rastafari, it was the Black Muslims who set a platform for post-war religio-political movement amongst the Caribbean diaspora in Britain.'[1] It can be argued that it is now once again Islam, and not Rastafari, which has the socio-spiritual dynamism to inspire Black people in their struggle for equality and justice in a prejudiced society.

The version of Islam Dr Beckford had in mind was a movement initiated by the late and much-maligned Michael de Freitas who, as Michael X, was arguably Britain's foremost Black leader in the 1960s and Britain's first high-profile Muslim convert.[2] Long before anyone in Britain had robust race-relations legislation or statutory bodies and organizations to champion them, this Black Islamic firebrand was at the forefront of the campaign for equality.

Michael de Freitas

Michael X was born Michael de Freitas in Trinidad in 1933, to a Black Bajan-born mother and a White St Kitts-born father of Portuguese origin.[3] His father abandoned the family while Michael was a boy, leaving his mother, Iona Brown, to raise a mixed-race son in a colonial society still obsessed with skin colour. The young Michael was raised as a Roman Catholic, and at one point was an altar boy at one of the many Catholic churches in Port of Spain, the island's capital. At seventeen he left home to search for his father on St Kitts, a move that did not realize the young man's dreams of reconciliation.[4] He subsequently opted for a life at sea and joined the merchant navy, a career move that enabled him to see most of the world before his mid twenties.

By the late 1950s he had settled in the Tiger Bay area of Cardiff, a place known for its ethnic diversity, poverty and vice.[5] He then moved to London where he settled in Notting Hill, which was then a culturally thriving but poverty-stricken African-Caribbean enclave. When not involved in drug-dealing, 'poncing' or pimping and petty crime, he was an associate of the Jewish landlord Peter Rachman. In his autobiography, de Freitas argues that he opposed Rachman's practice of using strong-arm tactics to obtain exorbitant rents from newly arrived African-Caribbean settlers.[6] Others have argued that he was in the pay of the notorious slum landlord. Either way, he was a well-known figure among the Black denizens of this deprived area of west London.

The X Men: Michael and Malcolm

What is certain is that his life changed when he met Malcolm X in London in 1965.[7] Like Michael, Malcolm X was rangy and light-skinned, but the African-American had no identity hang-ups and was keen to affirm his African heritage. Conversely, Michael had been encouraged by his colour-obsessed mother not to play with Black children and he had even once successfully passed himself off as an ethnic Jew.[8]

In 1965 Malcolm X was still at the spiritual and political crossroads in his life – he had broken from the Nation of Islam the previous year and was following orthodox or Sunni Islam. He was also keen to establish a socio-political organization which could campaign for Black rights in the USA and abroad.[9] When the two men met in the UK, Malcolm was on his way back to the USA after a tour of Africa.

Michael de Freitas was also at a junction in his life, looking for a legal and creative way to apply his tremendous energies to help his deprived Black brothers and sisters in London.[10] He saw in the charismatic Malcolm X a man whose Islamic faith had given him the fortitude and spirituality to overcome deprivations and suffering to become one of the great thinkers and activists of his generation.[11] Where Michael lacked discipline, Malcolm was focused; where the American was all urgency, the Trinidadian-born Briton displayed stereotypical Caribbean nonchalance; where Malcolm was a preacher and teacher, Michael was a hustler and con-man. However, Michael was no fool, and he was sharp enough to realize that Malcolm possessed something he did not: the X-factor was Islam.[12]

The two soon became friends, and Malcolm took to calling

the younger man 'brother', a typical African-American religious affectation. But some in the British media literally believed that Michael was the American's biological brother and dubbed him 'Michael X'. The name stuck, although his official Muslim name after he converted to Islam was Michael Abdul Malik. Speaking about his mentor he commented: 'I listened to Malcolm's speech on the problem of human – rather than civil – rights of the American Negro and heard the tumultuous applause which followed and then I ate with him and a number of the students in a Moslem restaurant. By the time we were in a train heading back to London I was completely convinced that a branch of his Afro-American Unity organisation should be set up in London.'[13]

Conversion and Controversy

One of the many controversies associated with Michael X was the genuineness of his commitment to Islam, and whether his conversion had more to do with opportunism or expediency than a sincere belief that Islam would transform his life. The Welsh writer John L. Williams' recent biography of Michael X is far more sympathetic to the charismatic Trinidadian than others, and presents him as a man of great contradictions and insecurities, both before and after his conversion. For him, 'There's no doubt that over the years Islam went on to play a big part in Michael's life.'[14] And Derek Humphry and David Tindall, whose biography *False Messiah: The Story of Michael X* is far more critical, admit that, 'The discipline of abstinence in the Muslim religion was good for him. He... admitted to having drunk too much, mainlining heroin and smoking marijuana, and told people he had since reformed.'[15]

When Michael X's name cropped up in my interviews with Muslim converts about Islam, the response was always negative. A typical comment is that of Hakim Ibrahim: 'He wasn't a Muslim. Not a real one. He was a man who pretended to be a Muslim to fool people. He was nothing more than a con-man who gave us a bad name.' Abdul Malik's comments are similar: 'A friend of my father knew him, and he said the man was someone who brought Islam into disrepute. He drank, took drugs and had all these women and did things that are prohibited in Islam. That's not being a Muslim.'

Michael X's new-found religious and political awakening resulted in the Racial Adjustment Action Society, or RAAS, one of the first serious grass-roots organizations to campaign for the rights of Black people in Britain.[16] The RAAS successfully campaigned for better working conditions on behalf of the largely Asian workforce at the Courtaulds textile factory in Preston, Lancashire, at a time when race relations law had not made it into the statute books. Michael's ability to court publicity through hyperbole ensured that the RAAS received considerable media coverage and increased its membership among those who were looking for someone or something to fight for their rights.[17]

Muhammad Ali

After Malcolm X's assassination in February 1965, Michael switched his allegiance to the Honourable Elijah Muhammad, who was then head of the Nation of Islam in the USA. According to one source it was the Messenger who gave Michael his Muslim name: 'Michael made contact with Elijah Muhammad and his son Herbert in Chicago… It was Elijah Muhammad who gave Michael his name Abdul Malik – Servant of God… At that point it gave him reason to live.'[18] Michael X's affiliation with the Messenger coincided with the meteoric rise of the pugilist Cassius Clay, and his subsequent announcement, the day after winning the world heavyweight boxing championship, that he wanted the world to call him Muhammad Ali.[19] Michael X had initially met Ali when he was in Sweden with his manager, Herbert Muhammad, the Messenger's son, for a series of exhibition bouts in Stockholm, and he sought to maintain his links with them via transatlantic correspondence.

When Ali came to London for his rematch with Henry Cooper in May 1966, Michael X assisted with security and administration for Ali's entourage. Ali was known the world over for his amazing boxing prowess and larger-than-life public persona.[20] Wherever he went fans mobbed him, especially Black ones. Ali, like Malcolm X, spoke with boldness about race issues and had a sense of Black pride at a time when Black Christian leaders were more reserved about race.[21] What made Ali unique was the fact that he was a famous sportsman who could also articulate the emotions of Black people across the diaspora in an uncomplicated yet insightful way. His more outrageous and trenchant comments would be made with a smile on his face, or in verse, which served to engage his supporters and wrong-foot his opponents.

Like Ali, Michael X would never overlook any opportunity to publicize his activities; Ali's arrival gave him a wonderful opportunity to bring himself and RAAS to an interested public. When Ali came to London to fight Henry Cooper, Michael X took his boxing brother around the capital, stopping off at the London Free School in Notting Hill where Michael orchestrated publicity shots of himself and Ali's entourage being mobbed by doting admirers outside the doors of the institute.[22]

Ali's visit served to stimulate greater interest in Michael X and his activities, and it also increased interest in Islam among Black people in Britain, at a time when the faith was regarded as the preserve of south Asians and a small but growing number of people from West Africa and Somalia.[23] It can be argued that Black Islam could have become a real force at this time had Michael X focused more on spiritual matters than political ones.

Unlike Malcolm X, who established both religious (Muslim mosque) and a political (Organization of Afro-American Unity) movement after his public falling-out with the Nation of Islam,[24] Michael X's interests were purely political. As a result, Black enquirers who wanted to know more about the religious beliefs that inspired him had no religious organizations in Britain to which they could turn for guidance.

Michael X and British Islam

There is little doubt that those Black Britons who were intrigued by Islam at this point were as much motivated by its spiritual ideas as by political teachings. However, many were focusing on a version of Islam based around the beliefs of the Nation of Islam, as well as idiosyncratic ideas and theories contributed by Michael X. There were very few, if any, mosques or 'temples' in Britain at that time which followed the Nation of Islam's 'Fardian' Islam, which frustrated such searchers spiritually and intellectually.

Those who were brave enough to venture into one of the many Sunni mosques in Britain's towns and cities would hear no mention of the Honourable W. D. Fard, the Messenger, Elijah Muhammad, Ezekiel's Wheel or the reckless scientist Yacub. And what they would hear would be largely meaningless to them since lessons were conducted in Arabic with smatterings of Urdu and other south Asian languages. These men would often be the only Black face in a sea of brown ones who would be confused by the preoccupation with 'race'. For many Asian Muslims, Islam is as much a lifestyle as a faith and is open to all of humanity, rather than being the preserve of particular ethnic groupings.

Long before the contemporary politicization of Islam in the form of 'Islamism', many conservative Asian Muslims had little time for the political agenda of Black religious activists. Even those Muslim brothers who followed Malcolm X's progression toward Sunni Islam wanted to hear the imam speak directly to their condition as Black people in Britain by applying the *ayahs* and *surahs* of the Qur'an to the situation they faced on a daily basis. These 1960s 'Muslims' considered themselves Black first, and then Muslim – whereas today Black Muslim converts provide a range of complex responses to the question of ethnic identity and race.

The 1960s were a time of upheaval and agitation when civil rights groups and Black Power activists were working to bring about racial equality and justice. In such a climate, even those espousing orthodox Muslim beliefs wanted a faith that could feed and inspire the political passions stirred up by Malcolm X, Stokely Carmichael, Huey P. Newton, Bobby Seale, Angela Davis and Eldridge Cleaver. These Black brothers did not want to attend mosques led by imams who spoke about perfection and the beauty of the Qur'an or the spiritual virtues of adhering to the Five Pillars of Islam.

So, although anecdotal evidence suggests that this period saw growing interest in Islam among Black Britons, very few became the type of practising believer who observes the Five Pillars of Islam or even regularly attends prayers at a mosque. Britain would have to wait at least twenty years for this phenomenon to occur. Most became cultural Muslims, who exchanged their European-sounding names for Islamic ones, read the Qur'an, mostly in English rather than Arabic, and steered clear of mosques. The more devout, like the BMCs, used their homes as places to gather and discuss religious ideas. The home or a community centre would prove a safe space for the sharing of faith and ideas.

Natural Religion of the Black Man

The emergence of Michael X and the increased interest in Islam within the Black community took place against the backdrop of the Black Consciousness movement, which began in the USA but soon spread to other parts of the African diaspora.[25] The 1960s saw Black people with an African heritage taking a keener interest in their culture, which had endured enslavement and colonialism to emerge battered and bruised but unbowed. And a number of Black academics began a task that continues today, of uncovering the great histories (and mysteries) of Africa and its people – histories which centuries of racism, ignorance and time had obscured. One such historian was Edward Wilmot Blyden, a Liberian-born statesman and educator whom many consider to be the father of Pan-Africanism. Blyden is also known for his seminal book *Christianity, Islam and the Negro Race* (1887), which elucidated his conviction that the effects of Christianity had been generally detrimental to Africans, whereas those of Islam had been largely beneficial.[26]

Blyden advocated Africans abandoning Christianity in favour of Islam, something he did himself. He arguably coined the phrase 'Islam is the natural religion of the Blackman', which became popular with the Nation of Islam in the USA. He also advanced the theory that Africans seeking to connect with their African ancestry must treat Islam as part of their heritage.[27] Adherents of traditional African religions would no doubt disagree with Blyden's assertion that Islam is the Black man's or African's 'natural religion': history shows that the same imperialist forces were at work in the spread of this faith in Africa as in the spread of Christianity.[28]

Islam and the Slave Trade

The bicentenary of the abolition of Britain's transatlantic slave trade in fact proved as awkward for Muslims as for Christians, because not only did Islam transform Africa culturally, 'Arab traders' helped to institutionalize slavery in many parts of the continent.[29] Although one cannot compare the trans-Saharan slave trade with the European-controlled Atlantic trade in terms of inhumanity and naked exploitation, it was far from being the benign institution many Muslim apologists would have us believe.[30] Indeed, in 2007, a number of slavery-related conferences and events included contributions from those adhering to traditional African religions, who were often critical of both Christianity and Islam.

A contributor to the Cross Community Forum meeting of 16 November 2006, Adje Kouakou said: 'It's hard for many

Africans to accept that they have their own religion because Islam and Christianity have been so promoted. It is equally hard for Africans even to acknowledge the existence of African religions before Christianity and Islam, but they predate these religions.'[31] Similarly, at Lambeth and the Abolition – The Big Debate, which took place in April 2007 in Brixton, Naa Akofor Omaduro II, a Ghanaian warrior queen, spoke about the role of traditional African religions in opposing slavery and made some cutting comments about the churches as well as criticizing Islam's relationship to slavery.[32]

For Afrocentrists and African cultural nationalists, a consciously 'African' man or woman can only adhere to a traditional African belief system, which 'is so much a part of everyday life it is virtually impossible to separate it from African culture. Most African languages do not even have a word for religion, because it is not seen as a separate element to life, in the way that religious and secular spheres of life are separated in western culture.'[33] Any other faith has been imposed upon Africans for the specific purpose of undermining their sense of balance, wholeness and well-being.[34] Paradoxically, Afrocentrists are not averse to speaking about indigenous African enslavement, which predates both Islamic Arab and Christian European enslavement by centuries, as an aspect of African culture that they assert was humane, dynamic and structured within societies. Indeed, in his seminal *Interesting Narrative* of 1789, the former enslaved African turned freedom fighter Olaudah Equiano speaks almost nonchalantly of his father's ownership of Africans in his village prior to his own enslavement as a boy.[35]

Some in the churches have been keen to use a 'you are no better than us' approach with regard to African slavery as a stick with which to attack Muslims. The few attempts by Black Christian leaders, as opposed to theologians, to address issues of 'Blackness' directly all mention Islamic slavery in tendentious ways, accentuating the Islamic or Arabic beginnings of African

129

enslavement and emphasizing the Christian role in ending this.

Black British Islamic Political Engagement

History shows that Black British Islamic political engagement can be traced to the 1960s, when the so-called race relations movement was in its infancy and protective laws were few, leaving the Black community vulnerable to state and street racism. Michael X, in his unique way, was someone seeking to fill this void through initiatives such as the Black House, a community arts and business collective aimed at empowering London's Black community. Like all of Michael X's activities, it was doomed to fail as a result of his paucity of organizational skills and inability to follow through ideas.[36] By 1971 Michael X, now known as Michael Abdul Malik, had relocated to Trinidad, which had a small but influential Black Muslim presence as a result of the growing Black Power movement in the Caribbean. There he established a commune to promote his ideas of Black economic empowerment.[37] Abdul Malik's return to the island of his birth had tragic consequences when the Black Power leader was accused of the murders of the British socialite Gail Ann Benson (who was also known as Hale Kimga) and Joe Skerritt.[38] Abdul Malik was subsequently convicted of the murder of Joe Skerritt and hanged in 1975 – an ignominious end to a man some considered a 'false messiah'.

History has not been good to Michael X. For many Black people he was a charlatan who took advantage of the Black community's need for leadership in the face of racism and structural inequality in Britain. Others regard him as an opportunist who benefited from society's desire to have a Black spokesperson who could articulate the needs and aspirations of the Black community.[39] He was also seen as a parasite who preyed on the guilt of White liberals. Muslims have some of the harshest words for the former Black Power activist, who remains a source of embarrassment, exemplifying the inability of Black Britons to produce a Muslim leader of the stature of Malcolm X and Elijah Muhammad in the 1960s and 1970s.

Renaissance

There has, however, recently been a reappraisal of Michael X's life, with a number of cinematic, theatrical and biographical accounts in 2008. The film *The Bank Job*, starring Jason Statham, is based on a real-life event and features an admittedly rather unflattering depiction of Michael X which alleges that he was being monitored by the British secret service and that his arrest for murder was the work of sinister forces.[40] This allegation sparked a minor campaign in the Black weekly newspaper *New Nation*, whose cover story on 24 November 2008 demanded 'Tell us the Truth about Michael X' and alleged that 'the Government refuse to release a file on race activist they hanged 30 years ago'. According to the newspaper, 'Whitehall want to keep the file secret until 2054'.[41] John L. Williams's *Michael X: A Life in Black and White* presents a more humane and rounded portrayal of Michael X, despite the phrase 'black and white' in the subtitle. The author, who is also a writer of crime fiction, casts doubt on the conviction of Michael X and alleges that the Black Power activist was a threat to national security.[42] Lastly, the one-man play *Michael X*, by Vanessa Walters, which opened at the Tabernacle Theatre in west London in November 2008, again reappraised the life of this dynamic but damaged figure.[43]

It is difficult to assess Michael X's legacy to the Black Muslim movement in Britain. By his own account, the movement had 'few followers' and 'no organisation'.[44] However, such a charismatic figure, who associated with other charismatic Muslims such as Malcolm X and Muhammad Ali, would easily attract the earnest and impressionable within the Black community. If one looks closely at the photographs of the time, especially of his meetings, it is evident that Michael X could draw a large crowd. And some of the expressions on the faces at his meetings display confidence and a sense of expectation that their leader could deliver the changes they desired.

Legacy

Michael X's real legacy is arguably his candour and courage, and the way he publicly articulated a lot of what the Black community thought, albeit in a rather crude and often insensitive manner. He advocated Black self-defence at a time when other leaders made little comment on the rising number of attacks on Black people.[45] He was the first, but not the last, Black Muslim to receive a jail sentence for comments made about race and religious issues. And his propensity for attracting media attention through sensational remarks and wild stunts anticipated the activities of radical Black and Asian Islamic clerics in Britain over the last ten years. On a deeper level, Michael X showed that Black Muslims were not frightened to speak their minds on issues affecting Black people in Britain. He never regarded himself as part of the establishment or wanted to ingratiate himself with them. He was the classic counter-cultural rebel who stood outside the camp and critiqued what was taking place inside, unconcerned about what those in power said.

Michael X's uncompromising, no-nonsense approach and his penchant for headline grabbing were reminiscent of the activities of another more recent Black Muslim convert, Abu Izzadeen. On Wednesday 20 September 2006 Abu Izzadeen, formerly known as Trevor Brookes, a Jamaican-born Muslim living in east London, achieved national notoriety by heckling the then Home Secretary, John Reid, during a speech about targeting potential Muslim extremists in Britain, accusing the minister of being an 'enemy of Islam'.[46] Such bravado and opportunism are straight out of the Michael X school of political engagement, and it can be argued that, were he living in the UK today, he would be denounced as an extremist.

Chapter 6

Towering Inferno: Muslim Converts, Radicalization and the Need to Walk the Straight Path

11 September 2001

The al-Qaeda bombing of the World Trade Center in New York on 11 September 2001 became one of those singularly defining moments in world history which changed ideas and perceptions for ever. From a purely historical standpoint, the attacks on the 'Twin Towers' in Manhattan, the heart of America's financial district – simultaneous with the attack on the Pentagon and a fourth, failed bombing attempt – have become 'where were you?' moments ranking alongside the fall of the Berlin Wall on 9 November 1989 and Nelson Mandela's release from prison on 11 February 1990. What made these events so momentous and pregnant with meaning was as much their lasting legacy as the events themselves. The fall of the Berlin Wall led to the end of the city's artificial partition, and contributed to the subsequent reunification of Germany, the collapse of European Communism and the end of the Cold War. Nelson Mandela's departure from Robben Island prison would ultimately lead to the end of South African apartheid, the election of the country's first Black President, and the birth of the Rainbow Nation promising equality and human rights to all South Africans.

In the case of 9/11 the world became aware of a small but extremely organized and ruthless group of terrorists who were willing to use extreme means to achieve their goals. The terrorists in question were members of al-Qaeda, a global terrorist network which seems to resemble something out of a James Bond movie. Its aims include the end of external influences on Muslim nations and the creation of an Islamic caliphate. It believes that the West is working to destroy Islam and that the killing of civilians is Islamically justified in the name of *jihad*.[1]

New York was an obvious target for any terrorist organization, given the socio-economic and cultural importance of the city and the iconic status of the Twin Towers. However, for Black people this multi-ethnic city is far from being the symbol of Western imperialism seen by al-Qaeda. Just a short cab-ride across Manhattan Bridge lies Brooklyn, with arguably the largest African-Caribbean community of the five New York boroughs. Caribbean people had been moving to the USA since the 1920s,[2] and there are parts of the Flatbush area which are devoid of American accents and resemble central Port of Spain or downtown Kingston. Labour Day in September is known for its annual West Indian carnival. Many of the 'West Indians' who have made Brooklyn their home for decades join other Brooklynites on the number 3 or 4 train to take the thirty-minute journey across town to jobs in Lower Manhattan, the scene of the bombings which killed 2,789 people.[3] Although the identities of all the victims will never be known, it is likely that a good proportion were Black and of Caribbean origin. Many Black Britons have family or friends in New York and would have been fearful for their loved ones when they heard about the bombings. They would have had little time for talk about the attack being a response to decades of misguided US foreign policy on the Middle East,[4] and even less time for the idea of the terrorists receiving a special welcome in heaven due to their actions.

7 July 2005

Britain also fell victim to 'Islamist' terrorism on 7 July 2005 when four young men, one of them a Black Muslim convert, used bombs in rucksacks to create mayhem on London's transport system. A few weeks later, the security services foiled the attempts of four Black bombers of Somali origin, who were again targeting the transport system in the capital.[5] As a result of these developments New Nation newspaper, which is aimed at Britain's Black community, ran the headline 'Why Are So Many Bombers Black?'[6] The article began: 'A new generation of Black would-be suicide bombers are being courted by radical clerics who prey on vulnerable converts.' The New Nation's comments struck a note with many in the Black community. Like most people in Britain, they found the notion of suicide bombing alien and horrifying. Most Black Britons describe themselves as Christians, and for these men and women suicide runs contrary to the belief that all human life is a gift of God, which is sacred and must be saved or preserved whenever possible. For them suicide is sinful; the few references to it in the Bible describe the actions of desperate and duplicitous individuals such as the fallen King Saul and Judas Iscariot.[7]

The 7/7 bombings were closer to home for people in the UK than the 9/11 attacks. Although Britain had become relatively desensitized to terrorist activity having lived through three decades of Irish Republican bombing campaigns, it was still unprepared for the events in London, when fifty-two commuters were killed by suicide bombings at King's Cross, Russell Square, Aldgate and Edgware Road Underground stations.[8] The four men strapped on explosive-laden rucksacks and boarded rush-hour trains and buses intent on causing carnage. By contrast with many Irish terrorist attacks, no coded warnings were sent to the police and these bombers were happy to suffer the same fate as their victims. As with 9/11 the victims represented the full diversity of the capital and included Muslims among their number. From a Black perspective, the fact that one of the suicide bombers was nineteen-year-old Jamaican-born Germaine Lindsay, who had converted to Islam during his teens, was new, disturbing information. Lindsay, who had been living in Buckinghamshire, detonated the explosives in his backpack at King's Cross Station, killing himself and twenty-six others.[9]

Black Community Concerns

Among those interviewed for this book, Black elders showed great concern that the involvement of Black Muslims in terrorist activities would collectively give the Black community a bad name. There was a sense of 'Black people don't do this sort of thing!' Extremist activities not only bring shame on the Black community, they are accompanied by unwanted media attention, and increased police and security service interest. A typical response was 'This behaviour don't belong in our community': the origins of these socio-political and religious struggles and their various motivations have nothing to do with Black Britons. 'What they were doing was wrong and should have no connection to Black people.' Several of those with long memories compared Black converts to the 900 Black believers whom the White American religious preacher Jim Jones brainwashed into committing mass suicide in Guyana in 1978.[10] Others had self-interested concerns about Black Muslim radicalization and how it could potentially impact them. Keeping in mind an article written by Darcus Howe in *The Voice*[11] on the shooting of Jean Charles de Menezes, the retired Brixton pensioner George Rowe suggested: 'Dem a mek tings bad fi wi. De police no mek joke fe arrest or shoot terrorist: look pon de Brazil bwoy here [he points to the newspaper article] – dem kill him ded and him not even Muslim.'

Many Black people reappraised Islam after the attacks. Most Black Britons are Christian and there is a general perception that all Muslims in Britain are of south Asian origin, and consequently the Black community can be forgiven for their lack of knowledge about Black Muslims.[12] Prior to 9/11 and 7/7 there was very little in the Black and mainstream media about the Black Muslim presence in Britain, apart from stories about the ongoing campaign of the Nation of Islam (UK) to overturn the ban on the Honourable Louis Farrakhan entering Britain.[13] For many, the fact that there was a growing Black Muslim population was new information which they tended to categorize alongside 'Osama bin Laden', 'jihad' and 'Islamism'. For the more informed, it was a case of reconciling what they knew about Islam and the efficacious work of Black Muslims within the community with the discovery that there were now also Black Muslims whose extreme interpretation of the Qur'an could result in danger and death.

Black Muslim Allegiances

The bombings not only made Black people look afresh at Islam, they also forced Muslims in this country and elsewhere to take a critical look at their own faith. For Black Muslims the primary issues were identity, allegiance and belonging; what does it mean to be Black, British and Muslim in an increasingly diverse, pluralistic society? Even the terms 'Black', 'British' and 'Muslim' required close examination. For instance, do Black Muslims consider themselves part of the Black community or the Muslim community? The easy answer would be both, as there is often a great deal of synergy between these communities on a range of socio-political and religious issues. However, this becomes less straightforward when their views and interests struggle to coalesce on issues such as British and Western foreign policy, and attitudes to the United States.

A test case may be America's first Black President, Barack Obama, who prior to coming to office enjoyed near-total support from

Black people on both sides of the Atlantic.[14] It will be interesting to find out whether he continues to enjoy this level of support among Black Muslims, in particular, if he focuses his efforts on tackling America's economic woes rather than on foreign policy concerns about the Middle East. He would probably soon lose popularity among some Muslims if he maintained the policies of his predecessor, George W. Bush, though Black people are likely to be more forgiving and accepting of a Black Commander in Chief, and temper their expectations with realism. Moreover, if a focus on economic policies resulted in an improvement in Black living standards (health, education, jobs and so on), many Black non-Muslims would regard his priorities as wise ones. In the end, it can be argued that the balance between 'Black' and 'Muslim' hinges upon the form of Islam adopted by the believer. Those adhering to a more moderate belief structure will acknowledge their Blackness and the fact that they cannot divorce this identity from the issues facing their non-Muslim brothers in Britain. Those with more extreme beliefs are encouraged to divest themselves of their ethnic identity in favour of a Muslim one. Writing in the *New Nation* newspaper, Birmingham-based lecturer Dr Garnet Parris explains: 'What we have to understand, especially with extreme brands of Islam where unbelievers are "kaffirs" is that even Black men see themselves as culturally and religiously different. They don't see themselves as Black first and foremost.'[15]

The issues surrounding Black Muslim identity mirror those encountered by the larger, more established Asian Muslim communities which have had longer to struggle with making sense of their faith within a changing British urban landscape. In his book *Young, British and Muslim*, Philip Lewis looks at the lives of Asian Muslims in Bradford, many of whom are of Pakistani origin, and investigates their growing sense of alienation and marginalization. These young people often do not share the socio-economic ambitions of their more conservative parents.[16] And they need their faith to give them a sense of belonging in a multi-ethnic city that experienced serious 'race'-related riots in 2001 and the resulting tensions between various communities.[17]

Community Cohesion

European Union research has discovered that, as a result of the 9/11 atrocities, Muslims across Europe are themselves 'increasingly likely to become targets of hostility and terror'.[18] In 2005, Hazel Blears, 'the minister responsible for counter-terrorism, said… that Muslims will have to accept as a "reality" that they will be stopped and searched by the police more often than the rest of the public'. Ms Blears told MPs that 'there was no getting away from it', because the terrorist threat came from people 'falsely hiding behind Islam'.[19] However, Black people (whatever their religion) were still more likely to be subject to stop and search measures than any other group.[20] This leads to a scenario in which Black Muslims may be targeted for being both 'Black' and 'Muslim'. As long as 'stop and search', which disproportionately targets Black people, is regarded as a legitimate tool to fight street crime,[21] there is an obvious fear within the Muslim community that certain policing activities unfairly target them.[22]

If the tabloid press are to be believed, there are Muslim extremists in this country who present a clear danger to British customs, values and ways of life; and Britain's Muslims are 'different from us and a threat to us'.[23] A study has shown that in any given week 96 per cent of tabloid articles focusing on 'Islam' are 'negative' – as opposed to a mere 89 per cent in the broadsheets. The study goes on to observe that 'combined circulation of the tabloids is about three times greater than that of the broadsheets'.[24] It discusses how these news stories shape people's thinking about Islam and often make Muslims defensive about their faith.

Moreover, 9/11 and 7/7 have witnessed the publication of a number of books which claim to unearth the hidden extremism which exists within Islam. In his controversial book *The Islamist*, London-born Muslim Mohamed 'Ed' Husain chronicles his descent from impressionable moderate Muslim teenager to militant Islamist.[25] He turned his back on his Brick Lane mosque for more radical Islamic organizations such as Hizb ut-Tahrir, and accepted the goal of a world Islamic state.[26] Husain's book reads like an Islamic version of the Italian-American confessional gangster film *Goodfellas*, and warns Britain to wake up to the dangers posed by radical Islamic clerics who believe the West is at war with Islam. These 'preachers of hate', as the media love to describe them, are hell-bent on subverting Islam and committed to winning over the youth, in particular, to the belief that violence and terror are a legitimate means to bring about an Islamic state.

Husain's book is not alone in suggesting a radical Islamic threat. The US investigative journalist Kenneth R. Timmerman, whose previous books included an exposé of the Revd Jesse Jackson, argues that:

> September 11 should have shown us that we can no longer ignore the preachers of hate and their rhetoric, nor can we continue to make excuses for their behaviour based on supposed 'cultural differences', 'oppression' or 'hopelessness'. We are not faced with a social problem which liberal policies and public money can solve. If we are to craft serious and effective policies to combat them, we must begin by recognising the uncompromising depths of their hatred.[27]

Other writers, such as the British journalist Melanie Phillips, continue this almost apocalyptic account of the threat posed to Britain by extremist Islam.[28] (Indeed, a fair proportion of the books published about 'Islamic terrorism' adopt this tone.)

Black Muslim Extremism

The whole issue of Islamic extremism is important to Black Muslims because, as we read in Ed Husain's book, radical Islamic groups target African as well as Asian students in east London. For him, it was not a question of ethnicity: 'there were only two divisions: Muslims and the rest.'[29] 'Black converts who had studied Islam in Saudi Arabia [were sent] to live and preach in the UK. They spoke passionately about the idea of one God, *tawheed* in Arabic, and ceaselessly warned against *shirk* or polytheism.'[30]

The issue of Black Muslim converts being targeted for extremism is best exemplified by Richard Reid, the so-called 'shoe-bomber'. Richard Reid was born in London in 1973 to a Jamaican father and an English mother. His parents split up when he was young and he drifted into a life of petty crime which led to a number of prison sentences while he was still in his youth. It was in Feltham young offenders' institution in west London that he converted to Islam. On release, young Abdel Rahim, as he was now known, went to Brixton mosque, which has been a haven for Black Muslim ex-offenders. However, after attending the mosque between 1996 and 1998, he found its teaching not 'radical enough and fell in with extremist Islamists'.[31] He is thought to have spent time in Egypt, Israel, Turkey, Pakistan, Belgium, the Netherlands, France and possibly Afghanistan. On 22 December 2001 he boarded American Airlines flight 63 from Paris to Miami wearing footwear laden with explosives.[32] A wary stewardess noticed Reid's failed attempts to ignite his shoes and the twenty-eight-year-old was detained. Reid subsequently pleaded guilty at his trial in the USA the following year and was given a long prison sentence.

Richard Reid remains a warning against the dangers of radicalization, especially among converts who display all the enthusiasm and susceptibility of a new believer. Ironically, Black Muslim converts have gained a reputation as being in the vanguard of extremism. Another, Abu Izzadeen, originally Trevor Brooks, was convicted of terrorist fund-raising and inciting terrorism overseas in April 2008. Abu Izzadeen was born in Hackney, east London, to Jamaican parents who arrived in the UK in the early 1960s. According to the BBC news he was 'born a Christian ... and converted to Islam at the age of 17'.[33] He is associated with the proscribed al-Muhajiroun group and was a spokesperson for Al Ghurabba, another group regarded as extremist.

Another convert who spent time in prison was the cleric Sheikh Abdullah al-Faisal, who was jailed in 2003 for 'soliciting the murder of Jews and Hindus'.[34] The sheikh was born Trevor William Forrest, in Jamaica, and was raised as a Christian by parents who were Salvation Army officers.[35] He became a Muslim after travelling to Saudi Arabia, where he obtained a degree in Islamic Studies. He moved to Britain after his studies and began preaching his own brand of Islam in London. A video of the sheikh showed him telling 'young British Muslims that it was their duty to kill nonbelievers, Jews, Hindus and Westerners, and urged them to adopt a "jihad mentality"'; the July 7 bomber Germaine Lindsay was said to have been influenced by him.[36] The sheikh was released from prison in May 2007, and was immediately deported back to his native Jamaica.

One of Sheikh Abdullah al-Faisal's students, Mohammed Hamid, was jailed in 2008 for organizing 'terrorist training designed to recruit, groom and corrupt impressionable young Muslims'.[37] Two of those who fell under the influence of the man known as 'Osama bin London' were Trinidad-born Roger Michael Figaro, who converted to Islam in 2004 and took the name Mohammed Zakariyya al-Figari, and Jamaican-born Kibley da Costa, who took the name Abdul Khaliq after he became a Muslim. Both men, who lived in London, were jailed alongside Hamid and three others for attending terrorist training camps.

When Black Muslims are interviewed about extremist converts their responses range from defensiveness and dismissal to passionate rants about the media's fixation with fanatical Muslims and terrorism. When the point was put to Jamal Brown he said: 'The trouble with you guys is that you're always going on about terrorism. The minute a Muslim opens his mouth and speaks the truth he's a troublemaker. The minute he stands up for what he believes he's a fanatic. Let me tell you this, Muslims won't stand for this treatment much longer. We demand respect for ourselves and our religion. It's time people laid off and left us alone.' Abdul Malik echoes his Muslim brother when he says:

Every day you pick up the paper there's all this stuff about Muslims arrested for this, Muslims arrested for that. They never tell you anything when they release the brothers without charges, which is always the case. But, they never let us forget about the few who get arrested and charged like the shoe bomber. I'm tired of seeing the brother's face on television. All the media want to do is presents us as terrorists. They should either tell the truth about us or don't write anything.

I made the mistake of asking Hakim Ibrahim the question about terrorism. Pointing in an animated fashion at me, he growled:

Look, you folks know nothing about Islam and that's part of the problem. A Muslim who takes his religion seriously is called a fanatic in the press. Plus, this hypocritical government keeps talking about moderate Muslims, how it wants to encourage Muslims to be moderate. You know what they mean by this, don't you? They want to create Muslims who don't believe anything; brothers who don't take Islam seriously. Brothers who drink alcohol and eat pork. That's *haram* [prohibited], my friend. I'm not one of

those Muslims. Look at me. [He points to his traditional
attire and beard.] They would like to cast me as a fanatic
because of the way I dress and follow my religion. I'm
not. I'm someone who loves Islam and wants to follow
Islam seriously, but they are threatened by this.

Black Muslims appear the first to encourage their brethren to
steer clear of extremism or Islamism and to adhere to the straight
path of Islam. Abdul Haqq Baker, the chairman of the Brixton
mosque,'began a campaign to root out the radicals from his
mosque. They often hung around the entrances preaching a holy
war against non-believers.'[38] Other Black Muslims are keen to
promote Islam's 'tolerance' and 'peace', and at gatherings it is
always fascinating to witness the theological jousting among
brothers about the 'true meaning of Islam'. All Black Muslims are
aware that the actions of those jailed or accused for their extreme
behaviour give the vast majority a 'bad name', and may feel
under scrutiny themselves, especially if they are new converts
or reverts. Moreover, as we shall see in chapter 8, they are often
keen to show not only how Islam has transformed their lives, but
that they are better people for embracing the faith.

Government Responses

Judging by the number of government-inspired initiatives on
this subject, it becomes obvious that many do not share the
confidence of mainstream Muslims that they can win the battle
ideas and define for themselves the essential teachings of Islam
and how to apply these teachings.[39] In the light of the 7/7
bombings in 2005, the government established the 'Preventing
Extremism Together task force', which 'canvassed the opinions
of more than 1,000 Muslims... to provide solutions to the
problems of disengagement and radicalisation among Britain's
Muslim youth'.[40] The taskforce, which included Yusuf Islam
(Cat Stevens) and members of the House of Lords, produced

a hundred-page report in November 2005 that 'concluded that extremists have found recruits among young Muslims "fuelled by anger, alienation and disaffection from mainstream British society"'. It also recommended setting up a road-show involving imams travelling around the country to disseminate a moderate form of Islam to young people and a more effective use of the internet to battle extremism.[41]

The government is the first to admit that it needs the assistance of the Muslim community in this battle for hearts and minds, and it has called upon Muslim leaders to do more to help eradicate extremism. Indeed, the former Prime Minister Tony Blair went as far as publicly chastising Muslim leaders for being complacent, and suggested that they 'had to do more to attack not just the extremists' methods, but their false sense of grievance about the west... Too many Muslim leaders gave the impression that they understood and sympathised with the grievances, an attitude that ensured the extremists would never be defeated. He insisted government alone could not root out extremism.'[42] The Muslim community naturally rebuffed these allegations of complacency. Likewise they have critiqued government attempts to create greater social integration and cohesion, especially in northern English towns and cities, as destined to fail due to their prescriptive nature and a lack of real grass-roots consultation in their preparation.

Black Muslim converts in their forties must feel a sense of *déjà vu* at the way government and other institutions are responding to the issue of Muslim extremism and looking for ways to steer the impressionable away from this path. Any major disturbance or 'outrage' involving Black and minority ethnic communities (BAME) invariably solicits the familiar responses and knee-jerk reactions. The uprisings in Brixton in 1981, which took place close to the Brixton mosque and the Nation of Islam (UK)'s headquarters, had their roots in heavy-handed policing as well as high unemployment, youth alienation and poverty.[43] The aftermath of this rebellion, and others elsewhere in England, resulted in the usual round of visits and interest from academics, politicians and liberal do-gooders seeking to explore the reasons for the disturbances.[44] The Conservative government, led by Margaret Thatcher, subsequently called upon the Venerable Lord Scarman to investigate the causes of the riots.[45]

The years that followed the disturbances saw a relative improvement in the infrastructure of the areas where they occurred, in the form of regeneration schemes, skills and training programmes, and general investment. Community leaders and spokespeople were sought by a government and media which were looking for answers. Unfortunately, many of those selected as leaders were not in fact representative of the community, or said what the authorities wanted to hear – namely that normality would soon return.

Predictably, the Black community was blamed for its role in the riots, with the youth denounced as lawless looters who used the riot to sack shops and businesses.[46] There were also suggestions that excessive consumption of marijuana was at the root of aggressive behaviour toward the police. Additionally, parents were castigated for not ensuring that their offspring were better behaved, and for allowing them to be out when the actual disturbances took place. The Black community was expected to shoulder much of the blame for what took place in April 1981. It can be argued that similar blame is being attached to Muslims in Britain today, only the majority of those affected are Asian. However, statistics reveal that some of these brothers and sisters are Black, and will probably find the current situation familiar, as it is one which their parents, or they themselves, faced under the 'sus' laws.[47]

The Straight Path

It is important to gain a sense of proportion on the issue of extremism within Islam. Muslim leaders and organizations (both the genuine ones and those selected by government as being 'responsible voices') have been at pains to argue that the vast majority of Muslims are law-abiding citizens who have no desire to harm Britain. They maintain that Islam is a peaceful faith which is tolerant and not incompatible with the vast majority of Western values. Black Muslim converts, for their part, share these sentiments.

It is important not to assume that the fervour of a convert will somehow lead him or her down the path of extremism. Religious conversion often involves working out your (new) relationship with a higher being or deity, and with the world and those who live in it. It requires seeing yourself and the world in a whole new light. If you hold to the belief that God is all-powerful, all-knowing and everlasting, any encounter with the Almighty should be life-changing. Moreover, if the Almighty is righteous and his people should be also, they should share God's passion for justice and truth. It is therefore quite natural for a person to display anger at poverty, injustice and inequality, especially if it involves his or her brethren. The great Malcolm X, a Muslim convert, was described as 'America's angriest man', not because he was a would-be bomber, but because he was angry about the treatment of his Black brothers and sisters and was willing to put everything on the line for this cause.

It would be natural for most Black Muslims to display real passion over matters of racism in the UK, and the lack of a meaningful resolution over the Middle East. The challenge these converts face is to galvanize themselves through the passion and ideas of great Black Muslim leaders who valued personal sacrifice over 'revolutionary suicide',[48] and used ideas and persuasive arguments to change hearts and minds.

Chapter 7

Black to the Future: The History of Britain's Muslim Convert Presence

The History of Britain's Black Muslims

According to the *Oxford Companion to Black British History* there is evidence of a Black Muslim presence in Britain which dates back to Tudor and Stuart times.[1] In 1596 Queen Elizabeth I ordered that 'blackmoores' and 'infidels' should be deported forthwith.[2] It has been argued that the Africans Her Majesty sought to eject from England were Muslim, practising a faith that many Christians in the country considered alien and threatening. It must be remembered that some of the queen's predecessors had almost bankrupted the country fighting against Muslims in the Middle East during the Crusades.[3] The queen's attitudes summed up the racial and religious prejudices that existed in England at that time. Records also show that 'three Moroccan delegations' visited London within a period of eleven years at the turn of the seventeenth century. 'The visitors were lodged at the Royal Exchange.'[4]

In his seminal book *Staying Power*, Peter Fryer explains how the transatlantic slave trade increased the numbers of Africans in Britain.[5] Many of these Africans arrived as enslaved men and women, though others had a free status and they usually worked. They usually worked in a range of menial tasks. It has been difficult to ascertain the religious affiliation of the Africans, especially if they were not Christian, because anyone who did not follow the Christian faith was dismissed as a pagan or infidel. What we do know is that according to a 1764 estimate, 'London was home to a community of about 20,000 freed slaves'.[6]

With the growth of the British empire around the globe, merchants and seamen from the Horn of Africa began settling in many British port cities. In the late nineteenth century, Somali men were a common sight on the docks of Cardiff, Liverpool, Bristol and London.[7] They were adventurous young men from the British protectorate of Somaliland who had left their homes to work in often atrocious conditions on the old coal-fired steamships that used to tour the empire.[7] Somalis also played a role fighting for king and country during both the First and Second World Wars. The beginning of multi-ethnic immigration from Britain's former empire saw a number of African Muslims arrive from Nigeria, Sierra Leone, Ghana and other places.

The Black Muslim Presence Today

According to the last census conducted in Britain, around 9 per cent of Black Britons describe themselves as Muslim, which makes Islam the second largest religion in Britain's Black communities after Christianity.[8] (No official statistics were available on religion from the previous census, taken in 1991.)

Black Muslims currently constitute around 7 per cent of Britain's overall Muslim population.[9] In London, where around 50 per cent of the Black population lives, it is estimated that 13 per cent of Muslims are Black.[10] The figures for other parts of the country are sketchy, but anecdotal evidence suggests that an increasing number of Black men in particular are converting, or 'reverting', to Islam.[11]

149

Very little has been written about the Black Muslim movement in Britain and what exists is relatively limited. Both the authoritative *Oxford Companion to Black British History*[12] and Peter Fryer's *Staying Power*[13] mention Black Muslims, but fail to provide a chronology of their presence in the UK. There is nothing about Black converts to Islam, although they are often the most conspicuous and controversial representatives of the faith in Britain.

If the division in world Islam is between those who follow Sunni and Shii traditions,[14] within a Black British context, as in the USA, the division lies between followers of the Nation of Islam's 'Fardian' teachings and those of Sunni or 'orthodox' Islam. Why both these branches of Islam are increasingly attracting Black people under forty – men in particular – should have been the subject of a whole school of academic research.

For the purposes of this book, a number of Muslims were asked for their suggestions as to why many Black people had, like them, turned to Islam. They appeared very pleased with the fact that their faith was increasingly being chosen by people in the West, both Black and White, but they applied a particular caution to this sanguinity. The 'orthodox' Muslims interviewed showed varying degrees of concern over the way that an increasing number of 'seekers', and a few converts, regard Islam as socio-religious and a political force which can solve problems around the globe by acts of aggression and bellicosity.[15] Many have been attracted by the perception that Islam is a combative faith which is prepared to confront Western hypocrisy head-on in the name of 'truth'. Abdul Best, a Muslim living in Tooting, said:

> Many are new to the faith and not familiar with the teachings of the Qur'an on mercy, brotherhood and most importantly peace. For me, Islam is not a faith taken up with discussion about flowers and mountains and the

ideas one associates with Omar Khayyam. But, it is also
not about *jihad*, *fatwa*s and repelling the infidels either.
The problem is that these brothers became interested in
the faith for particular reasons and their thinking and
belief systems have not changed since they made their
commitment.

In June 2008 the Black weekly publication *New Nation* laid the
blame for Black radicalization squarely at the feet of 'radical
Islamic clerics' who, it argued, 'prey on the vulnerable'. Quoting
Abdul Haq Ashanti of the Islamic Cultural Centre and Mosque in
Brixton, the article went on to suggest that: 'Some irresponsible
clerics target new converts who are eager to learn and who are
still quite gullible. We know that these extremist clerics have bad
intentions. They dupe a significant mass of young Black males by
bolstering their Islamic credentials.'[16]

The issue of vulnerability and being impressionable among the
young remains important within Black communities, where almost
50 per cent of youths grow up in single parent households headed
by women, and contact with a positive male role model is often
non-existent.[17] The last few decades have witnessed a number of
phenomena appearing to fill this vacuum by providing young
people with comradeship and protection, with the most troubling
of these being gangs. Estimates suggest that there are around 170
gangs in London alone, which provide their young members with
friendship, protection and support at the expense of alienation and
criminality.[18] Both the church and the mosque have sought more
positive solutions to the issues affecting Britain's Black youth, with
varying degrees of success. When this work is efficacious, lives are
transformed and communities change, but when it goes awry, as
in the case of the 'Black Islamic bombers', lives are destroyed and
entire communities are held to blame.

Evidence suggests that the Black Muslim convert population
in Britain during the 1970s and 1980s was small, and that many

who called themselves Muslims practised their faith privately, sufficing with a name change, abstinence from alcohol and adherence to dietary rules. But it can be argued that Islam's profile was raised by the *Satanic Verses* furore in 1987. In towns and cities such as Bradford, Burnley and Oldham Muslims found their voices and confidence to speak out, not only against Salman Rushdie's book, but also against the prejudice that Muslim communities were facing in Britain.[19] A further political flashpoint was the first Gulf War, which saw the USA and its allies fight to eject Saddam Hussein's armies from Kuwait in the name of democracy, even though no such system existed in the country. And there was also the West's reluctance to act as honest brokers in relation to the Israel and Palestine situation.[20]

In the last few decades Muslims from Britain, as in other parts of the globe, have been increasingly expressing their grievances over apparent US and European inertia in the Middle East, over interference in Afghanistan, and over what they perceive as the West's modern-day crusade against world Islam.[21] At the same time the re-emergence of Black consciousness and Afrocentrism within the Black diaspora has been evidenced in popular culture (hip-hop music and the Five Percenter movement), in the popularity of books and videos by African-American academics such as Leonard Jeffries, John Henrik Clarke and the Trinidadian Garvey expert Tony Martin, and the growing influence of the Honourable Louis Farrakhan.

Popular culture, history and religion found a perfect synergy in filmmaker Spike Lee's *Malcolm X*, an account of the life, death and legacy of the late, great Muslim activist. Although not a Muslim himself, Spike Lee was sympathetic toward the faith, even meeting with Minister Farrakhan prior to filming.[22] Equally, in struggling with the Hollywood film studios to get his movie completed, Lee displayed a charisma, self-sufficiency and sheer bloody-mindedness that recalled Marcus Garvey and his ideas of Black self-help.[23]

The movie played to packed cinemas on both sides of the Atlantic. In Britain, those who had been inspired by reading Malcolm X's autobiography now saw a cinematic transformation of the one-time hustler and prison inmate into a sharp-talking, no-nonsense Black man.[24] For some Black Britons, *Malcolm X* represented what their life could be if they acquired the transformational knowledge proffered by Islam. For those to whom Malcolm X was only a name, the film put flesh on the bones of a man whom the great African-American actor Ossie Davis described as 'our manhood, our living, black manhood!... our own black shining prince! Who didn't hesitate to die, because he loved us so.'[25] Black Londoners started to appear in T-shirts bearing slogans such as 'By any means necessary' or 'You wouldn't understand, it's a Black thing!' or 'No sell-out!'[26] Others put away their gold medallions and chains and opted for leather pendants, brass amulets and woven bracelets with images of Africa, beads or cowrie shells.

Birth of a Nation

At this time it was possible to see clusters of young men from the Nation of Islam (UK), dressed neatly in dark suits and bow ties, selling copies of the *Final Call* in areas of London with a sizeable Black population such as Brixton, Croydon, Peckham and Tottenham. They would congregate outside a tube or train station or shopping centre on a Saturday, looking to engage men of a similar age in conversation about social and religious matters. I first came across the Nation of Islam (UK) during my student days, when its adherents congregated outside the shopping centre in Dalston, east London, selling newspapers. I used to make regular visits to Dalston from my digs in Stoke Newington on Saturdays to buy African-Caribbean food, records and other items from the Ridley Road street market, which was adjacent to the shopping centre. It was impossible to miss these Muslim brothers and even more difficult to avoid all conversation with them. At this point the Nation of Islam (UK) had a mosque at 2B Prince George Road, which adjoins Stoke Newington High Street and is a stone's throw from Dalston.

Converts to the Nation of Islam (UK) in Britain tend to be people who have had some connection to the churches, so they are aware of the basic tenets of Christianity as well as Christian doctrine and practices. During their Friday evening study and discussion times they often spend as much time perusing the Bible as they do the Qur'an for spiritual answers. All Muslims display a certain respect for the Bible,[27] but the Nation of Islam (UK) appear to have a deeper reverence for it. Nation of Islam (UK) adherents are known for their knowledge of the Bible and their religious instruction requires adherents to know what Christians call the Old Testament and the New Testament. This approach is highly practical, as most of the Black people they talk to probably have some working knowledge of the Bible but little of the Qur'an. As a result, the Bible is often used as a reference or starting point for religious street discussions.

The Nation of Islam (UK), like all Muslims, are of course fully conversant with the Qur'an and quote freely from it whenever the need arises. Hence, it is always interesting to observe their religious discussions with Christians; both tend to be on firm ground when discussing biblical matters, but the moment the conversation switches to the Qur'an, the Christian is suddenly on shaky ground. Most Black Christians have never even looked into the Qur'an out of curiosity, and spoken to those for the purposes of this book did not possess one for reference.[28]

As well as the Qur'an and Bible, the other text of special interest for the Nation of Islam (UK) is the Honourable Elijah Muhammad's *Message to the Blackman*, a book which is littered with biblical references and prophecies. Although history suggests that Elijah Muhammad passed away in 1975, many within the Nation of Islam (UK) believe he is 'still alive' – a revelation that was first made known to the current leader, Minister Louis Farrakhan, in the early 1980s.[29] Hence, the *Message to the Blackman* takes on special resonance for many Black Muslims, as do the writings and speeches of Louis Farrakhan, which are sometimes used as material for group discussion.

The re-emergence of Black consciousness and Afrocentrism among Black Britons in the late 1980s occurred alongside the growth of Black entrepreneurial initiatives which combined the desire to 'recycle the pound' within the Black community with that of spreading knowledge. This resulted in the emergence of arts and crafts and bookshops throughout London and in the Black enclaves of cities such as Birmingham, Manchester, Leeds, Huddersfield and Bristol. Dalston had a number of these shops, which had the express aim of celebrating Africa's glorious past and its current potential through the retail of items such as African carvings, paintings and religious symbols. It was possible to buy books on anything from the ancient Egyptians being Black to the African discovery of the Americas. Religious subject matter usually consisted of books on traditional African belief systems, the African roots of the Bible, Rastafari and Islam.

It was in shops such as these that the Honourable Elijah Muhammad's *Message to the Blackman* and *How to Eat to Live* could be purchased by would-be interested parties. The shelves of these bookstores displayed numerous videos and tapes of the Honourable Louis Farrakhan's speeches and talks in the USA. Due to Louis Farrakhan's exclusion from the UK, in the early days the faithful and the fascinated had to make do with this technology in order to hear from the Supreme Minister. The advent of satellite technology and the growth of the internet have enabled the Nation of Islam (UK) to circumvent the proscription,[30] and their Sunday gatherings in Brixton often involve a live video stream of Minister Farrakhan's talks from the USA.

For many people, the Nation of Islam (UK)'s best-known adherent is Leo Muhammad, who was born Leo Chester in Jamaica in the late 1950s, but raised in the UK. I first became aware of his comic prowess in 1990 when he supported the comedy duo Curtis and Ishmael at a gig at the now defunct Cave venue on Moseley Road in Birmingham. In the late 1980s a new, cutting-edge Black British comedy emerged, which left behind the old stereotypical humour of comedians such as Charlie Williams and even the young Lenny Henry in his first stand-up routines of the 1970s. Alongside Sheila Hyde, Miles Crawford, Curtis (Walker) and Ishmael (Thomas), Llewella Gideon, Felicity Ethnic, and (Geoff) Aymer and (Marcus) Powell, Leo Chester was in a vanguard that sought to transform the nature of Black comedy in Britain.

By the early 1990s Chester had embraced Islam and his comedy was now 'edutainment' – a combination of humour and education. His performances were a curious mix of comedy, teaching and preaching, with the first part of the show containing gags and the second part serious teaching. There was always a strong Black Muslim presence at these events, with women, dressed in white, seated at the front on one side of the hall while their menfolk sat on the other.

The Nation of Islam basked in the worldwide publicity surrounding the Million Man March on Washington in the US, which demonstrated the influence of Louis Farrakhan on a world stage. They were also helped by the British-born, US-raised boxer Michael X. Bentt winning the World Boxing Organization heavyweight belt in October 1993. In the USA, the Nation of Islam has always enjoyed the benefits of recruiting championship boxers, starting with Muhammad Ali in 1964.[31] In the late 1970s a number of Muslim boxers such as Eddie Mustafa Muhammad (Eddie Gregory), Dwight Muhammad Qawi (Dwight Braxton) and Matthew Saad Muhammad (Matt Franklin) held world titles at light heavyweight.[32]

By the 1990s Britain was desperate to have its first heavyweight champion since Bob Fitzsimmons in 1897,[33] and Bentt, although no longer resident in Britain, fitted the bill for some. The new champion carried out a number of interviews on sporting programmes such as the BBC's *Grandstand* and *Sportsnight*, and even made an appearance on Channel Four's *Big Breakfast* magazine programme, when he refused to be interviewed by the late Paula Yates reclining on her bed. He spoke to the presenter about his boxing career and his Islamic faith, which was one of the reasons why he refused to lie next to her, along with a concern to avoid ridicule. Although Michael X. Bentt was no Muhammad Ali, either in the ring or outside it, he conducted himself with dignity and spoke well in interviews, and was often seen flanked by Fruit of Islam bodyguards.

Unfortunately for the Nation of Islam, Bentt's tenure as champion was fleeting. Herbie Hide knocked him out in a title fight in London in March 1994, which saw him struggle to regain consciousness from a coma. As a result, Bentt was forced to retire from the ring and, like many of his peers, turned his attention to Hollywood, where he appeared in a number of boxing roles as Michael A. Bentt, the most notable being Sonny Liston in the film *Ali*, where he starred alongside Will Smith. It is not known whether he is still active within the faith.

The Nation of Islam (UK) was involved in its own version of the Million Man March in the late 1990s when it organized a 10,000 Man Atonement March in London as part of the Black United Front, an amalgamation of various Black religious and secular groups. This event, which took place in a rain-drenched Trafalgar Square on 17 October 1998, attracted Black men in their thousands.[34] Black Majority Churches were undecided about how to respond to the Nation of Islam (UK)'s invitation to be part of this event. One church leader, Kingsway's Matthew Ashimolowo, argued that it was 'an insult to Christ' for his church 'to march or speak under the crest or star of Islam'.[35] Others, such as former African-Caribbean Evangelical Alliance director Ron Nathan, believed that Christians could best serve God by being part of the gathering.

The Nation of Islam (UK) hit the headlines through its intervention at the Stephen Lawrence inquiry, an attempt to piece together events surrounding the racist killing of a Black teenager.[36] Like a number of other Black groups, the Nation of Islam (UK) had taken an active interest in the Stephen Lawrence case, which was seen as a testing ground for racial justice in the UK.[37] According to the BBC news, 'Members of the black supremacist group confronted policemen, shouting "You are stopping the public from coming into the inquiry. You are disrespecting black people."' As a result, 'the inquiry... was temporarily suspended... after action by members of the Nation of Islam'.[38] The BBC followed up this news item with a critical profile that expressed doubts over the Nation of Islam (UK)'s size, secrecy and beliefs.[39] Like its US counterpart, the Nation of Islam (UK) is reluctant to provide information on its membership, but it is estimated to be in the thousands.

Black Muslims and London

Since the capital is home to 60 per cent of Britain's Black population, it is inevitably the city where most Black Islamic activity takes place. Within London there are certain areas with a historic Black population that have now become known as centres of the Black Muslim presence, such as Brixton, in south London.

The Nation of Islam (UK)'s headquarters are located in Brixton, in a former industrial building that has been converted for worship purposes. These 'change of use' properties have become the preferred homes for the flourishing African Pentecostal churches in south London, and the road on which the main mosque is found also contains several such churches. Although Leo Muhammad is arguably the Nation of Islam (UK)'s most high-profile adherent, its current leader is Hilary Muhammad, whose official title, 'Student Minister', makes him the UK representative of the Honourable Minister Louis Farrakhan.

Student Minister Muhammad is a charismatic individual, and his talks and debates seamlessly weave the religious with the socio-political in a way not unlike one of the better Black Christian preachers. As one would expect, Hilary Muhammad is fully conversant with both the Qur'an and the Bible and his words are punctuated with appropriate verses from each in answer to questions.

He says that the Nation of Islam (UK)'s 'work in this country is primarily aimed at peoples of African and Caribbean descent and indeed involves imparting knowledge and performing community activities that can benefit a wide range of peoples'.[40] Like all Black Muslims he believes that knowledge is power and wants to liberate Black minds from the 'mental deadness' caused by centuries of enslavement, colonization and other forms of degradation. As a result the Nation of Islam (UK) takes a keen interest in formal and informal education for all age ranges. It has also been involved for over a decade in the New Mind School, an independent institute which began as a supplementary school, but has now developed into a full-time school for children between the ages of three and eleven. The New Mind School gives its pupils a 'holistic education, teaching a knowledge of God, oneself, and respect for others'.[41] It is not just the building, or the use of Bibles or its sermonizing that makes the Nation of Islam (UK) very reminiscent of a church; unlike most orthodox Muslims, Nation of Islam (UK) members hold their main meeting on a Sunday afternoon, while Friday's meeting takes place in the evening rather than at lunch time for the traditional *jumah* or Friday prayers.

A short walk from the headquarters of the Nation of Islam (UK) is the Masjid ibn Taymeeyah, better known as Brixton Mosque and Islamic Cultural Centre, which has gained something of a reputation in the media because of a number of 'radicals' who have at one time worshipped at the mosque.[42] Based in a Victorian terraced house, the mosque is renowned for its work with those who have become Muslims while incarcerated at the nearby prison in Brixton Hill.[43] The mosque is very much a multi-cultural establishment, with many of its Black adherents being converts or 'reverts' to Islam from Christianity and other faiths. For many years Abdul Haqq Baker, a British-born man in his early forties who converted to Islam in 1989, has chaired the mosque and has had to deal with the rising numbers of young Black people interested in Islam.[44]

Brixton mosque is part of the Salafi or Salafiyya movement, which is a version of Sunni Islam that believes the faith was complete during the days of the Prophet Muhammad*. Various developments have been added over later centuries because of materialist and other cultural influences, and Salafism seeks to return or restore Islam to being the religion it was during the time of Prophet Muhammad*.[45]The mosque is at pains to argue that its teachings are orthodox and in no wise encourage radicalism among converts or seekers. It seeks to teach the basics of the religion and to assimilate those on the margins back into society.[46]

The mosque was initially established almost two decades ago by a group of people, some of whom have now moved to East Anglia, who were interested in finding out how Islam could bring greater spiritual fulfilment to their lives as young Black men in inner-city London. Most of these young men, such as Amari Douglas, were drawn toward Islam's teachings on peace, mercy and forgiveness as well as the brotherhood it offered believers who submitted to the will of Allah. For many, conversion was not a rejection of Christianity, as they never believed what they read in the Scriptures to be the truth; it was more the case that reading the Qur'an and speaking to fellow believers and observing their lifestyle eventually led to conversion.

The Role of Women and Modesty
What all (Black) Muslims have in common is the placing of women in what many would consider subservient roles within

the faith. Like Christianity and Judaism, Islam is a patriarcha
faith which has afforded traditional roles to men and women
within society.[47] For instance, within the Nation of Islam (UK)
one would never see a woman selling copies of the *Final Call* on a
shopping precinct in Croydon or outside an Underground station
in Brixton. This activity is the preserve of men; it is the women's
role to carry out the nurturing of children and maintaining the
family home. Women are expected to conform to strict religious
norms concerning behaviour, conduct and dress, and are
generally expected to accept the headship of their menfolk.[48]

A frequent criticism made against some Black women
converts is that their attitude to dress is a matter of extremes.
Before they become Muslims, their clothes are often revealing;
and afterwards they become exaggeratedly modest. However,
there is evidence that many Black British Muslim women
regard dressing modestly, or *hijab* (covering the head, arms and
legs), as liberating, since it frees them from the pressures and
expense of a fashion consciousness which is linked to the sexual
objectification of women.[49] Interestingly, many of the women
interviewed for this book were very critical of the way society
has always portrayed women, and were concerned that girls
were being 'sexualized' very early by what they were wearing,
reading in magazines and learning at school. Brixton-born Aisha
Joseph, who became a Muslim a decade ago, is someone who
takes pride in both her faith and her identity. When I met her at a
library in Lambeth, she was dressed in a beautiful *salwar kameez*,
which is considered traditional attire for women and men from
south Asia. She looked sophisticated and dignified, and said
that dressing in this way was both comfortable and inexpensive.
During the course of our conversation, Aisha mentioned that she
had once been a follower of the dance-hall music scene, which
would suggest that she formerly dressed quite differently. When
we discuss women's attire in Islam, she says:

loing is going back to our roots. You read
ory [she points to the section of the library
ick history material] and you'll see that
;o our women were dressed like this [she
points to her garment]. This was at a time when the
peoples elsewhere were wearing next to nothing. Look at
how things have changed. Instead of going forwards, our
people have gone backwards. My sisters feel no shame
going out on the street with little more than their birthday
suits, and the worst thing is they don't feel any shame
about this.

Patriarchy and Emasculation

The issue of patriarchy within African-diaspora families is
riddled with contradictions and ironies. Men, the supposed
heads of the households, actually play an equal role to women for
a number of socio-economic and historic reasons. In her seminal
publication, *Black Macho and the Myth of the Superwoman*, Michele
Wallace explored the ways in which migration, structural racism
and other economic pressures forced Black women to become
the *de facto* head of the home.[50]

But some Black Muslim women appear keen to empower their
menfolk, whom they regard as having been emasculated by
centuries of African chattel enslavement, which denied them the
roles usually assigned to men in patriarchal societies.[51] For women
such as Shahida Muhammad, from Wandsworth, south London,
Islam gives a man the opportunity to exercise his manhood and
play out the roles defined by the Qur'an. She says, 'The Black man
is by nature strong and forceful. Slavery took that away. It wanted
him to be a boy; to act like a boy rather than the strong Black man
that he is and whose job it was to provide and protect his family.
Allah has provided such a man for me – so who am I to argue?'

Not every woman, or man, would agree with this rather
phlegmatic response to the roles of women within 'Black' Islam.

162

Historically, African-American feminists or 'womanist' academics and activists have always been critical of the notion of Black emasculation during centuries of chattel enslavement.[52] They have also been wary of the attitudes of the Black nationalist and Black Power organizations in the 1960s, including the Muslims, to the role of Black women in the civil rights struggle and in society *per se*. The late, great Malcolm X, who was regarded as the embodiment of 'Black manhood', had some rather barbed comments to make about women. According to the academic Michael Eric Dyson, 'Malcolm X went to extremes in demonising women, saying that the "closest thing to a woman is a devil".'[53] And the African-American writer and academic bell hooks suggests that 'Malcolm often blamed black women for many of the problems black men faced... '.[54] She adds that Malcolm's advancement of 'black patriarchy...afforded 'Black men the right to dominate black women'. This 'was part and parcel of the conservative ideology underlying the Black Muslim religion and both reformist and radical approaches to black liberation'.[55] According to Michele Wallace, 'the most important reason the Black Movement did not work was that black men did not realize they could not wage struggle without full involvement of women'.[56] The apparent Muslim desire to sideline women in relation to issues affecting the Black community was arguably exemplified by the historic Million Man March in 1995. Prominent African-American feminists such as Angela Davis and Julianne Malveaux denounced the deliberate exclusion of women from the mobilization, 'arguing that Farrakhan's reactionary concepts of women were patriarchal and misogynist'.[57]

Did Black women in the diaspora struggle so valiantly alongside their menfolk to end centuries of White chattel enslavement, which used the Christian religion to subjugate them,[58] only to find themselves subjugated once again by another religion, Islam, that claimed to liberate them? And can it be argued that some Black men are attracted to Islam because Muslim women appear 'surrendered' and are willing to put the socio-economic and spiritual requirements of their men first? Among the individuals I interviewed, no Muslim woman looked as if she was under the thumb of her spouse or was a religious 'Stepford Wife' who lived and breathed for his pleasure. The Black women interviewed were intelligent, confident and not lacking in self-esteem; and there is no way anyone could call them naïve or impressionable. The majority were qualified to degree level and were familiar with the criticisms levelled against Islam by Black and White detractors; they had well-rehearsed answers to the usual arguments. It was obvious that their decisions to become Muslims owed as much to the head as the heart; they were aware of the exigencies that the religion placed upon them as Black women, and of possible responses of others to their decisions.

On the few occasions that I interviewed Muslim couples together, their body language displayed love and respect, with couples looking to one another for accord or a sign of agreement in responding to my questions. Moreover I never gained the impression that women's views were not taken seriously or given the opportunity to be heard. However, I tended to notice that, during conversations with couples, it was often the man who responded first to questions, with the woman only responding first when a question was primarily female-orientated. These women also seemed slightly more hesitant and restrained in their responses as opposed to those who were interviewed on their own. While it would be wrong to read anything sinister into this, it was noticeable. Having said that, the women interviewed on their own were no less open in their praise of their menfolk, and there were never any critical voices. [59]

Black women have a well-documented history of fighting oppression both alongside their menfolk and on their own. It is often difficult to reconcile a history of strong African warrior women, whether on the continent of Africa or in the diaspora, whether it be Queen Ngola Ann Nzinga in Angola or Nanny of the Maroons in Jamaica, with the image of women wearing *hijabs* for the sake of modesty as defined by men. The wearing of such conservative attire does not preclude women from struggle, as the two things have little direct connection, but one can argue that modesty was not uppermost in the minds of these women who fought for their freedom and equality.[60]

No man would even allow me to suggest that one of the reasons he was attracted to Islam was that it is patriarchal. Most of the married men spoke about their wives in terms filled with both religious and practical affection. One brother, Jamal Brown, spoke about his wife as being like a 'hand which complements his'; another, Abdul Malik, said his spouse was a 'blessing from above'. When asked about their role within the family none was under any misapprehension that the man was not the head of the home and a protector for the family.[61] Jamal said that his relationship with his wife was one of partners whose love and commitment to one another had been blessed by the birth of two children, and that it was his divine responsibility to provide for his family. He did not appear to entertain any notions of the deferential wife nor the need to assert a hypermasculinity over his wife and family. Abdul Malik confessed that prior to his 'reversion' and subsequent marriage he had had a number of broken relationships, and he was committed to making his current relationship work as a Muslim believer. He spoke about his wife in rather reverent terms, which were endearing, but also reminiscent of the way many of the Rasta men I knew spoke about their 'queens'. This was always complimentary, but it did not stop them from showing disrespect through their own sexual promiscuity. This behaviour is typified by the Rastafari reggae artist Bob Marley, who fathered numerous children with different mothers while married to his 'queen' of fifteen years, Rita Anderson Marley.[62]

The whole issue of marriage within Islam is fascinating, as the faith makes provision for polygamous (or polygynous) marriages under certain circumstances, though it limits the number of wives to four.[63] This practice, which is no longer common (or lawful in the West) is inevitably weighted in favour of men.[64] It has also been regarded by ill-informed detractors as one of the reasons why many Black men are attracted to Islam. There are instances of non-religious Black men marrying women from Muslim backgrounds and continuing their promiscuous ways in the mistaken belief that Muslim women are used to their men having other women, but these marriages usually end in a predictable divorce. The institution of polygamy also exists within some traditional African societies, and similar accusations are also made against men within these cultures.[65]

There is little doubt that Muslims could benefit from better public relations to debunk the long-held misconceptions and untruths that many people take a pleasure in disseminating. If this happened, more would be aware of the fact that Black Muslim families display a stability and cohesion that the Black Majority Churches had previously regarded as their preserve.[66] As the result of conversion men who were formerly on the margins of society or at risk have often become 'model citizens' whose discipline, focus and integrity make them ideal role models for today's Black youth. The recently launched Reach initiative 'is a key Communities and Local Government project aimed at raising the aspirations, attainment and achievement of Black boys and young Black men, enabling them to reach their potential'.[67] Among other activities, it has brought together a number of Black men who are deemed ideal role models for Black youth. It would have been useful to have had prominent Black Muslims among them to highlight their contribution to the Black community. Likewise, given the excellent work Muslims are doing among ex-offenders, it would have been useful to have included a Muslim man who had lived a similar life to these young people, but had been able to turn his life around, as an inspiration for those looking to change their lives.

The project of raising the aspirations of Black youth needs to use all available resources. Black Muslim men who have overcome a range of adversities to lead lives as upstanding citizens are a resource the Black community, and society in general, can ill afford to ignore.

Chapter 8

Telling Tales: Black Muslims Speak

Conversion Stories

People's views of Muslim converts, and of Islam in general, are often dependent on a personal contact with Muslims and knowledge of Islam. This is particularly the situation with the Black community. Without generalizing too much, it would be true to say that those who have relationships with Muslims and have first-hand knowledge of the faith tend to have a more favourable estimation and are less inclined to rely on the usual negative sources for their opinions or fall back on stereotypes. Having said that, this does not mean that those with Muslim sons and daughters, partners or parents are immune from prejudiced words or behaviour.

Research for this book has shown that some of the most critical opinions of Islam come from people, usually with their own strong beliefs, who feel betrayed by their friends' or relatives' choices. Just as some of the most racist views can be found among those whose relatives or friends are involved with a person of a different ethnicity, so those with Muslim relatives often hold bigoted opinions about Muslims.

In recent years the Black Muslim movement in Britain has gained a reputation for 'cleaning up' Black people who have been failed by society or have fallen foul of the law. A lot of this work goes unheralded and is low key, but has been efficacious for many of the beneficiaries. Yet even those who can see the differences Islam has made in the lives of loved ones often remain sceptical about the faith and those connected with it.

Jamal Rahman

One of those who have benefited from Islamic rehabilitation work is Jamal Rahman, a gangling Brixtonian who, by his own admission, was a wayward youth. He confesses: 'I was wild, man! Totally out of control. You couldn't tell me anything. I knew it all – or I thought I did.' By his early twenties he had drifted into what he describes as 'petty crime', which was connected to his cannabis intake. Such activities landed him with several short, almost concurrent, prison sentences. It was while he was serving time in HMP Brixton that he encountered Islam. In a classic conversion, Jamal renounced drugs and nearly all aspects of his former life. On release, his now weary and wary parents received him back into their nearby family home with reluctance, and paid very little attention to their son's protestations about being a new man. He takes up the story: 'After my incarceration, I came out a new man. I was determined to show everyone how I was a different person because of Islam. At first they thought I was playing some sort of game. Then they thought I was mad, especially when I told them about my Muslim name. It was really crazy at first.' Jamal's birth name was Milton Seymour Davidson, and his father initially insisted on continuing to use Milton (Milton being the family's traditional name for the first-born male). According to Jamal, his mother, a Christian in the New Testament Assembly denomination, was a little more sympathetic, but everyone in his large family remained sceptical of his new beliefs and resulting lifestyle. He believes that his father reckoned his conversion was a scam – invented to inveigle his way back into the house. His younger brother thought he was insincere: in the past he had claimed he had 'turned around his life' through the martial arts.

Over the months he managed to win over his family and earn their respect for his faith. His parents noticed that most of his time was spent in prayer at home or in the local mosque, rather than on the streets with friends whom his parents regarded as a bad influence. His mother said that she could now get a good night's sleep, safe in the knowledge that he was in bed rather than cruising some of south London's more perilous streets. Jamal's preference for simple Islamic clothing is also respected. According to Jamal, 'My parents think it's great that I don't show so much interest in clothes – I was always someone who had to wear the latest style. I always wanted the latest fashions but I never had the cash to buy them. I think that's why I got into the dodgy stuff. That's over now.' Likewise, his abstinence from smoking marijuana, always a cause of constant argument in the family, has been welcomed by all, and even his refusal to eat his mother's noted garlic pork is no longer treated with contempt or ridicule.

Although it would be wrong to suggest that Jamal's parents are now fully accepting of his conversion to Islam, they are no longer hostile and are willing to accept him and his beliefs as part of the family. He concludes, 'You know what, I can't say they are totally happy with my beliefs' – he points to his Qur'an – 'but compared to what things were, I would say things are OK.' Jamal is now considered a 'positive' influence on his siblings – as opposed to a negative one as before – and is often heard encouraging his brothers to avoid drink, drugs and a 'carnal' lifestyle. He is currently studying at college and wants to become a teacher.

Abdul Yusuf

Jamal's experience is in direct contrast to that of Abdul Yusuf, formerly Joseph McClean, a shaven-headed, squat thirty-something with a beaming smile. Abdul's parents are committed Christians; his father is one of the pastors at a Pentecostal church in Dalston, east London. Like Jamal, Abdul first came into contact with Islam while serving time in prison, for fraud. Abdul admits that he has always had a testy relationship with his father, and takes up the story: 'Me being a Muslim has nothing to do with it. His beef has to do with me refusing to go to church when I was a youth. He couldn't believe I could turn my back on his beloved church.' Abdul's father refused to visit him while he was incarcerated because he saw his prison sentence as a consequence of his abandoning Christianity.

Abdul's father regarded his embrace of Islam as a betrayal of his own Christian upbringing and background, and a failure on his own part. According to Abdul, his father's religious beliefs mean that he's forced to treat him with 'love', but he feels there is little real affection. He says, 'I think my old man loves me in his own way. What he doesn't like is Islam, which he thinks is devil worship. He reckons Christianity is the only way and he tells me he prays for me every night. He wants me to become like him!' Abdul believes his father has a particular dislike for Islam, which he believes 'is corrupting the hearts of Black men in Britain'. Abdul's pleas for his father to judge him by his 'actions rather than words' have fallen on deaf ears. He continues, 'What I can't understand is his refusal to see the truth. He keeps going on about "truth this", and "truth that". Well, the truth is I went to church and it did nothing for me. I got into trouble. I'm not blaming anyone there, but in all truth, prison was the best thing that happened to me. While I was inside I became a Muslim. Look at me now. Totally changed. I can see it, the world can see it, everyone can see it, except a certain Pastor McClean and his wife!'

His conversion has seen Abdul become a 'real' father to his three children (he previously had little contact with them, and his father used to call him 'worthless'); he now runs his own business, a small Islamic shop in a south London market (he was previously unemployed) and has plans to purchase the house he currently rents. Encounters between father and son invariably result in animated discussions about theology and epistemology, and the efficacy of their respective faiths. Although father and son discuss religion, Abdul has been told not to speak about it among his three siblings, two of whom are teenagers, for fear of making further 'pagans'. He is also forbidden to carry out any religious practices in the family home. He adds: 'It's a good job I don't live there no more. The Qur'an teaches you that if you live in a place where there is persecution you must remove yourself from that place. I hope that they will come to their senses and see things for what they are – Insha'Allah.'

Hakim Ibrahim

Another Muslim convert, Hakim Ibrahim, believes that his conversion to Islam has caused real damage to a once-close relationship with his parents. Unlike the previous interviewees, Hakim (formerly Timothy Jefferson) was a model child whose doting parents were extremely proud when he passed ten GCSEs and obtained two 'A's at A level. Hakim says, 'I first became interested in Islam when I was a student at university. We had these freshers' fairs and I got speaking to two guys from the Islamic Society. I was never that religious – I mean, I went to church now and again for weddings and the like.' Hakim is an only child, and his parents noticed the subtle, yet frequent, changes in their son every time he returned home during term breaks. The first was his insistence that he did not eat certain foods (for health reasons). He then began growing a beard, without a moustache, and a copy of the Qur'an was always to be found with his academic books. He started refusing to accompany his parents to church at Christmas and Easter, preferring to spend his time watching DVDs of Islamic clerics.

It should have come as no great surprise to Hakim's parents when he announced that he had converted, or reverted, to Islam and taken on the name 'Hakim'. He says, 'They went ballistic – both of them. They were acting like I'd let the side down. It was totally irrational.' Hakim reckons he's faced nothing short of persecution since he broke the news to his parents. 'My mum hopes I'll grow out of it and that I'll leave it all behind once I graduate in 2009. My dad, well, he's another story! The man has taken leave of his senses. It's all *jihad* this, and *sharia* that! I wouldn't mind but he knows nothing about Islam. He gets all his information from the *Daily Mail* and Wikipedia.' Hakim admits that he has yet to have a meaningful discussion with his father, and can only try to persuade him that there is more to his faith than terrorism, radicalization and suicide bombers. In his father's eyes, his level-headed, studious son has been brainwashed by radicals at university. His father contacted the university to complain about the Islamic Society's activities and even threatened to cut off funding for his son if he continues 'with this nonsense'. At the time of writing, Hakim's father has not made good on the funding threats, but has refused to attend the graduation ceremony if his son insists on using his Islamic name and dressing in religious attire. There is little doubt that Hakim finds this situation very distressing, and would not want his faith to be the cause of trouble between family and friends. But he is mindful of the sacrifices a believer has to make for Islam and sees this as one.

Raheem Hasan

Another believer who is willing to make these sacrifices is Raheem Hasan, a burly Jamaican-born brother with a scar on his eyebrow, probably the only reminder of his former career as a prize fighter. Unlike the others interviewed for this book, the forty-three-year-old refuses to divulge information about his 'real name'. When asked he quickly responds: 'It's not important. I no longer answer to that name because I am no longer that person.' Raheem first became interested in Islam after he shook the hand of his former idol, Muhammad Ali, when the 'greatest' visited his native Hockley in Birmingham in the early 1980s.

Raheem not only took up boxing, he also began reading about Islam, via Malcolm X's autobiography. For most of the 1980s and early 1990s Raheem says he closely identified with the teachings of the Honourable Louis Farrakhan, whom he still describes as the 'bravest Black man in the USA'. However, he never joined the Nation of Islam (UK) because, he says, 'I always thought they looked down on sports. I had a tape of Minister Farrakhan speaking about basketball players and he seemed to think that Black youth should concentrate more on education and things. At that time, boxing was all I knew. I couldn't give it up so I decided to follow [Islam] from a distance.' About a decade ago Raheem found himself increasingly drawn toward the more spiritual aspects of 'Sufi' Islam and made the full reversion or conversion at the turn of the millennium. When asked what Islam means to him, his answer is curt: 'Everything! It means everything.' About his conversion's impact on his family he says: 'They're cool with it. My wife's now a Muslim as well as my boys. I didn't face any issues whatsoever. You should try it, my brother!'

Waheed Ogunkoye

Another brother whose family embraced his beliefs is twenty-five-year-old north Londoner Waheed Ogunkoye, who is from a Nigerian and Jamaican background.

I became a Muslim about three years after my older brother Kareem, back in 2005. He used to have these CDs around the house and I'd listen to them on my way to work. They used to talk about all kinds of things like life, health, the Middle East – all sorts really. They really made me think. When I asked him about them he gave me some books to read which spoke about the Prophet Muhammad* and how he received the Qur'an by divine means and how Islam requires us to submit to the will of Allah. I didn't become a Muslim straight away. My brother got married to an Arab woman and moved to Turkey. After that I became a Muslim. My mum's cool with that. We always talk about religion at home because my brother was a Muslim and she's used to the religion.

Although Waheed's father lives in Nigeria his parents are not separated. He says, 'My dad knows about my conversion and he's OK with it. We have Muslims in our family in Nigeria. I plan to go and see them next year.'

Jameel McClintock

Another interviewee was forty-year-old Jameel McClintock, a mixed-race brother who became a Muslim after almost fifteen years as a Marxist. He states, 'For years I was one of those who swallowed the *Communist Manifesto* totally. I believed in dialectic materialism, which basically means I was an atheist – God didn't exist – there were no universal truths, religions and spirits. It was all about a battle of ideas based around the class struggle to overthrow global capitalism and the bourgeoisie.' When he speaks about his old Marxist days there are flashes of the old revolutionary fire. He continues:

I first became interested in Islam when I carried out a comparative study of Islam and Communism using Afghanistan as a focal point. Both Marxism and Islam are worldviews; there is a Marxist interpretation or analysis of nearly everything, just like Islam. The major difference was a belief in a supreme being and this was a deciding factor in Afghanistan when the Mujahaddin fought against the Russian communist insurgents. All this study showed me Islam was more than ideas; it was about brotherhood and justice and love. I travelled to Egypt and Saudi Arabia to study Islam and became a Muslim in 2002.

175

When asked to compare Islam to Marxism he says, 'We used to say that the essence of human beings is to work to bring about change. As a Muslim, it's about submission to the will of Allah.' Jameel's parents split up when he was a boy and he has not seen his father in over a decade. He is also estranged from his mother and younger sister, who live in Wiltshire. As a result, his conversion had no impact on family members. He says that his family are now his brothers at the mosque in south London.

Maryam Saddique

The conversion of Maryam Saddique (formerly Mary Taylor) to Islam has met with a positive reception from family and friends. Her mother was largely enthusiastic (her father is deceased), and her siblings are generally very supportive. Like so many of her generation, Maryam became interested in Islam after watching Spike Lee's seminal *Malcolm X* biopic in the early 1990s. She says:

> Before I saw that film I didn't know anything about
> Malcolm X. He was just a name. The movie totally
> changed everything. I remember going down to the
> library the next day – it was a Sunday but it was open –
> and I took out these three books on Malcolm X and read
> them off. Up to that point I knew little about Black history,
> slavery and Islam. A few years later I went to Senegal
> with friends and stayed with their family in Dhaka. We
> went to this place called Goree Island, and saw where
> they kept the slaves. The family I stayed with were
> Muslims and I felt drawn to the people and their beliefs.
> I know that might sound strange but that's how it felt.
> When I got back I started talking to a Muslim colleague at
> work about Islam and it all happened from there.

Maryam's mother is very complimentary about her daughter's new faith; she's pleased that her wardrobe no longer contains items that are 'short and tight' and describes her new choice of clothing as dignified. Her mother is also cheered that Maryam's love life no longer involves a series of 'handsome rogues' and that her daughter is saving herself for a 'good Muslim husband'.

It has been suggested that some Black women are attracted to Islam because Black Muslim men have gained the reputation for being responsible, hardworking and law-abiding, thus making them ideal marriage material and excellent fathers. However, all of the women interviewed were keen to point out that this factor played no part in their decision to convert. When this point was put to Maryam Saddique she was adamant that the idea of finding a suitable husband played no role in her conversion. For her, a husband would be a consequence of her choice, not the primary rationale.

Safia Ahmad

Maryam Saddique's views are echoed by Safia Ahmad, whose decision to become a Muslim a decade ago meant she had turned her back on her Methodist Sunday school upbringing and Church of England education. The woman who was formerly known as Sharon Thomas says: 'There was nothing mysterious about becoming a Muslim. It's really pretty straightforward, to tell the truth. But I can tell you this: once you make that confession that's it. You're a different person.' Although Safia met her husband, Rasoul, several years after converting, she claims that she was never fixated on finding someone special; her relationship began and grew in circumstances she describes as divinely inspired.

Gender Issues

Much has been written about allegedly feckless Black men, who are everything from serial philanderers to irresponsible fathers who do not take sufficient responsibility for their children.[1]

An apparent consequence of the latter propensity is that a lone female parent heads almost 50 per cent of Black households in the United Kingdom.[2] Black men are several times more likely to receive custodial sentences than their White peers for similar types of crime.[3] And they are three times more likely to be formally detained ('sectioned') under the Mental Health Act. They are also over-represented on mental health inpatient wards and more likely than White men to be taken by the police to a 'place of safety' under section 136 of the Mental Health Act.[4] Moreover 50 per cent of Black men are romantically involved with White women, which means that for Black women there is an ever-shrinking pool of good, available Black men. These scenarios give the impression that a 'good' Black man is hard to find and any Black woman in a relationship with such a Black man is extremely fortunate.

From a gender perspective, the major difference between mosques and BMCs is that the former have far more men among their membership. Whereas BMCs are predominantly female domains, apart from their leadership, which still remains a male-dominated sphere,[5] mosques are predominantly male environs. This has to do with the process of how Black people become Muslims, and also with the patriarchal nature of mosques, which rigidly separate male and female in worship and have an inflexible demarcation of leadership as male. As a result, it is male 'seekers' who tend to have direct interactions with Muslims, and they are the ones who invariably find their way to mosques. There is a tacit strategy of targeting men, whose womenfolk and children usually come in tow. This has been the situation for many of the Muslim converts interviewed for this book: I did not come across any instances of Black Muslim couples in which the woman found the Muslim faith first and then brought her husband on board. A scenario where male conversions can become awkward occurs when spouses hold strong religious beliefs of her own, and there are instances of tensions between

Muslim men and their Christian wives – see Chapter 9 for a more in-depth discussion about this issue.

There is still a real controversy about whether women can serve as imams in mosques and lead men (as opposed to women) in congregational prayers; Islamic scholars still continue to debate about the Qur'an and the Hadith's interpretation of women's roles.[6] Suffice it to say, it is very difficult for women to assume leadership roles within mosques, even in a superficial way. This is not to suggest that mosques are anti-female or unfriendly spaces for women, but such is the nature of Islamic tradition and related conservative practices that women play deferential roles within these places of worship.

Taking the Word to the Street

Where the church and the mosque are at one is in their desire to win over people to the cause. Like church folk, Black Muslims are not shy of proselytizing, and can be seen handing out religious tracts on high streets. London also has a number of Black Muslim shops, usually found in markets, which sell books, DVDs, CDs and incense, and which are run by those eager to engage with would-be 'seekers'. Although Black Muslims are keen to add to their number, they are also wary of those who may have ulterior motives for joining their organizations. Muslims know to their cost that their mosque will be cited as a centre for fanaticism if a current or a former worshipper is associated with a proscribed group or linked to terrorist activities. Also, the media are always ready to believe that mosques are hotbeds of radical extremism and are keen to expose unsavoury goings-on. Lastly, certain mosques in Britain have come to the attention of the police, and it is alleged that under-cover operatives have infiltrated them to monitor activities. I spoke to two Black Muslim converts who stated that they had left a particular London mosque because they became aware of official surveillance activities and no longer felt comfortable in such an environment.

Notwithstanding these reservations, many converts are keen to share their new faith with friends, and with anyone prepared to listen. Indeed, some of the Muslim converts interviewed for this book often faced a real conundrum about how to express their faith in ways that could be understood and would engage rather than repel. For instance, when Abdul Yusuf was released from Wandsworth Prison he was keen to tell everyone about his new faith. He says, 'Listen, my brother, when I got out I wanted to tell the whole world, but no one wanted to know, not my parents or friends, no one!' Only his children, who now get to spend time with their father, and his former partner showed a little interest. His friends still remain sceptical, years after his reversion/conversion, especially those with whom he spent time in prison. The latter believe that his conversion was typical of what happens in prison. Most of his peers also left prison as 'reformed' characters, determined to change, only to find themselves back behind bars within a few years of their release.

It is within this context that Abdul finds himself judged; his friends believe that he will inevitably succumb to the temptations of the street now he is free. This is unfair, since Abdul has steered clear of trouble since his release. However, doing so has meant disassociating himself from some of his more wayward friends, whose lifestyles are now incompatible with his. Before his last conviction and his subsequent conversion, Abdul was comfortable with a happy-go-lucky existence which involved no long-term plans. When he returned to the community after his release Abdul felt uncomfortable associating with careless 'bredren' (as he calls them) who smoked 'weed'. He says, 'I don't do any of those things now. I'm a changed man. I don't have any time for clubs or dances or any of those activities I did before I went inside the last time. I spend my time praying and reading [the Qur'an]. I encourage everyone to do this as well. It's a great thing.'

Whereas Abdul turned his own back on his erstwhile friends, Hakim Ibrahim's appear to have distanced themselves since his reversion/conversion. According to Hakim, 'I think they view me with a mixture of suspicion and ridicule. My parents say they've heard them call me "head-case Hakim" and "Timothy the ticking time bomb". That's their issue, not mine. I know what I believe; they believe nothing. In the final analysis, something always beats nothing; especially when that something is Islam.'

Family Matters: Relative Values of Islam

Inevitably, the media's portrayal of Islam has helped to promote negative opinions about the faith in the Black community – as well as in other communities.[7] A number of the Black elders interviewed for this book, especially those from the Caribbean, who have obtained their knowledge about Islam from such unsympathetic sources made some very unhelpful comments about Islam that verged on Islamophobia.

When older church folk were questioned about their sons' or daughters' conversions to Islam, many displayed an attitude that was similar to that of a previous generation with regard to Rastafari. Some thirty years ago, it was Rastafari that presented the major challenge to the church for the hearts and minds of young Black people in Britain. And one of the greatest fears of any respectable Black Christian family was seeing a son let his neat Afro hairstyle 'go to seed' in anticipation of dreadlocks.[8] A whole generation of Black girls and women were warned by concerned parents that they would face expulsion from the family home if they brought home a 'ganja smoking Rastaman' as a boyfriend.

Although there are fundamental doctrinal and socio-religious differences between Islam and Rastafari, it appears from this research that some Black families have drawn parallels between the oppositional stances of faiths which, they believe, call for adherents to denounce Western society and its values.[9] In the 1970s and early 1980s, reggae became the musical mouthpiece for the mass dissemination of Rastafari through the records of leading Rasta singers and groups such as Bob Marley, Dennis Brown, Burning Spear, the Mighty Diamonds and Culture. Their songs were full of phrases such as 'Beat down Babylon', identifying the West as Babylon – a corrupt place from which all true believers must flee before it is destroyed (or destroys itself).[10] For many Rastas Ethiopia or Africa is 'Zion', the 'homeland' where the righteous will dwell.

The parents of Hakim Ibrahim, Gladstone and Muriel Jefferson, hold very negative views about Islam, although they have Asian Muslim neighbours with whom they are on good terms. Indeed, Hakim has suggested that his parents speak to their neighbours about Islam to discredit the misinformation and nonsense that they believe about the faith. Such a conversation has yet to take place. Often when those interviewed were asked about Islam and Black Muslims they appeared not to make the connection between this faith and that of their Asian work colleague, local shopkeeper, doctor or dentist. It appeared as if one were talking about a different faith altogether. For some of these men and women, it is incongruous for Black people to become Muslims. And some adopted attitudes similar to those of Abdul Yusuf's parents – that Muslims should keep their beliefs to themselves.

Negative Feedback

It can be argued that there is a fundamental reason for the socio-religious ignorance and prejudice displayed by some of the Black people interviewed in this book which cuts across science, economics, philosophy and culture. Crudely put, Islam is regarded as an 'Eastern' or Asian faith in the UK (despite the fact that a third of Muslims in the UK are not Asian),[11] that lacks the complexity, rationality and compassion of Christianity. The argument goes that the spread of Christianity throughout the globe went in tandem with a range of developments that led to the hegemony of the West.[12] As a result, societies that are seen as economically and technically advanced, respect civil liberties and promote democracy are Christian. Although such a worldview is consonant with White supremacy, many Black people have tacitly accepted it.[13]

This argument suggests that Islam has very little of a 'progressive' nature to offer Black people – or anyone who considers themselves enlightened. The celebrated Trinidadian writer Sir V. S. Naipaul wrote:

> Islam, going by what I saw of it from the outside, was
> less metaphysical and more direct than Hinduism. In this
> religion of fear and reward, oddly compounded with war
> and worldly grief, there was much that reminded me
> of Christianity – more visible and 'official' in Trinidad;
> and it was possible for me to feel that I knew about it.
> The doctrine, or what I thought was its doctrine, didn't
> attract me. It didn't seem worth inquiring into; and
> over the years, in spite of travel, I had added little to
> the knowledge gathered in my Trinidad childhood. The
> glories of this religion were in the remote past; it had
> generated nothing like a Renaissance. Muslim countries,
> where not colonized, were despotisms; and nearly all,
> before oil, were poor.[14]

These comments are not dissimilar to those made by the former Labour MP and chat-show host Robert Kilroy-Silk in the *Daily Express*: 'Apart from oil – which was discovered, is produced and is paid for by the west – what do they [Arabs] contribute? Can you think of anything? Anything really useful? Anything really valuable? Something we really need, could not do without? No, nor can I.'[15]

Kilroy-Silk's sweeping generalizations are not only racist but factually incorrect. History shows that Arabs and Muslims have been responsible for a range of scientific, cultural and technical developments that have transformed the world, in mathematics, language, astronomy, medicine, chemistry and physics as well as other areas of the applied sciences.[16] Yet, this contribution is not common knowledge, just as the glories of Africa and the huge contributions of Africans have been written out of history. In both instances, there is a persistent Western desire to present the 'other', whether in terms of ethnicity, culture or religion, as 'primitive and inferior' to the West itself.

It can be argued that many from the Judaeo-Christian tradition surreptitiously or unwittingly harbour a sense of moral and ethical superiority over Muslims, which may be manifested in a variety of ways. The media are content to give a platform to people such as Robert Kilroy-Silk, who are more interested in reinforcing stereotypes than engaging in serious debate about Islamic theology and religious practices. They implicitly promote an attitude of 'I bet you're glad you don't live over there', which implies that Muslim societies are bereft of the systems and structures that we in the West take for granted. The flip-side of this condescension is self-congratulation at Western tolerance when Muslims take to the streets to demonstrate, as if to suggest that they would not be allowed such freedom of expression in their countries.

It would be interesting to know how many non-Muslims prior to 9/11 and 7/7 had even looked at the Qur'an. After those events many began to dust down copies of the holy book, or purchase it online, but only to tell Muslims what their faith says about *jihad*.

Life-changing Decisions

When the parents of Muslim converts were asked about their offspring's religious choices many appeared initially reluctant to see them as a positive development. Interestingly, there was little difference between the responses from parents with or without religious beliefs. Sometimes when they were encouraged to juxtapose 'before and after' conversion scenarios, they reluctantly admitted that the change had been positive. But this was always accompanied by the concern that their children should not 'get involved with the wrong crowd' – speaking of fundamentalists or extremists in the same language they might use about street gangs. Their responses always damned with faint praise, though many remained supportive of family members and wanted 'the best for them'.

Many of the Muslim brothers and sisters interviewed for this book had been on a spiritual journey over a number of years which resulted in their finding faith in Islam. There was no one route to Islam: some found faith while in prison, others while studying at university and for some it was almost serendipitous. Most had had very little direct contact with Islam or Muslims during their formative years and their conversion or reversion had usually taken place within the last ten to fifteen years. None appeared to have become Muslims after some emotional or psychological crisis. Their decisions, which appeared rational and almost hard-headed, were never impulsive. Fascinatingly, none mentioned 9/11 or 7/7 as a catalyst or stimulus in their decision-making – although these events were deemed important with regard to how Muslims were now viewed by others.

No one interviewed felt coerced or shepherded into becoming a Muslim – both men and women said that their decisions were of their own volition. Their conversions had a profound effect on family members, many of whom struggled to come to terms with these new beliefs; the more prudent adopted a 'wait and see' approach. However, in a few cases family members have been obdurate and are hoping (and in some cases praying) for the converts to drop their new beliefs. However, there seems little chance of this happening, as all the converts believed that Islam had transformed their lives and that negative attitudes to their conversion were to be expected from those without a knowledge of God.

Chapter 9

Race, Religion and Rap

Race Matters

Any religious conversion usually results in a change of ideas, attitudes and behaviours, either immediately or over the course of time. Within Islam, the external manifestations of this usually involve a change of name, adaptation of appearance, and an abstinence from certain practices. For the most part, those Muslims interviewed had relatively few problems making these changes. The challenges they faced came from a society that is increasingly wary of formalized religion. If the faith is Islam, the pressure is increased because of a perception, in part derived from the media, that this faith is dogmatic and incapable of allowing believers to integrate into a non-Muslim society. Yet evidence suggests that Black Muslims are not an insular community with a bunker mentality who view the world as threatening and oppositional.

Most Black Muslims live in London, but it is possible to find them even in towns with a tiny Black population such as Norwich. The writer met with a small but growing number of Black Muslims in the East Anglian city who had relocated from London to establish a community of believers. Over the last decade this community has grown and has brought some welcome diversity to Norwich. It appears that the city appreciates this enrichment; when I went to interview these Muslim brothers I only had to mention the name of the mosque (Ishan) to the taxi-driver at the station, and he knew exactly where I wanted to go. He spoke very positively about the mosque and its worshippers.

For the Black believers in Norwich, the issue of race remains an important aspect of their identity, although Islam transcends matters of race, and their mosque includes believers from all ethnicities. What really impressed me was the way the diverse Muslim brothers (I did not meet any women during this visit) appeared to interact with a naturalness and ease that would put many churches to shame. This reminded me of one of the fathers of Pan-Africanism, Edward Wilmot Blyden, who argued that, because of its history, Islam was not subject to the racism and anti-Black ideology found in Christianity.[1] One prominent Christian writer, Steven Tsoukalas, whose book on the Nation of Islam (UK) remains one of the better attempts by US Christians to explore the faith, has argued that a reason why African-Americans are increasingly drawn to Islam is the church's reluctance to tackle racism and structural inequality.[2] But has Islam found a way of overcoming the ethnic tensions that still plague society and the Christian church? Certainly when Malcolm X visited Mecca he was astounded at the universal brotherhood of Muslims during the *hajj* and believed that White Americans could be 'cured' of their racism if they embraced Islam.[3]

However, before one gets carried away it is important to listen to Muslim dissent about this apparent religious colour-blindness. If Malcolm X's visit to Mecca changed the way he looked at race matters, the Honourable Louis Farrakhan's certainly did not. In conversation with the African-American film director Spike Lee, Minister Farrakhan stated:

> I first went there [Mecca] in 1977. There was a ghetto
> there in Mecca and Blacks were in that ghetto in Mecca,
> the Holy City. And I saw little Arab boys right around the
> Ka'Ba, white Arabs throwing bread to Nubian women
> like they were feeding pigeons, throwing the bread in the

air, and these Black women had to run and scrape for that
bread. I know what I saw and I talked about it to them
– I don't wait to get behind their backs, I talk straight to
them, so you can't tell me nothing about Islam removing
racism, not *that* Islam. It ain't happening, brother. It can
happen, but it hasn't happened.[4]

A little closer to home, an article in the *New Nation* newspaper
highlights the problems some Black men face when looking for
spouses in UK mosques. Because there are more Black Muslim
men than women, and Black Sunni Muslims are often open to
mixed marriages, many Black men are seeking partners from
within the Asian community. Abdul Rahman, an African-
Caribbean convert from the Brixton mosque, states: 'I know
one brother who is still looking for a wife after ten years. His
white friend has been offered hundreds of wives from the Asian
community, but he has been completely rejected.' Abdul says
prejudice can be overcome, but often arises when converts look
for partners. 'Any Black who tries to marry an Asian woman is
going to experience discrimination. I'm now married to an Asian.
Believe me, it rarely happens smoothly.'[5]

The Black Sunni Muslim openness to inter-ethnic relationships is
not shared by the Nation of Islam (UK). Although it has modified
some of its more doctrinaire attitudes to race and intermarriage,
the Nation of Islam (UK) still regards mixed marriages not as
progressive race relations but as evidence of Black self-loathing and
self-distrust.[6] Many Black nationalists would agree with the Nation
of Islam (UK) that the tendency of so many African-Caribbean
people to opt for White partners is symptomatic of a propensity to
value White more than Black.[7] Like bleach cream, hair-straightening
products and plastic surgery, the choice of a Caucasian partner is
seen as a rejection of one's Blackness. In his satirical book *The Black
Anglo-Saxons*, which deals with the pretentiousness of some within
the Black community, Black academic Nathan Hare questions the

disproportionate number of Black sports stars, entertainers and celebrities who have White partners.[8]

Inter-faith relationships, usually between Muslims and Christians, are also a source of tension. A Black south London pastor, the Revd Clinton Small, spends a lot of his time counselling women whose spouses have become Muslims while in prison. Small says:

These men often went inside as agnostics or nominal 'Christians'. While inside their wives and partners were praying for their redemption, earnestly hoping they'd find God, only to discover the God they found was Allah. When these men are released they've got this zeal and want to convert their wives. They have nothing but criticism for their wives' faith and lifestyle choices. They start laying down all these demands. They must get rid of all the Christian symbols in the house, crosses, pictures of Jesus and Bible plaques. The wife must not cook certain foods and all alcohol must be got rid of. These women find it hard to be with these men after they become Muslims. I tell them to stick at it and pray for patience and peace.

Not everyone shares Pastor Small's experience, and one Black Muslim brother, Tony Muhammad, who lives in Chapeltown, Leeds, suggests that his marriage has not only survived his conversion, it has thrived. He says:

Before I became a Muslim I was someone who went to church every now and again, but my wife was a Christian. After I became a Muslim things really changed. For one, our discussions about religion have made my wife look again at what she believes and why. We now have some heavy talks about faith, especially on Wednesdays after she comes back from her evening church group. I respect her religious choices. I know what she believes and how this has helped her. More importantly, she knows what I believe and she respects that. It's all about love and respect.

With regard to race, it is difficult to glean whether conversion to Islam has truly led the orthodox Muslims who were interviewed to a post-race sensibility about ethnic difference, or to pragmatism. They are a religious minority within Islam and, as converts, they may simply want to keep their heads down and not upset the religious status quo by addressing the topic of race. It might be refreshing to believe that there is truly a brotherhood of believers within Islam, that no longer sees skin colour but faith as the defining attribute. Many of those interviewed spoke about their bonds of brotherhood with fellow believers throughout the world, and they took a keen interest in the Middle East, Iraq, Iran, Afghanistan and other countries where there is conflict involving Muslims. I once worked with a young Black Muslim man who took part in an aid mission involving a convoy of vehicles from London to Bosnia to assist the Bosnian Muslim population during the crisis in the 1990s. At the time, none of this man's work colleagues could understand why he was prepared to take a leave of absence to involve himself in what many described as a European-inspired conflict, albeit one with a religious subtext. He was told that he would be better spending his time helping to support brothers and sisters in Africa who had been suffering for centuries under European-inspired tyranny. Ironically the man's sharpest critics thought nothing about giving money to Christian charities and churches who were carrying out relief and development work in the same part of the world.[9]

Muslim Communities

Particular minority ethnic Muslim communities have a preference for certain mosques. For instance, within inner London there are mosques for sections of the Turkish and Somali communities,[10] as well as others catering for the spiritual and cultural needs of south Asian believers. As with Black Majority Churches, one cannot put this development down to ethnic tensions; it is an expression of the unity in diversity that enables Muslims to connect their religion with their cultural heritage. Those interviewed for this book often pointed out that as new believers they had specific spiritual and cultural needs that were not often catered for by their local mosques. These mosques were usually full of adherents from lifelong Muslim backgrounds who were unaware of the socio-cultural and religious challenges faced by converts. For instance, a new convert to Islam with only a smattering of Arabic finds it difficult to keep up with prayers and other religious activities delivered in Arabic. Equally, some of the activities taking place in mosques owe as much to cultural traditions of Britain's south Asian Muslim communities as they do to the teachings of the Qur'an. This is particularly true with regard to the attire of women; the *burqa*, an outer garment which covers their entire bodies, is not expressly mentioned in the Qur'an, which only suggests that women should dress and behave modestly.[11] Equally, the custom of Muslim women being forbidden to work outside the home and notions of the totally submissive wife are cultural baggage rather than purely religious practices. As a result, some converts, especially women, spend a lot of time distinguishing what is truly Islamic and pertains to the Qur'an from what is cultural and belongs to the traditions of a particular worshipping community.

One way of circumventing these religious and cultural inconsistencies is to establish or attend mosques catering for new converts' requirements. The Brixton mosque is a case in point, as are others found in houses or based in community centres. Black Muslims living in south-east London can worship at the Old Kent Road mosque, with its large Nigerian Muslim congregation and its reputation for good community relations and openness toward seekers.[12] Many progressive mosques are aware that an increasing numbers of 'seekers' are coming to their doors and organize orientation classes and activities for those who may not be aware, for example, that shoes need to be removed and body parts washed prior to prayer, or that mosques demand a separation of genders at all times.

Theological Differences among Black Muslims

One area of controversy that Black Muslims were wary of discussing was the relationship between the Nation of Islam (UK) and Sunni Muslims, and whether the latter regarded the former as 'authentic' believers. Interestingly only two orthodox Muslims were willing to provide anything like a serious response to this question, and in both instances the responses were negative. One came from Bilal Hussain, a Streatham-based man who had obtained a degree in theology from King's College, London, prior to his conversion. He explained the theological situation like this:

> You're a church man [gesturing toward me]. Would you consider the [Jesus Christ of the] Latter Day Saints or [Jehovah's] Witnesses as Christian? Aren't they seen as heterodox groups or sects that have moved way from biblical truths? Well, I see these brothers the same way. They have moved away from the truths found in the Qur'an. Any real Muslim knows that and should be prepared to tell you as such. No, my brother, they are in error, they must know as much as we do.

The other response came from Raheem Hasan, the Jamaican-born boxer who had initially studied 'Fardian' Islam. 'You know I read a lot of stuff from the Nation when I first got interested in Islam. But then I read some other Islamic material which didn't correspond with the Nation's take on Islam. I then moved towards Sunni Islam.'

This guardedness may be due to the fact that some of the converts interviewed for this book first became interested in Islam after reading Malcolm X's autobiography and/or hearing a tape of the Honourable Louis Farrakhan. It was this introduction to 'Fardian' Islam that first whetted their appetite for the faith. As a result, far too many responded with a shrug that said 'They believe what they believe.' However, I felt that many interviewees were irked that for many people, in the Black community in particular, the Nation of Islam (UK) is the 'face' of Islam in Britain. The first image of 'Black Muslims' that comes to mind for many people is a man in a dark suit and a bow tie rather than a *kufi* cap and *throbe*. This is despite the fact that, as in the USA, in the UK Sunni Muslims far outnumber members of the Nation of Islam (UK).[13]

Although many accusations have been levelled against the Nation of Islam (UK), from Black supremacy to anti-Semitism,[14] it has never been linked to acts of violence or terror. Hence, it would be totally wrong to compare the Nation of Islam (UK) to White supremacist groups on either side of the Atlantic who are known for their racist violence and intimidation. By contrast, the Nation of Islam (UK) is known for its discipline and order, and one of the characteristics of the Million Man March in Washington in 1995 was the lack of police activity. No Black Muslim convert to the Nation of Islam (UK) has been linked to a terrorist plot or speeches that have led to them being censured or incarcerated.

As we saw in Chapter 8, the families of Muslims responded in various ways to news of their conversion. Some converts said that their families gave their decision to follow Islam the proverbial 'six months', not expecting it to last. And obviously not everyone who professes a faith in Islam either stays the course or is genuine. There is evidence of recidivism among those who find faith while in prison. While some Muslims welcome the moral absolutism and strictness of Islam, which give order and focus to their once chaotic lives, others find the strict religious practices onerous and they wander away from the faith. Islam, like all major faiths, is not immune from apostasy, and some zealous converts soon find themselves going back to the behaviours and practices they had formerly renounced.

Muslim Chic

As well as recidivism and bogus conversions, there is a phenomenon I would describe as 'Muslim chic', which is similar to what took place within the Rastafari movement in the 1970s and 1980s, when many latched on to aspects of the movement for reasons of fashion. Spike Lee's film *Malcolm X* not only generated a greater interest in the iconic Black Muslim activist, it also created a greater interest in all things Islamic. A whole generation of young Black adults who were born in the early 1990s have Muslim first names such as Jamal, Abdul, Raheem, Bilal, Amani, Khadeeja and Rasheeda. These Islamic names, like the African ones that many parents were also choosing around this time, have beautiful meanings which serve to inspire a child for his or her later life. However, many of the parents who opted for these names had very little interest in Islam and chose the name because it sounded good rather than even being aware of its meaning.[15]

Around this time some brothers began greeting one another with the Muslim greeting *al-salaamu alaykumu*, or a version of this, rather than with the familiar 'respect', followed by fist-bumping or a handshake. There were also the obligatory Malcolm X T-shirts, and apparel bearing Arabic writing. Subsequently some brothers, who were clearly not Muslims, took to wearing skull caps and white, loose garments (long sleeved tops and three-quarter-length trousers). This righteous look was often spoilt by a penchant for jewellery and for activities that most Muslims would frown upon. Many of these brothers were also known for adopting slogans that borrowed heavily from the lyrics of Muslim hip-hop artists and from Black Power revolutionaries, such as 'Fight the Power' (from Public Enemy), 'Too Black – Too Strong' and 'Keep it Real'. Like the clothing, all this revolutionary talk was mere style over substance.

In America, which is often said to be ahead of Britain in terms of fashion, Muslim chic has resulted in situations like this one described by the African-American academic Dr Nathan Hare:

> It is not unusual to have an old friend walk up, unrecognizable in his African getup and beard, and declare that he is ready to 'get down' with the White man. After you discover that Muhammad Akbar Karim Ali is none other than old Willie V. Jackson from Money, Mississippi, he invariably follows you home to sit up all night, drinking your whiskey… Intermittently he will spell out the parlour strategy of a fiery declaration of the war on the [White man] until four o'clock in the morning, or until the whiskey is gone. Should you later solicit his aid in some revolutionary skirmish, he is likely to express his revolutionary regrets that he has to help his wife shop for groceries or some similar tale.[16]

Although imitation is proverbially supposed to be flattering, no serious Muslim would appreciate this hijacking of Islam for trendy purposes, as it is another way of bringing the faith into disrepute. There is no suggestion that Islam will suffer as badly as the Rastafari movement, but it will be interesting to see how Black Muslims deal with these challenges.

The Power of Hip Hop

The conversion or commitment of several high-profile US rap artists to Islam, such as Nas, Busta Rhymes, Mos Def, Snoop Dogg and Jurassic Five, has opened up the faith to a new audience, some of whom will go beyond being fans to take on board the music's religious message. The relationship between hip-hop culture and

Islam is fascinating, and it can be argued that over the last thirty years they have become almost inextricably linked. The academic Mattias Gardell has suggested that 'what reggae was to the expansion of the Rastafarian movement in the 1970s, so hip-hop is to the spread of Black Islam in 1980s and 1990s'.[17] Interestingly, the small but influential Islamic religious sect known as the Five Percenters has been crucial for this dissemination.

Hip hop is an aspect of Black culture that has its roots in the African-American tradition, rising out of New York to conquer more or less the entire world. It initially consisted of the four elements of MC-ing (formerly MC meant Master of Ceremonies, but within a hip-hop context it has come to mean a 'rapper' – someone who uses a speaking voice to articulate a message rhythmically, with or without music); DJ-ing ('disc jockeying' or spinning records for the backing music); writing (graffiti); and b-boying (breakdancing).[18] It is common to hear people use the terms 'rap' and 'hip hop' interchangeably, but the legendary MC and hip-hop artist KRS-One was right when he suggested that 'rap is something you do, hip-hop is something you live'.[19] As a consequence, hip hop has moved beyond the initial four elements to embrace a whole lifestyle.

Hip-hop fashion is now a multi-million dollar industry pumping out apparel by Phat Farm, G-Unit, Rocawear and so on – these clothing labels are often owned by hip-hop artists or people connected to the music. The penchant among many young people for baggy or oversize clothing is directly attributable to hip hop, as is the common phrase 'bling-bling', the ostentatious display of wealth through jewellery and other valuables. Hip hop has conquered Hollywood in the person of Will Smith, formerly the rapper known as the Fresh Prince, who had chart successes as a solo artist as well as with DJ Jazzy Jeff. Will Smith's films *I, Robot, Shark's Tale, Hitch, The Pursuit of Happyness, I am Legend* and *Hancock* have grossed over one billion dollars between them at the US box office alone.[20] Hip hop is also responsible for a series of 'hood' films starring, directed or produced by hip-hop artists such as Dr Dre, Nas, Snoop (Dogg), Ice Cube, Ice T, Queen Latifah, 50 Cent, DMX and others.

Mainstream popular culture is increasingly being dominated by rap music to such an extent that 'from 1997 to 1998 rap music sales showed a 31 percent increase, making rap the fastest growing music genre [in the USA], ahead of country, rock, classical and all other musical forms. By 1998 rap was the top selling musical format, outdistancing rock music and country music, the previous leading sellers.'[21]

Islamic Ska

Although hip hop is seen as the primary musical genre for US and UK Muslim artists to disseminate their religious message, it was Jamaican music that first brought the musical message of Islam to Black Britons as early as the 1960s. Long before the term 'hip hop' had been invented, the Jamaican singer Prince Buster had embraced Islam (the Nation of Islam) and was making records with explicit Islamic meanings. During the 1960s Prince Buster was 'Mr Jamaican music' – the island's answer to Bob Dylan, the Beatles and Sam Cooke rolled into one. The pioneering British reggae music presenter David Rodigan went as far as to suggest that 'before Bob Marley there was only Prince Buster – no one else on that scale'.[22] It is not possible to quantify the importance of music as a cultural form among Africans in the diaspora and on the African continent. Suffice it to say, for many it was the only opportunity for cultural expression. It is within this context that the significance of someone like Prince Buster must be measured.

According to the writer Sebastian Clarke, Buster converted to Islam from Christianity in the mid 1960s,[23] after reputedly meeting his hero, Muhammad Ali. Conversely, Lloyd Bradley, author of the authoritative chronicle of reggae music, *Bass Culture*, suggests he converted in 1961/62 as a result of 'his distaste at the roles Black people were forced to play in Jamaica due to slavery and its colonial successor'.[24] Buster believed the Nation of Islam would fulfil his desire to see real Black solidarity and empowerment in his beloved Jamaica. Curiously, like today's hip-hop artists, whose albums often mix socially conscious songs with others extolling murder, misogyny and drugs, Buster's embrace of Islam coincided with his producing what the academic Dick Hebdige describes as 'some of the wittiest, lewdest and most ungodly Ska records' typical of the 'rude reggae' era of the late 1960s and early 1970s.[25]

When one looks at Buster's musical output during the 1960s, it is evident that Islam influenced his recordings. One of his biggest hits 'The Ten Commandments' [of man to woman] (Blue Beat Records, 1965) is a humorous, but male chauvinist, look at the supposed behaviour of women toward their menfolk. But this track owes more to Elijah Muhammad's teachings than those found in the Bible. Equally, other hits such as 'The Prophet' (Blue Beat Records, 1966), 'The Drunkard's Psalm' (Blue Beat Records, 1967) and 'Black Soul' (FAB Records, 1969) have clear Islamic themes that many Jamaican listeners ought to have easily detected – the 'Drunkard's Psalm', for instance, warns against the dangers of alcohol.

One of Buster's biggest hits, 'Shakin' Up Orange Street' (FAB Records, 1967) has the B-side 'Black Girl', which praises submissive Black women who do not eat pork, use bleach cream or drink alcohol. Likewise, on 'Kings of Old' (FAB Records, 1968), which discusses the importance of knowing the true history of Black people and Africa, the singer thanks Elijah Muhammad 'for taking him out of slavery and teaching him his history'. Buster has stated that, 'After sitting down and talking to Elijah Muhammad, you don't really back down from anybody. Not if what you're saying is the truth. I have a letter written to me by Louis Farrakhan, offering support. And when [Muhammad] Ali, the heavyweight champion of the world come to Jamaica, instead of staying uptown away from the poor people, he walked up and down in West Kingston with me. That really shook the Government.'[26]

From the mid 1960s, one of Buster's main Jamaican record labels was Islam Records, and discs issued on this label such as 'Prince of Peace', 'Light of the World' and 'Africa is Calling' were big hits in Britain. By the late 1960s Melodisc established Prince Buster Records in Britain, which featured Islamic iconography such as crescents and stars on the label's centrepiece. Equally, the album *The Ten Commandments*, which charted in the US (RCA Victor Records, 1967), featured a cover image of Buster with arms held out in the Islamic posture of prayer. And on his seminal *I Feel the Spirit* LP (Blue Beat, 1963), Buster and a woman friend are wearing traditional African Islamic attire.

Interestingly, many of Prince Buster's biggest hits, such as 'Judge Dread', 'The Ten Commandments' and 'Al Capone', feature the singer using a speaking rather than singing delivery, which has led to some US music critics to describe him as a 'rapper' rather than a singer.

The Birth of a Musical Giant

Jamaican popular music owes a great debt to its US cousin. At the same time, hip hop is indebted to Jamaica, since one of its pioneers came from the Caribbean island. Jamaican-born Clive Campbell, aka Kool Herc, DJ Kool Herc and Kool DJ Herc, is regarded as the godfather of hip hop, having left Jamaica to set up a sound system in New York in 1967. His sound system was 'of Kingstonian proportions, the like of which New York had never seen... So deep did he involve himself in the Bronx disco world that he is universally accredited as one of the founding fathers of hip-hop, scratch-mixing and rap.'[27] Rap developed in part because DJs playing at dances realized that they needed to do something to get the crowd moving and would speak over the music to fire up the audience.

According to the legendary social commentator on Black music, Nelson George, 'most of the youngsters who do this [hip hop] in

America [are] ignorant of the Jamaican precedent, yet the raps serve the same purpose in both these African-derived cultures'.[28] Another seminal figure of Jamaican ancestry is Afrika Bambaataa, whose Zulu Nation organization championed the cultural and political cause of hip hop.[29] When not philosophizing, Bambaataa span records at dances and parties in various neighbourhoods of his native New York which invariably drew large crowds of adoring fans. The Zulu Nation caught the attention of journalist turned music entrepreneur Tom Silverman, who owned Tommy Boy Records. Silverman was to release Bambaataa's 'Planet Rock', which he described as 'one of the most important hip hop records of all time'.[30]

New York and New Jersey became the home territory of this musical form, with DJs such as Gary Byrd using 'conversation', or rap, over pre-recorded music in their shows, though it was travelling DJs who originated 'scratching', manipulating the stylus on a record to produce new sounds.[31] What we now know as rap music came to national, and later international, prominence in October 1979 with the successf of the Sugarhill Gang's 'Rapper's Delight'. This record borrowed heavily from the tune 'Good Times' by the US funk group Chic.[32] Over the music, 'Rapper's Delight' featured the nonsensical phrase 'hiphop-de-hibby-dibby', from which the term 'hip hop' is reputedly derived.[33] The single sold well and record-label owner Sylvia Robinson recorded 'The Message' from Grandmaster Flash and Furious Five in 1981 – a social commentary on the 'ghetto life' of many African-Americans in the inner city. It was reminiscent of the material produced by the African-American poet and performer Gil Scott-Heron, whose work with the 'Last Poets' in the 1970s used the spoken word to analyse the social and political spirit of the time.[34] 'The Message' set the tone in the early 1980s for 'conscious' rap, with Robinson's Sugar Hill Records releasing Melle Mel's 'White Lines' in 1983, a massive US and British chart hit, which railed against the dangers of drugs, especially cocaine, which was beginning to wreak havoc in African-American communities.[35]

At this point very few believed that the hip hop phenomenon would last. As in the early days of rock 'n' roll in the USA, the 'Mersey Beat' in Britain, and ska in Jamaica, sceptics soon began prophesying that the form would be a summer craze.[36] One college graduate who was convinced of hip hop's potential, and who was determined to see the music last longer than a season, was the New Yorker Russell Simmons. Around the same time as 'Rapper's Delight' was taking the US charts by storm, a young Simmons teamed up with concert promoter and rapper Curtis Walker, aka Kurtis Blow. By the early 1980s, Simmons had recruited his brother Joseph to spin the decks to accompany Blow's raps. The result of the partnership was 'Christmas Rappin', a record which charted in the US in late 1979.[37] Simmons's next move was to team up with White New Yorker Rick Rubin, with whom he established Def Jam, a record label that would become the hip hop equivalent of Motown Records – the musical home of the genre's leading artists.

Figures now considered legends such as L. L. Cool J and Run DMC were just starting to become international stars. Run DMC's 'Walk this Way', a hip-hop version of an old Aerosmith song, became rap's first crossover success.[38] Just as groundbreaking was the success of three White middle-class rappers, the Beastie Boys, who achieved critical acclaim among Black hip-hop devotees, as well as millions of record sales.[39] It was not until the emergence of Eminem at the turn of the millennium that another White artist would sustain a similar following among critical Black hip-hop aficionados.

Up until this point, Def Jam's success had involved artists renowned for humour or comedy rather than social commentary – the Beastie Boys' 'Fight for Your Right to Party' was a good example. But this was to change with the emergence of Public Enemy, an East Coast hip-hop collective headed by lead rapper

Carlton Ridenhour, aka Chuck D. Public Enemy often dressed in army fatigues and used the image of a soldier in a target as a logo, and their music matched the confrontational image by taking aim at the injustices facing African-Americans in contemporary, racist America. Albums such as *Yo! Bum Rush the Show* and *Fear of a Black Planet* were a potent expression of Black cultural nationalism which scored chart and critical successes among Black and White alike.

The late 1980s and early 1990s saw the rise of West Coast hip hop, based in California (and in the African-American dominated neighbourhoods of South Central and Compton in particular) and typified by groups and artists such as NWA, Snoop Dogg, Nate Dogg and Warren G. This new form of hip hop was known as gangsta rap and drew on gangland themes; it was notorious for its misogynistic, homophobic and nihilist material.

The Five Percenter Movement

Centrally important to the emergence of hip hop was the Five Percenter Islamic religious movement, also known as Nation of Gods and Earths, which has its roots in the US Nation of Islam through the enigmatic Clarence 13X. Clarence 13X was born Clarence Smith in Virginia in 1928. Little is known about his early life, but it is on record that he served in the Korean War in the early 1950s, receiving numerous military decorations for his courage under fire.[40] After military service he joined the Nation of Islam and attended the Muslim temple in Harlem, New York, where Malcolm X was the serving minister. As a new convert he took the surname 13X because he was thirteenth person called Clarence within the Nation of Islam. The Nation of Islam was not slow to recognize the newly named Clarence 13X's military experience and martial arts ability, and drafted him into the advance ranks of the Fruit of Islam.

Clarence 13X was regarded as an intelligent individual with a keen interest in finding ways to improve the Nation of Islam's religious and philosophical approach to the problems facing the African-Americans he encountered daily on Harlem's streets. Unfortunately Clarence 13X persistently struggled with the Nation of Islam's strict moral codes, and he constantly clashed with Malcolm X over his gambling, drinking and sexual infidelity, which resulted in periodic suspensions from the temple.[41] Clarence 13X's keen mind was also for ever questioning the Nation of Islam's theology, especially the deification of Master W. D. Fard, whose divinity Clarence 13X doubted because he was an 'Arab' and not a Black man like the Creator.[42] He also queried the way Master Fard had become a mysterious figure within the Nation of Islam, with few adherents knowing much about his origins and even less about his departure. It was not long before Clarence 13X resolved that Master Fard had become like the 'mystery god' or 'spook' that the Nation of Islam accused Christians of worshipping.

An already bad situation became even worse after Clarence 13X witnessed the treatment of Malcolm X for revealing the alleged infidelities of the Honourable Elijah Muhammad. The Messenger had apparently broken his organization's own behavioural code, but his sexual indiscretions, unlike those of Clarence 13X, had gone unpunished and were not criticized by the Nation of Islam. As a result of these disagreements, Clarence 13X left the organization around the same time as Malcolm X was suspended for his 'Chickens coming home to roost' speech.

Clarence X chose to call himself 'Allah', and set up his own religious movement whose teachings fused aspects of the Nation of Islam's teachings with numerology, Kemetic or Egyptian symbolism and Black nationalism.[43] The group was initially known as the Five Percenters, because in its view the world could be split into three groups: 85 per cent mindless sheep, who are being led astray by 10 per cent, who know the truth, but merely wish to create chaos, and 5 per cent, Clarence 13X or Father Allah's group, 'enlightened divine beings' or the 'poor righteous teachers' as 13X described them. The fixation on percentages is part of Five Percenter theology, which seeks to find meaning or enlightenment through numbers as part of the 'Science' of 'Supreme Mathematics'.[44]

Like the Nation of Islam, the Five Percenters believe that God is not a spirit or 'spook', but Black. Unlike the Nation of Islam, the Five Percenters also believe that each Black man is a God; Clarence 13X broke down the letters that make up the word 'Allah' to signify 'Arm, leg, leg, arm and head' to show that God was indeed human. Consequently, Black men are described as 'Gods', their women 'Earths' and their offspring 'Seeds'.[45] Because each man is a God he has the capacity to make his own decisions about what he eats and drinks, and his general behaviour and demeanour, so he is not bound by strict religious guidelines. And although they refuse pork like most orthodox Muslims, Five Percenters are known to consume alcohol, dabble with drugs and display a relaxed attitude toward moral issues. This is in keeping with Clarence 13X's own disposition; he had been disciplined by the Nation of Islam while he was a member for attending meetings in shorts, rather than the standard suit and bow tie, and for his penchant for extra-marital relations. This relaxed attitude is still to be found in the conduct of many of the hip-hop artists who are members of the movement, and are known for their outrageous antics and the 'parental advisory warning' stickers on their CDs. These relaxed Five Percenter mores do not apply to women, or 'Earths', who remained bound by patriarchal regulations relating to family responsibility, dress codes and overall demeanour.

Five Percenters do not consider what they adhere to as a religion but a way of life, leading the writer Pen Black to suggest that they are more interested in Islamic culture than religion.[46] Five Percenters do not follow the Five Pillars of Islam – acknowledging no God but Allah, daily prayer, fasting, alms giving and *hajj* or pilgrimage to Mecca – because for them each man is the God of his own world and can make up his own rules. They prefer to adhere to the slogans 'Show and prove' and 'Each one, teach one', and the nine doctrinal lessons outlining core Five Percenter beliefs.[47]

Like all radical Black groups in the 1960s, the Five Percenters' activities did not go unnoticed by the FBI, and J. Edgar Hoover placed surveillance teams on Clarence 13X, or Father Allah, and his 'gang'. During the mid 1960s, the FBI regarded the Five Percenters as a 'gang of subversives' whose rhetoric and overall behaviour was 'anti-White'. The New York Police Department's Special Unit began a crackdown on Five Percenter activities in Harlem (which they called Mecca), Brooklyn and the Bronx.[48] Clarence 13X, by virtue of his military training and his time spent in mental health facilities for what was diagnosed as 'delusions of grandeur' (calling himself God), was seen as a threat to President Lyndon B. Johnson.

Although the media presented the Five Percenters as seditious and anti-White, African-American New Yorkers in particular were curious about the new kids on the block and attended their academies or schools in Harlem and Brooklyn. America at that time was awash with Black nationalist and religious groups.[49] Tragically, violence was never too far from this landscape, and the victims were often leaders. Like his namesake Malcolm X, Clarence 13X was murdered, in June 1969; his assailants were never caught. The movement continued without Father Allah, choosing to function with no designated leader.

By the 1970s Five Percenter groups were a constant presence at the Bronx and Brooklyn-based dances held by DJ Kool Herc and other DJs, where they acted as unofficial security guards. DJs and dance promoters often welcomed their presence, as they not only ensured that there was a full house, but also guaranteed a relatively safe environment for patrons. During the 1970s, what would become known as hip-hop dances were occasionally violent affairs, and a Five Percenter presence would often guarantee relative peace. This led to DJs acknowledging these unofficial security groups from the microphone, giving the movement particular status among music fans. It was this interaction between culture and religion that led to such a profound Five Percenter influence within what would become hip-hop culture. It was therefore natural that many of the earliest hip-hop exponents were sympathetic to the Five Percenter message, even if they were not actually part of the movement. By the 1980s and 1990s, when hip hop was a mainstay in the music industry, some of its biggest names, such as Public Enemy, KRS-One (whose name is derived from the Five Percenters' Supreme Alphabet and Supreme Mathematics), Brand Nubian, Poor Righteous Teachers, the Jungle Brothers, X-Clan, Queen Latifah, Busta Rhymes, Nas, the Wu-Tang Clan and Mos Def, had close connections with the movement.[50]

In the excellent book *Five Percenter Rap*, Felicia Miyakawa explores the deliberate way in which these artists used their music to support and publicize their beliefs, including the 'sampling' of leaders' speeches in their records and the use of religious imagery and iconography on CD covers, leading to the term 'God Hop' being used to describe this genre. As a result, numerous hip-hop-related singles and albums feature references to Five Percenter theology. US writers such as Miyakawa and Michael Muhammad have shown how many converts to both the Five Percenter movement and the Nation of Islam first became interested in 'Islam' by way of hip-hop music. Chuck D, the former front man of legendary hip-hop outfit Public Enemy famously described rap as 'CNN for Black people', expressing the power and influence of hip hop within the Black community. The Five Percenter greeting, 'salaam' or 'peace', soon became *de rigueur* within hip hop, especially among the youth.

Islamic Hip Hop

The relationship between hip hop and Islam has been symbiotic, with the Nation of Islam in particular not slow to use the power of the music to advance aspects of their faith, and also to tackle some of the social ills within the Black community. Throughout the 1980s rap artists had been making references to Farrakhan on their records, and one of hip hop's first musical and cultural forces, Afrika Bambaataa, suggests that only the Honourable Louis Farrakhan and the Nation of Islam could speak to the alienated youth: 'They held the teachings of "You're not a 'nigga.' You're not colored. Wake up Black man and Black woman and love yourself. Respect your own. Turn back to Africa." That started sticking with a lot of the brothers and sisters.'[51] Moreover, the emergence of Public Enemy, who were open supporters of the Nation of Islam, had a powerful effect on Farrakhan's profile. They made clear reference to him on hit records such as 'Don't Believe the Hype', and included 'An urgent speech' by Nation of Islam 'hip hop minister' Dr Khalid Abdul Muhammad on 'Night of the Living Baseheads'.[52] Both Chuck D and Richard Griffin, aka Professor Griff, Public Enemy's 'Minister for Information', often quoted the Honourable Louis Farrakhan liberally during interviews. Professor Griff would wind up in trouble, both in and out of the group, for 'misinterpreting' the Nation of Islam's supreme leader on comments relating to African-Americans and the Jewish community.[53]

The Nation of Islam's entrance into the heart of hip hop came through the arrival of African-American activist and former clergyman Benjamin Chavis Jr in the mid 1990s. Chavis had long been interested in the connections between music and social activism, and his work within the United Church of Christ, in which he was an ordained minister, combined these passions. During the 1980s and early 1990s he went from being a leader within his church to someone with a high profile on the national stage. It came as no surprise when, in May 1993, the respected National Association for the Advancement of Colored People (NAACP) chose to elect him as its executive director and CEO. Dr Chavis was seen as the man to restore the fortunes of what had been the US's premier civil rights organization – until a financial and sexual scandal led to his departure the following year.[54] During these events Chavis was working with Russell Simmons's Hip Hop Summit Action Network, which brought together rappers, academics, politicians and religious leaders to push for social change.

When Chavis parted company with the church he joined the Nation of Islam in the mid 1990s, becoming Benjamin Chavis Muhammad. He gave the organization a platform within the Hip Hop Summit Action Network, where he was CEO. As a result Louis Farrakhan has spoken at the Summit and organized convocations which attract some of hip hop's biggest artists, where he has attacked forms of rap that he regards as degrading.

Hip hop remains a powerful tool for the transmission of the Nation of Islam's message. The *Final Call* for 5 August 2008 had an image of the best-selling, award-winning hip-hop artist Nas, next to the words 'hip hop – the Voice of the Youth'. Nas, himself a supporter of the Honourable Louis Farrakhan, was interviewed in an exclusive covering several pages of the newspaper, which also had an article on the power of the musical genre.[55] As hip hop continues its inexorable rise to world music domination, many movements and organizations will continue to use the cultural form to propagate their message, with Islam at the forefront.

British Islamic Rap

Within the UK, Muslim artists use hip hop as a means of disseminating their message as well as encouraging other artists to use the genre for more positive purposes. Practically all the leading Muslim hip-hop artists are converts to the faith, and their music often speaks about how Islam has transformed their lives, and how it can change others, as well as society. The leading British Muslim hip-hop group Mecca2Medina describe their aim as to 'educate, entertain and enlighten through the music of conscious hip hop', quite contrary to the usual fixation on money, misogyny and murder. According to Ishmael South from Mecca2Medina, 'What's missing in most Western nations today is a viable cultural alternative for Muslim youth... that's why Islamic hip hop is growing. What I'm noticing is that a lot of the UK hip hop artists are turning up at Muslim hip hop events because they're seeing that there is a better turn out of fans at these events.'[56] Another prominent Muslim rapper is the south London born and raised Muslim Belal, who converted to Islam in 2002. After a period of travel and study in Egypt he now uses his skills to talk about his conversion to Islam.

The Islamic establishment is also aware of hip hop's power, and the now annual 'Eid in the Square', which is hosted by the Muslim Council of Britain in Trafalgar Square, invariably features hip-hop artists. At 'Eid in the Square' 2008, which took place on Saturday 11 October, there were musical contributions from Muslim Belal and the female rap group Pearls of Wisdom.[57] These artists not only represent a credible and relevant face of Islam to youth, they also display the inclusiveness and diversity of the faith. It was the inclusion of Pearls of Wisdom in this line-up which shows how radical and counter-cultural Muslim hip hop is, and how it is able to challenge stereotypes and question women's roles from within Islam. According to the Pearls of Wisdom, 'When we first started out it was such a new idea, not just Islamic hip-hop music, but also the idea that Muslim ladies are able to do so. There are these silly misconceptions about Muslim ladies.'[58]

According to the journalist Jerome Taylor, 'Female [Muslim] acts have begun using their position as artists to try and persuade their Muslim "brothers" to give women a greater voice. Poetic Pilgrimage, a powerful vocal duo consisting of two sisters, whose motto features a veiled woman holding a Kalashnikov with a flower in the barrel, are one of the major bands who rap as much about encouraging social change within the Muslim community as they do about the religion itself.'[59]

Why hip hop has become the music of choice for Muslims is a matter of some debate. It is often argued that because the genre revolves around the speaking voice and beats, it avoids the controversy about the legitimacy of music in Islam.[60] According to the writer Alveena Salim, 'Some [Islamic] scholars allow any sort of singing, be it accompanied with musical instruments or not, and even consider it recommended. A second group of scholars allow singing only when it is not accompanied with a musical instrument. A third group declare it to be forbidden whether it is accompanied with a musical instrument or not; they even consider it a major sin.'[61]

There are now Islamic club nights at venues in west London where crowds of believers and interested parties get to listen to a variety of hip-hop artists rap about everything from being Muslim and British to Guantánamo Bay. In early 2008, UK and US Muslim rap artists took part in the Dangerous Minds tour, which played to sell-out audiences around the country: 2008 also saw the launch of the first national magazine dedicated to Islamic hip hop.[62] The development of the genre is reminiscent of the Christian gospel music scene, primarily in London, which has a number of venues with 'Gospel Nights' offering open mike sessions. The major difference between the two is the timeframe: British gospel music is over thirty years old, but the appearance of 'Gospel Nights' is relatively recent.[63]

British Black Christians have been reluctant to embrace hip hop, as they were reggae music a generation before, and British Christian hip hop only came of age in the late 1990s. Without wanting to fall into clichés, it would be true to suggest that there has been a reluctance among Christians to use genres which are considered 'unsanctified' music. Reggae was seen as 'Rasta' music,[64] while hip hop belonged to 'gangstas from the 'hood'.

Because of its origins and subject matter, Muslims have been swift to latch on to this musical genre and claim it as their own. In July 2006 the writer and broadcaster Ziauddin Sardar suggested:

'Cool Islam' expresses its identity through hip-hop and
rap, and is heavily influenced by an underground Muslim
hip-hop movement in the US. Followers listen to British
Muslim groups such as Mecca2Medina and American
crews such as Native Deen. They wear urban-style Muslim
clothing, their hooded tops and T-shirts sporting such
slogans as 'Property of Allah', '1 Umma' and 'Islam 4 Real'.
Cool Islam uses hip-hop to convey a political and religious
message: all Muslims are united; Islam is a pragmatic and
rational faith; Muslims are not helpless victims, but have
creative ways to resist and subvert imperialism'.[65]

However, not every British Muslim artist is using hip hop for
constructive or redemptive purposes, and there is evidence
that some use the genre to advance an Islamist agenda of
change through violence. In 2004 British rappers Sheikh Terra
and the Soul Salah Crew released the infamous rap tune 'Dirty
Kuffar', praising Osama bin Laden and the attack on the World
Trade Center in New York.[66] And in November 2006 *The Times*
newspaper ran the headline 'Islamic Hip-Hop Artists Are Accused
of Indoctrinating Young Against the West', which went on to
argue that 'hip hop and rap artists are teaching young Muslims
the ideology of radical Islamism through songs about the war in
Iraq, the oppression of Muslims and the creation of an Islamic
state governed by Sharia, or religious law'. The piece went on to
quote Madeleine Gruen, an American intelligence analyst, who
'highlighted the lyrics of a British [rap] group called Blakstone
as a possible gateway to extremist politics'.[67] In both instances,
British Muslim hip-hop artists were not slow to release material
which challenged these interpretations of Islam.

Hip-hop music, rightly or wrongly, has been blamed for many
of the problems currently plaguing Black youth in Britain.[68]
However, what we do know is that if it is united with a particular
interpretation of Islam one is left with a powerful force with the

potential to cause immeasurable damage. Hip hop's power to educate as well as indoctrinate leaves British Muslims with a tremendous responsibility to ensure that the musical genre is steered in the right direction.

Chapter 10

Fast Forward

Black Muslim Converts and the Church

Research for this book revealed that the majority of Muslim converts come from Christian backgrounds: in many instances the individuals had attended church on a regular basis. What it did not discover were men and women who had been active or 'born again' Christians and had abandoned the cross for the crescent. Indeed, most were never at that point where they seriously considered committing their lives to Jesus. What this research did find was that a number had family members, parents in particular, who were committed Christians – in many instances they were leaders or pastors in churches.

Bearing in mind the closeness between Christianity and Islam in the lives of these individuals, it is astonishing that there is so little contact between Black Muslim organizations and BMCs. The relationship has largely been characterized by a mutual wariness that verges on distrust. From a Muslim convert perspective, this is exemplified by, and connected to, a rejection of and dissatisfaction with the church. Some of the Black Muslims interviewed in this book are somewhat ambiguous about Christianity and regard it as a former factor in their lives which, along with other behaviours and attitudes, they have subsequently renounced. The church is considered as an entity they were associated with on their way to finding the true path. When the subject was raised directly during interviews, it mostly solicited a shrug of the shoulder and a 'that was then, and this is now' response. There does not appear to be any ire or passion, rather an indifference born of disregard. For a few it produced more extreme responses that suggest a history of rejection eliciting anger and pain. These individuals took a conscious decision to walk away from Christianity for clear spiritual and/or socio-political reasons and, as a result, they do not have fond memories of the faith. At best the churches are regarded as outmoded and lacking in credibility, and at worst racist, reactionary and irrelevant.

For some in the BMCs the whole Black Muslim presence is a temporary phenomenon: the older church pastors and leaders who lived through the Rastafari movement suggest that Islam attracts those individuals who would have at one time gravitated toward Rastafari before its decline. And pastors such as Clinton Small regard Islam, like Rasta, as a faith which attracts the type of person who would never feel comfortable within the churches because of their conservatism. But Pastor Small believes that the church is still the 'solid rock' that has always been there to support and guide Black people. For him, it is going nowhere because it is the 'rock of ages'. As a result of this kind of thinking, some in the churches have adopted a bunker mentality; they believe they can keep their heads down and see out the Muslim storm.

This apparent confrontation does not mean that there have been no occasions for engagement. One of the first opportunities for mutual cooperation came during the Black United Front's '10,000 Man March' in London on 17 October 1998. The Black United Front, which was an amalgamation of groups such as the Society of Black Lawyers, Operation Black Vote, Exousia Fellowship and the Nation of Islam (UK), had the aim of 'highlighting the disproportionate numbers of Black people languishing in prisons and mental institutions, and the high rates of unemployment, homelessness and school exclusions among the UK Black population'.[1] In truth, the Nation of Islam (UK) were the key players in this organization – the march was based on the US Nation's Million Man March on Washington in 1995, and this fact split the Black Christian community about whether they should march 'under the crescent of Islam'. It can be argued that some used the Nation of Islam (UK)'s presence as a pretext for not demonstrating around Nelson's Column; Black Christians only really began taking to the streets in a concerted way after the millennium.

In an edition of *Focus* magazine which also looked at Black Muslim/Christian relations concerning the atonement march, the news pages ran a story about the launch of the Black Christian Civic Forum (BCCF) which 'aimed to put across the Christian message in a way that grapple[d] with socio-political and racial issues facing Black people (including Christians) in the UK'.[2] The article mentioned that the 'Forum is careful not to be seen as a firebrand Christian version of the Nation of Islam, but a group that will provide a faith perspective on issues such as justice and equality'.[3] Dr R. David Muir, a one-time Rasta who became a stalwart in the New Testament Church of God, was the BCCF's executive director. Dr Muir, who for many years lectured at a number of London universities, has been one of the few church leaders to have actively engaged with Black Muslims and Pan-Africanists on a range of socio-religious and political matters, and the BCCF was a further opportunity to display those combative credentials.

The Forum was launched in January 1999 to coincide with what would have been Dr Martin Luther King Jr's seventieth birthday – a man who epitomized Christian civic engagement and social activism. Despite this rather auspicious start, and the real need for such an organization, the BCCF never captured the imagination of the vast majority of Black Christians, for whom social-activism was regarded as an oxymoron. As a result the BCCF suffered a slow and sad demise, terminally neglected by the very people it was there to help.

The Persecution Issue

Muslim–Christian relationships are also affected by the frequent reports and news stories from Christian organizations working with the 'persecuted church' that highlight the alleged maltreatment of Christians in Islamic countries. A generation of Black and White Christians read Bilquis Sheikh's moving and inspiring autobiography, *I Dared to Call Him Father*, which spoke of her conversion to Christianity in Islamic Pakistan and the travails she faced as a result.[4] Within Islamic law, the charge of apostasy ('riddah' or 'irtidad), which is a rejection of Islam 'in word or deed' by a believer, is punishable by death under certain circumstances.[5]

The problems Christians face in Muslim countries have been brought to wider attention by groups such as Christian Solidarity Worldwide, a human rights organization which works on behalf of 'those suffering for their Christian beliefs and promotes religious liberty for all',[6] while the Barnabas Fund, another Christian organization, aims to assist Christians facing persecution in Muslim environments.[7] It would be true to argue that since the fall of Communism in the East, where state-sponsored atheism or materialism resulted in believers facing harassment, Christian organizations have focused on the fate of fellow believers in Islamic countries. A good example of this is the Open Doors organization, established by Brother Andrew, which was formerly active behind the Iron Curtain, but is now very energetic in Muslim countries. Likewise, the Christian media have also disseminated information about persecution, with the popular Christian monthly *Christianity* running a feature on Christian converts from Islam or Muslim Background Believers or MBBs, which explored the way they often 'have to choose between keeping their faith a secret and facing severe persecution for what is considered a betrayal of culture, nation and family'.[8]

Ironically, some of Islam's sternest Christian critics are former Muslims or those born in Islamic countries such as Patrick Sookhdeo, whose books, including *Islam the Challenge to the*

Church, often strike an alarmist tone when they explore the relationship between Islam and Christianity.[9] Another detractor is Dr Michael Nazir-Ali, the Bishop of Rochester, who has suggested that there is a 'need to convert Britain's Muslims', and has argued how radical Islam is filling the 'moral vacuum' left by the decline of Christianity. Dr Nazir-Ali, who was born in Pakistan to parents who had converted from Islam, has also argued that 'Muslims had created "no-go" areas for people of different faiths or races'.[10] Moreover, Black Christian attitudes have also been informed (and hardened) by stories of British Asian Muslim converts facing persecution by former religious brothers on British streets. In April 2008, *The Times* newspaper ran a story about Nissar Hussein, an Asian Christian from Bradford, who was 'subjected to a number of attacks and, after being told that his house would be burnt down if he did not repent and return to Islam, reported the threat to the police'.[11] Equally, the Christian Solidarity Worldwide report *No Place to Call Home* highlights alleged abuse by Muslim staff working for the Home Office and other statutory bodies of Muslim background believers claiming asylum in Britain.[12]

The Common Interest and the Need for Interaction

These situations have served to obstruct good relations between Black Christians and Muslims on matters where there is common interest and mutual concern. For instance, there are a number of issues, primarily those which affect their constituencies, Black people, on which they ought to come together, such as family structure, young people, education, health, the criminal justice system, employment and poverty.

Formal education is regarded by many as the lever to improve the socio-economic standards of Black people in the UK, and in recent years there have been numerous interventions to ensure Black school pupils make the grade within the British education system.[13] The Christian response to this phenomenon has been patchy and is typified by a flurry of conferences offering reports and resolutions that are rarely followed up. Admittedly, there are worthy initiatives such as the National Black Boys Can Association[14] and a handful of faith schools, but these are the exception rather than the rule within the church.

Many within Black Muslim and Christian communities have expressed the desire to play more of a role within the education system, either through more effective lobbying of government on school exclusions or, more assertively, by entering the faith school debate. On a more mundane level, the Black faith communities have a key role to play in Parent Teacher Associations, as school governors and as teachers, to ensure ethnic balance and Black representation within education.

Moreover, there are many other issues where Black Christians and Muslims have a common interest, such as the need to acquire suitable buildings in which they can worship and meet. Many Muslim groups are finding it difficult to obtain properties in London because of the inflated rent or purchasing costs; they also have problems finding premises that accommodate a complete separation of the genders and have facilities for youth. Like churches, Muslim congregations are seeking to corner the 'change of building use' market for buildings where planning permission has been granted by councils for religious use. The increasing number of Muslim converts has resulted in the need to find suitable premises for mosques that double as places of worship and community centres. (Most mosques are multi-functional spaces which cater to the myriad needs of communities in education, advice and work with children.) Bearing in mind the ways in which Black converts often come to Islam, these buildings must be able to offer space for various forms of counselling, on addictions and emotional issues, as well as education in foundational Islamic teachings to ensure a correct understanding of the faith and deter misunderstandings that extremists can exploit.

Up until now, what dialogue has taken place between Black Muslims and Black Christians has largely been adversarial, taking the form of debates about the efficacy of each faith and its relative advantages in addressing the social issues affecting Black people. There is a need for greater interfaith dialogue between Black Muslims and Christians on the same scale and with the same frequency as between mainstream Christian and Muslim bodies, where it has produced publications such as *The Road Ahead: A Christian-Muslim Dialogue*.[15] This book is a useful result of the dialogue facilitated by forums such as the Christian Muslim Forum and the Interfaith Network. As the book recognizes, 'there is much that Christians and Muslims share and also much which divides them'.[16]

Undoubtedly, the formation of a Black Christian and Muslim forum would be an opportunity for engagement on areas of common concern, such as the dynamics and ramifications of faith conversions and how they affect both communities. For instance, the impact of Muslim conversions on families of a Christian background has yet to be fully explored, but there is evidence that this growing phenomenon can create tensions within families, especially when spouses are involved. Currently, such families are left to their own devices, and the *ad hoc* support they receive can often do more harm than good. A first step would be for both parties to concur that such families are common and in need of support and affirmation. A further step would be some form of ministry offering advice and counselling to them.

Black Muslims can learn from the BMCs by establishing representative bodies which speak for them on a regional or national basis. No such organization currently exists, which means churches, statutory bodies and the like have no way of gathering wider Black Muslim opinion. Such a body would be a clear sign of maturity within the Black Muslim community, showing that Black Muslims have the confidence to take their place alongside other faith groups who are comfortable engaging in dialogue with politicians, the police, academics and the general public. It could also lobby those in decision-making positions on issues affecting Black British Muslims, as well as working alongside other faith and political groups in making their voices heard on issues of common concern.

Such an organization ought to have the further function of promoting greater understanding among fellow Muslims, especially between converts to Sunni Islam and those within the Nation of Islam (UK). The differences between these two groups result in many non-Muslims becoming confused about theological matters and doctrine, and leave some Muslims unable to provide a coherent response on their theological differences.

Obviously, the establishment of such an entity would be dependent on how some Black Muslims view themselves within the body of Islam, and whether they perceive the need for such separate identity groups. Some Black Muslims, especially Sunnis, appear disposed to fuse or subordinate 'racial' or ethnic identity within the broader, all-encompassing concept of faith. As a result, they see all talk of representative organizations or forums that address 'Black' concerns as failing to recognize the all-embracing nature of Islam.

Black Masculinities

The churches could learn much from the dynamism and energy of the Black Muslim movement in the UK, and the way it seeks synergy between spiritual, socio-political and cultural issues affecting those within its orbit. One major factor in this approach is the way Black Muslim structures acknowledge and affirm Black masculinity and male comradeship, in ways which are rarely seen within BMCs or in many sections of the Black community. This is not the type of hyper-masculinity one associates with certain hip-hop artists or nihilistic gang members which is rife with homophobia and deeply misogynistic.[17] Nor is it the kind of masculinity that makes men afraid to show their emotions or vulnerability in the company of peers; rather it is able to provide the types of support that men, when they strip away the macho veneer, often yearn for. This support is crucial, especially when one reads reports from doctors suggesting that 'young men may be more vulnerable to suicide and serious mental health problems because their ideas about masculinity prevent them from seeking the help that they need'. This research, which focused on a section of north London, also identified 69 per cent of African-Caribbean men as 'at risk' because 'they believe that masculinity is about self-reliance and finding your own solutions. They are uncomfortable talking about feelings and prefer to talk about stress and coping, as these ideas are more compatible with their ideas of being a man. Mostly they feel that sharing problems with peers or seeking professional help is a sign of weakness.'[18]

However, far too often this male affirmation and support is at the price of female deference, and men should not get the opportunity to demonstrate their manliness by preventing women from asserting their talents outside the home and during motherhood. This is especially the situation in mosques, which appear to typify the patriarchal nature of Islam and the subordination of women. As one writer has suggested, 'all the functions of an imam, such as religious teaching, spiritual and social counselling, have always been open to Muslim women, they are not allowed to lead prayers where men are in the congregation (although they may lead women only)'.[19] Having said that, there are mosques solely for women in countries such as China, and efforts are being made to set up similar establishments in India and Iran. Amina Wadud, who was the first woman in South Africa 'to deliver Friday "khutbah", at the Claremont Main Road Mosque in Cape Town', has also led a congregation in Friday prayer in New York.[20] One wonders how soon such initiatives will become a reality in Britain.

By contrast women experience relative gender equality within British churches, where an imbalance exists in their favour, which has arguably led to a feminization of Christian places of worship.[21]

The lack of men in the churches has prompted the publication *Christianity* to dedicate two issues (February and March 2008) to this matter, and over the last two decades numerous resources and ministries have been dedicated to making churches male friendly and redressing the gender imbalance.[22] Within BMCs there is the phenomenon of what some sarcastically call the 'Domino Widows', women whose spouses prefer to spend their Sundays either sleeping in or playing dominoes or cards rather than attending church; they only darken the doors of God's house for births, deaths and marriages. These 'widows' are the stalwarts of churches, but one would never know that they had husbands if one only met them at church.

Although men often hold vital positions in BMCs as leaders they are strikingly absent from the pews, and several of the Muslim converts from Christian backgrounds interviewed for this book described how, as children, they always felt strange accompanying their mothers to church while their fathers were still sleeping off Saturday night's excesses. When one Muslim brother, Sheffield-born Jamal (James) Thomas, reminisced about this experience, he disdainfully mentioned that he was particularly irked that his father insisted that he and his sister attend the local Baptist church as teenagers while he listened to the omnibus edition of *The Archers* on Radio 4. He said that his father reckoned that church was more for his mother than him and the preacher wasn't saying anything of interest to him. Jamal deduced that if church had little to offer his father, it had little to offer him, and at the age of sixteen, when Sunday school classes officially ended for young people, he stopped attending altogether. Ten years later, after a change of city, he became interested in Islam after reading material given to him by Muslims in Tooting high street, south London. He subsequently converted and became Jamal. By contrast, his sister Jennifer continued at the church, becoming a Sunday school teacher and then a worship leader, a role she currently carries out with her Scottish husband.

The Black Female Response

There is a vital need for places of worship which affirm men, but not at the expense of women. For some, the rise of the 'womanist' theology which has emerged over the last two decades to challenge church and society in relation to women is a Godsend. The term 'womanist' was popularized by the US author and academic Alice Walker in the 1980s to describe Black women's 'particular history of racial and gender oppression in the United States, but has developed to become a gender-progressive worldview that emerges from black women's unique history and focus around a vision of black empowerment.'

In the influential *Black Theology: An International Journal*, the Jamaican academic Marjorie Lewis makes a cogent argument for a theology which acknowledges that: 'Systems of domination have combined to marginalize the Black woman historically, through the experience of slavery, and in contemporary forms of sexism, classism and racism. The dominant social structures have not often recorded, acknowledged or valued the Black woman's perspective, but Black women have found creative ways of sharing wisdom within and across generations.'[23] And in Britain, the BMCs have a number of Black women such as Lorraine Dixon, Maxine Howell, Hyacinth Sweeney-Dixon, Valentina Alexander and Cecilia Cappel whose critical thinking and agitation for female empowerment have challenged the churches' basic assumptions.

Within the Black British Muslim movement there is no equivalent of womanism, which would use the prism of theology to address gender equality in the mosque and society. But interestingly, there is a growing international Muslim feminist movement which provides a critical space to discuss gender equality, social justice, freedom of conscience and culture. In October 2008 Muslim women attended the Third International Congress on Islamic Feminism, which focused on the problems of Muslim women in the era of globalization, who are facing a double oppression from economic neo-Liberalism and religious fundamentalism.[24] However, many Black academics and theologians have argued that feminism is a Eurocentric concept, and, unlike 'Womanism', it has been 'criticised for ignoring racism and classism, and in some instances advocating a separatist position that is unacceptable to Black women who are committed to the struggle of the entire Black community against racism and poverty'.[25]

It would be interesting if Black Muslim women could tap into the rich female heritage of courage and dissent which has recently been expressed through womanism to achieve leadership roles as imams within mosques. Such a movement would be able to contextualize the contentious issue of female Islamic attire, and differentiate where Islamic law ends and cultural tradition begins. As converts, these women have not come from a background in which religion and cultural tradition have been melded so seamlessly that they are difficult to unpick or critique. And it would be equally valuable for Black women to take a lead in helping their sisters in the faith to grapple with this important theological and cultural problem. Admittedly, the Black Muslim movement in Britain is relatively new, and it has taken Black women in the churches literally centuries to get where they are today. However, many of the women interviewed for this book have the savvy, intelligence and integrity to take forward this work and it is hoped that they will have the confidence and support to do so.

Perceptions of Converts

In the previous chapter, the examination of romantic relationships between Sunni Black Muslim men and Muslim women of different ethnicities suggested that British Islam had not become a post-race faith. But when Sunni converts were interviewed about how they were perceived by their non-Black brethren, responses were invariably positive. For instance, Jamal Thomas was given his first Islamic literature by two Muslim brothers, one Asian and the other Black. When he eventually converted he found himself attending the Tooting mosque, which is largely south Asian with a smattering of Somalis, West Africans and converts like himself. He takes up the story: 'It's been cool. I feel like one of the brothers and I'm accepted as one. They've got to know me at prayers and other activities we do at the mosque and they know I'm sincere.'

His conclusion is echoed by the Streatham-born theology graduate Bilal Hussain, who says, 'I think the mosque had a "watch and see" policy with me. When I first attended there was some curiosity from the [Asian] brothers. But I was serious and read up beforehand about mosques, so I knew what happened inside and how to behave. There's a lot of useful information on websites about mosque etiquette to ensure you don't make *faux pas*, if you catch my drift! I'm totally comfortable with everything and feel a real sense of peace.'

The fact that both men hinted that it took time for them to integrate into their respective mosques suggests that they were initially viewed with a modicum of suspicion by fellow worshippers. When asked if this had anything to do with colour both were quick to explain that the present religious climate has created a sense of wariness among Muslims, especially of new believers with the convert's zeal. There has been no shortage of sensational news stories on this particular issue. It is no wonder converts sometimes appear a little defensive, and Bilal Hussain remarks 'I often end up defending myself and Islam from charges of terrorism and fanaticism, both of which have nothing to do with our faith. Even if there is Islamophobia and US foreign policy that's been anti-Islamic, most Muslims do not respond with violence like the media suggest'. Bilal Hussain's comments mirror those made by non-Black Muslim converts in the national press, many of whom 'are growing increasingly anxious about anti-Muslim sentiment'. In the *Daily Telegraph* article 'Islamic Converts Defend Their Faith against Terrorism'

Nicole Martin suggests that '"New Muslims", in common with recruits to any faith or philosophy, are sometimes suspected of being more committed than those who are born Muslim. But many are anxious to distance themselves from the fanaticism of such converts as Richard Reid, the shoe-bomber.'[26]

When Muslims from a south Asian background, who still compose the majority Muslim community in Britain, are questioned about Black Muslim converts the responses tend to be affirmative. For instance, Pakistani-born Khalid Shah, a taxi-driver in Leeds, was keen to tell me how Bilal, an enslaved African who was a companion of the time of the Prophet Muhammad*, was clear evidence that Islam is a religion for Black people. He went on to state, 'Bilal had this wonderful voice and could sing really well and the Prophet Muhammad* chose him to lead prayers. His colour didn't matter. He was chosen because of his goodness and lovely voice.' Shah's colleague, Iqbal Shaffi, showed me his bare forearm and placed it alongside mine, saying, 'In Islam there is no difference, we are all the same. In Islam we are all brothers, simple as that. Muslims aren't like the rest of society; we treat our own with respect.'

In Reading Mansoor Ali, a student of Pakistani origin at Thames Valley University, suggested, 'We have Black people in my country; we call them "Sidis". They're Muslims like me and treated as equals. So, those Black people in my mosque are just Muslims. We don't notice their colour.' However, fellow student Tariq Rahman, who was present during the interview, added, 'I think we do notice their colour at our mosque, but it doesn't mean we treat them any differently. The Qur'an doesn't allow it, so we don't do it. Besides, [Black] Muslims aren't like other Black people; they're different because of Islam. Look at Malcolm X.'

North London library assistant Mehmet Beyaz points out: 'If all races turned to Islam there wouldn't be these problems. Islam breaks down all barriers, including those of colour. Once a person becomes a Muslim they're part of this family or community, and everything else is secondary. The mosque is full of people from all over the world.' His colleague Hasan Patel argues: 'You shouldn't apply those judgments or values to Islam. Just because you Christians have those problems, don't go thinking that we do. We've people in our mosque [Clapton, east London] who went to church when they were kids and they told me about all the racism and crazy behaviour that exists there. They say they experience none of this in the mosque.'

Across the city in Hillingdon, the views of two other Muslims were more troubling. Ishtiaq Ali, a library worker, stressed the unity of those who call themselves Muslims:

I think it's a good thing when anyone becomes a Muslim, Black, White or Yellow, because Islam is the true religion. You know, we're soon going to take over this country because a lot of people are turning their backs on false religions and becoming Muslim. I know a lot of you guys [Black people] are becoming Muslims. I read something in the papers about Islam becoming more popular to you guys than the church. That doesn't surprise me. The church believes in rights for women and homosexuals and you guys don't believe in those things, do you? No wonder you're walking away from those places. Muslims don't change the Qur'an to suit people's ideas.

His boss, Aftab Khan, said:

It doesn't surprise me that Black people are becoming Muslims. I read this book that said Black people love religion and it doesn't matter what religion, or how kooky it is; you'll always find some Black people following it. Look at that mad man [David Koresh] in [Waco] Texas. Half his followers were Black! This same book also said Mormons used to believe Black people were cursed and

227

hadn't got souls. They don't believe that any more and spend their time recruiting Black people. If you don't believe me just look yourself, they only target those places with Black people. Around here they only stop Black people. I don't know why they stop to talk to them. They've never stopped me. At least when Blacks follow Islam they're worshipping the one true God, Almighty Allah, and not false Messiahs or infidels. We Muslims know how to treat people fairly and any Black man who becomes a Muslim gets the respect they don't get in the rest of society.

It was bracing to hear such comments end in an affirmation of Black converts. However, within the context of Islam, I have not been in a position to accurately assess whether this picture of racial harmony is a reality. That would involve scientific observation of behaviour and a rigorous analysis of institutional structures, which I had no opportunity to carry out. The question also needs to be asked as to whether my 'race' was a major factor in these face-to-face interviews, as well as the fact that respondents wanted to present Islam in a positive light to an avowed Christian. All seemed candid and genuine in their responses. A great many appeared initially puzzled by the question of 'race' and Islam, as if the subject had no place within the faith and the mere mention of the term polluted the purity of Islam. Likewise, none of the interviewees even considered the notion that Black people could not be Muslims or made the connection between converts and terrorism.

The Way Ahead
In his seminal *Souls of Black Folks*, the legendary African-American intellectual, activist and leader William Edward Burghardt DuBois prophetically suggested the 'problem of the twentieth century is the problem of the color-line'.[27] Du Bois was undoubtedly correct in his analysis, not only in the United States of America,

but around the globe. It has been argued that, with the first Black President in the United States, the advance of equality and racial justice initiatives, greater ethnic diversity, and rising instances of interracial relationships, we now live in a 'post-race' society, in which the old fixations on race and identity are no longer paramount.[28]Conversely, the US Indian Muslim academic Dr Eboo Patel has argued that 'the twenty-first century will be shaped by the question of the faith line'. Dr Patel goes on:

> On one side of the faith line are the religious totalitarians.
> Their conviction is that only one interpretation of one
> religion is a legitimate way of being, believing, and
> belonging on earth. Everyone else needs to be cowed, or
> converted, or condemned, or killed. On the other side
> of the faith line are the religious pluralists, who hold
> that people believing in different creeds and belonging
> to different communities need to learn to live together.
> Religious pluralism is neither mere coexistence nor forced
> consensus. It is a form of proactive cooperation that
> affirms the identity of the constituent communities while
> emphasizing that the well being of each and all depends
> on the health of the whole.[29]

The context of Dr Patel's analysis is the events of 9/11 in the USA and 7/7 in Britain, which put religion on the agenda in a way that was previously reserved for race.

Although Dr Patel's arguments are persuasive, they do not mitigate the importance of 'race' in either the USA or Britain. The beginning of post-race society cannot be determined by the election of one man; and statistics are open to manipulation. Religion and race are still major factors in a country such as Britain which is still grappling with issues of social cohesion and integration.[30] The rise of the Black Muslim presence in Britain is a crystallization of race and faith, and as for all Black people in the diaspora, the issues of 'belonging' and identity remain ones with which Black Muslims continue to wrestle. This struggle takes place against the background of a society which constantly forces individuals into categories or places labels on them.

It is not my belief that the increase in the numbers of Black people turning to Islam is a phenomenon that will wax and wane like the Rastafari movement a generation ago. For one thing, Islam is not a faith that took root in Jamaica less than a century ago and sought to address the socio-religious and cultural yearnings of an oppressed Black majority; Islam is a world faith which has existed for over a millennium and has more than a billion adherents. And although Islam currently attracts the type of Black person who may have been drawn to the counter-cultural rebelliousness of Rasta, there is less symbolism and iconography within Islam to make it susceptible to appropriation by mere trendsetters. In the Qur'an, the Hadith, the Five Pillars of Islam and Islamic law in general there are set rules and regulations that govern the way a good Muslim ought to live. Many Muslim converts welcome the strictures of Islam as a stabilizing influence in lives which had often lacked a sense of order and focus. This was never the situation with Rastafari, which lacked a fixed credo and whose doctrines and practices were open to interpretation and abuse. And as a result of a lack of rigorous theological scholarship and analysis, it was difficult to denounce behaviour as 'un-Rasta' apart from the flouting of dietary laws and obvious licentious behaviour.[31]

It is my contention that neither society nor church can 'sit this one out' in the hope that growth of Islam within the Black community will subside and the situation will go back to normal. The rise of the Black Muslim presence over the last two decades has been informed by a range of religious, political, cultural, economic and social factors around the globe that show no signs of going away. Despite the advance of science, the emergence of rationalism and the efforts of committed atheists such as Richard Dawkins, religion, or rather spirituality, is in rude health. This book is not the place to examine what appears to be the innate desire or need of human beings to seek out a higher power or deity whom they believe exerts force over their lives and the world about them, and to whom they are willing to make a commitment. But suffice it to say that within Black communities this has been a reality since time immemorial, and shows no signs of change. And while the 1980s and the 1990s were characterized by huge growth within BMCs, it can be argued that the simultaneous emergence of 'prosperity teaching', which became popular within many BMCs,[32] allied to their natural conservatism, allowed them to disregard a neglected community. At the same time there remained the real desire of many for faith to make sense of what it means to be Black, young and voiceless in a society that often views these traits as a threat, and that uses the apparatus of institutional racism to curtail equality, justice and rights.

In this soil the Black Muslim movement took root, feeding on the spiritual hunger of those with a natural thirst for truth and justice and a craving to make a difference in the lives of their brothers and sisters. And, to quote Malcolm X, these Muslims are prepared to use 'any means necessary' to achieve their aim. The previous chapter has shown how hip hop, which has become the foremost force in popular culture, has close links with Islam and has been used by Black Muslims to disseminate their message, especially to youth. Equally, Muslim brothers are not shy of hitting the streets with their message of redemption and transformation, with a zeal that often puts other missionary faiths to shame.

But the events of 9/11 and 7/7 have altered perceptions of the power of faith and the way it can be misinterpreted and ultimately exploited by those whom the media label fanatics and extremists. They have given rise to a perceived 'war on Islam'[33] which has served to galvanize the hearts and minds of those who believe their faith is under attack. Some Muslims have sought to make Islam the 'religion of the oppressed' – the faith of the world's righteous poor who are victims of a rapacious, irreligious economic and political system controlled by those with a vendetta against God's people. Such a mindset suggests that Islam is the religion of the developing world, which is populated by Black and Brown people, and is opposed to the 'West' or the 'North', which is White, Christian and exploitative. Budding Black devotees in Britain, who face institutional racism and discrimination, are encouraged to stand with their oppressed brothers and sisters in the developing, Islamic world.

It would be wrong to suggest that Britain's Black Muslim presence is a threat to either church or society. Current statistics reveal that BMCs still continue to grow in numbers and show no signs of falling into the malaise affecting other churches. Likewise, the Muslims interviewed for this book did not harbour any hostility against Britain; what they did want was a society that would let them practise their faith free from malice and interference, and one that would respect the rights of Muslims in Britain and abroad.

Many of Britain's Black Muslim leaders are men who attract followers with their dazzling oratory and ability to tap into the hopes and concerns of a range of individuals. Their 'street' credentials give them a kudos among the young – many of the leaders are young themselves – and their willingness to take advantage of hip-hop culture is often powerful for those who want greater meaning to their lives than Play Stations and Facebook. And because many Sunni Muslims in particular do not over-emphasize issues of 'race', Islam is likely to attract people from other ethnicities. Anecdotal evidence suggests that there are now more non-Black adherents of Rastafari than Black ones, with Japan, the Netherlands, Germany and the Scandinavian countries being real growth areas. A similar diversification could take place with Islam; it might start with people being drawn to Islam because of popular culture, but it will invariably result in conversions, since Islam by its nature demands 'the total surrender of oneself to God'. It is difficult for a convert to become a cultural or nominal Muslim.

This religious development would present a challenge to the churches, since both Christianity and Islam would be drawing on the same 'pool of unbelievers'. For society, this new Muslim presence would bring people of various ethnicities together, forging a much-needed unity in diversity. And society would welcome this development if it followed the religious pluralism advocated by Dr Eboo Patel, in which believers 'affirm the identity of the constituent communities while emphasizing that the well being of each and all depends on the health of the whole'.

Black Muslim converts are a relatively new presence in the diverse religious tapestry of modern-day Britain. This presence is to be welcomed and affirmed as it enriches Britain's faith community and belies the notion that Islam is the sole preserve of south Asians in Britain. Indeed, many converts can also be found within Britain's White population; books by writers such as Kate Zebiri[34] and Lucy Bushill-Matthews[35] explore the experiences of White British converts to Islam.

Black British culture has transformed and enriched Britain in ways which were unimaginable in 1948, when the SS *Empire Windrush* first docked at Tilbury with its Caribbean passengers. Academics and observers would be wise to watch the way in which the increasingly influential Black Muslim convert presence shapes the experiences and identities of Britain's Black communities over the next few decades. History has shown that any changes within the Black community will undoubtedly influence mainstream British culture, especially popular, youth-related culture, over which it has had a disproportionate sway. This cultural influence has worked to dispel misconceptions, break down barriers and build bridges across communities. It can be argued that it is probably the most efficacious method of generating much-needed cohesion and unity within Britain.

Notes

Introduction

1. *The Oxford Companion to Black British History*, edited by David Dabydeen, John Gilmore and Cecily Jones, Oxford University Press, 2007, p. 54.

2. 'Somalis in Cardiff', *The Guardian* (23 January 2006), p. 6.

3. Writers such as Joel Edwards, Mark Sturge, Joe Aldred, Io Smith, Selwyn Arnold, Ron Nathan, Robert Beckford, Anthony Reddie, Robinson Milwood, Wilfred Wood, Glynne Gordon-Carter, Roswith Gerloff and Valentina Alexander among others have all written about Black Majority Churches in Britain over the years.

4. *Oxford Companion to Black British History*, pp. 54–56.

5. Many Rastafari worship the former emperor of Ethiopia, Haile Selassie I, as a deity.

6. *The Search for Common Ground: Muslims, Non-Muslims and the UK Media*, Greater London Authority, 2007, p. 18.

7. E. U. Essien-Udom, *Black Nationalism: The Rise of the Black Muslims in the USA*, Penguin, 1966, p. 53.

8. Equally, there is also a debate about whether Black people in this country are 'Black' or 'African'. An increasing number are opting for the term African-British as a more apt way of describing themselves.

9. *Black British Culture and Society: A Text Reader*, edited by Kwesi Owusu, Routledge, 2000, p. 1.

Chapter 1

1. Chris Horrie and Peter Chippendale, *What is Islam? A Comprehensive Introduction*, Virgin Books, 2003, p. 3.

2. It is common for Muslims to use the term 'Peace Be Upon Him', which is often reduced to 'PBUH', as a sign of reverence to the Prophet Muhammad. For the purposes of this book, when referring to the Prophet Muhammad I will use an '*', not only to denote Muslim respect for the Prophet, but also to differentiate between the numerous other Muslims with the name Muhammad.

3. Matthew S. Gordon, *Understanding Islam: Origins, Beliefs, Practices, Holy Texts, Sacred Places*, Duncan Baird Publishers, 2002, p. 6.

4. Nabil I. Matar, *Islam for Beginners*, For Beginners Books, 2007, p. 12.

5. Horrie and Chippendale, *What is Islam?*, p. 14.

6. John Esposito, *Islam: The Straight Path*, 3rd revised edition, Oxford University Press, 1998, p. 112.

7. Matar, *Islam for Beginners*.

8. The translation of the Qur'an used here is that by M. H. Shakir, Tahrike Tarsile Qur'an, Inc., 2006.

9. Matar, *Islam for Beginners*, p. 15.

10. Ruqaiyyah Waris Maqsood, *Need to Know? Islam: Understand the Religion Behind the Headlines*, HarperCollins, 2008, p. 38.

11. Jamal J. Elias, *Islam*, Prentice Hall, 1999, p. 19.

12. Esposito, *Islam*, p. 112.

13. Gordon, *Understanding Islam*, p. 51.

14. Ibid., p. 14.

15. Maqsood, *Need to Know? Islam*, p. 6.

16. Gordon, *Understanding Islam*, p. 37.

17. Esposito, *Islam*, pp. 6–12.

18. Horrie and Chippendale, *What is Islam?*, p. 46.

19. Matar, *Islam for Beginners*, pp. 29–35.

20. Esposito, *Islam*, p. 93.

21. Ibid., p. 43.

22. Elias, *Islam*, p. 24.

23. Gordon, *Understanding Islam*, p. 37.

24. Elias, *Islam*, p. 24.

25. Matar, *Islam for Beginners*, p. 5.

26. Horrie and Chippendale, *What is Islam?*, p. 7.

27. Ibid., p.9.

28. *The Oxford Illustrated History of Christianity*, edited by John Manners, Oxford University Press, 1996, p.174.

29. Gordon, *Understanding Islam*, p.17.

30. Matar, *Islam for Beginners*, p. 89.

31. Ibid., pp. 84–85.

32. Horrie and Chippendale, *What is Islam?*, p.133.

33. Ibid., p.137.

34. The term Shii or Shi'a derives from *shiat Ali*, which means followers of Ali.

35. Elias, *Islam*, p. 36.

36. Esposito, *Islam*, pp. 109–110.

37. Gordon, *Understanding Islam*, p. 52.

38. Maqsood, *Need to Know? Islam*, p. 108.

39. Elias, *Islam*, p. 39.

40. Shaykh Fadhlalla Haeri, *The Thoughtful Guide to Sufism*, O Books, 2003, p. 11.

41. Ibid., p. 12.

42. Horrie and Chippendale, *What is Islam?*, p. 63.

43. Gordon, *Understanding Islam*, p.14.

44. Hugh Kennedy, *The Great Arab Conquests: How the Spread of Islam Changed the World We Live In*, Da Capo Press, 2008, pp. 66–98.

45. Ibid., pp. 200–25.

46. Ibid., pp. 296–324.

47. *Oxford Illustrated History of Christianity*, p.172.

48. Ibid., p. 173.

49. See Ali A. Mazrui, *The Africans: A Triple Heritage*, Little Brown & Co., 1986.

50. John Reader, *Africa: A Biography of the Continent*, Penguin, 1997, p. 282.

51. *The History of Islam in Africa*, edited by Nehemia Levtzion and Randall L. Pouwels, James Currey Publishers, 2000.

52. *Taking Back Islam: American Muslims Reclaim Their Faith*, edited by Michael Wolfe and others, Rodale, 2002, p. 133.

53. Molefi Kete Asante, *The History of Africa: The Quest for Eternal Harmony*, Routledge, 2007, p. 115.

54. Robin Walker, *When We Ruled: The Ancient and Mediaeval History of Black Civilisation*, Every Generation Media, 2006, p. 491.

55. John Iliffe, *Africans: The History of a Continent*, Cambridge University Press, 1995, pp. 53–56.

56. Walker, *When We Ruled*, pp. 469, 470, 471.

57. Tatah Mentan and Moye Bongyu, 'Promise and Perils of Politicised Islam in Africa', in *The Homeland Security Handbook*, edited by Jack Pinkowski, CRC, 2008, p. 179.

58. Asante, *The History of Africa*, p. 129.

59. Robert O. Collins, *Africa: A Short History*, Markus Wiener Publishers, 2006, p. 59.

60. Richard Reddie, *Abolition! The Struggle to Abolish Slavery in the British Colonies*, Lion, 2007, p. 60.

61. *Taking Back Islam*, p. 131.

62. Ibid., p. 130.

63. *African Presence in Early America*, edited by Ivan van Sertima, Transaction Publishers, 1992.

64. Michael Bradley, *The Black Journey of America: The Amazing Evidence of Daring Voyages by Ancient West African Mariners*, Personal Library, 1981.

65. C. Eric Lincoln, *The Black Muslims in America*, 3rd edition, Africa World Press, 1994, p. 48.

66. See Sylviane A. Diouf, *Servants of Allah: African Muslims Enslaved in the Americas*, NYU Press, 1998.

67. Michael Muhammad Knight, *The Five Percenters: Islam, Hip Hop and the Gods of New York*, Oneworld, 2007, p. 11.

68. Ibid., p. 11.

69. David Paterson, Doug Willoughby and Susan Willoughby, *Civil Rights in the USA, 1863–1980*, Heinemann, 2001, pp. 48–72.

70. John White, *Black Leadership in America: From Booker T. Washington to Jesse Jackson*, 2nd edition, Longman, 1990, pp. 1–3.

71. *Garvey: Africa, Europe, the Americas*, edited by Rupert Lewis and Maureen Warner-Lewis, Institute of Social and Economic Research, 1986, pp. 200–205.

72. Colin Grant, *Negro with a Hat: The Rise and Fall of Marcus Garvey and His Dream of Mother Africa*, Jonathan Cape, 2008, pp. 61–68.

73. Ibid., pp. 367–373.

74. *Garvey: Africa, Europe, the Americas*, p. 181.

75. Quoted in Felicia M. Miyakawa, *Five Percenter Rap: God's Hop Music, Message, and Black Muslim Mission*, Indiana University Press, 2005, p. 11.

76. Lincoln, *The Black Muslims in America*, p. 48.

77. Steven Tsoukalas, *The Nation of Islam: Understanding the 'Black Muslims'*, P&R Publishing Company, 2001, pp. 11–12.

78. Ibid., p. 11.

79. Miyakawa, *Five Percenter Rap*, p. 11.

80. Ibid., p. 12.

81. Lincoln, *The Black Muslims in America*, p. 50.

82. Elijah Muhammad, *Message to the Blackman in America*, Secretarius Memps Publications, 1965, 1973, p. 21.

83. Martha F. Lee, *The Nation of Islam: An American Millenarian Movement*, Edwin Mellen Press, 1988, p. 31.

84. According to Mattias Gardell, Fard's birthplace may also have been New Zealand, Barbados, Jamaica, Syria, Palestine, Turkey or Oregon. See Mattias Gardell, *Countdown to Armageddon: Louis Farrakhan and the Nation of Islam*, Hurst and Company, 1996, p. 55.

85. Elijah Muhammad, *Message to the Blackman*, p. 21.

86. According to Felicia M. Miyakawa, 'Under the leadership of W. D. Fard the spirit of Black American Islam evolved from joyful race pride into a more aggressive black supremacism.' Miyakawa, *Five Percenter Rap*, p. 21.

87. Paterson, Willoughby and Willoughby, *Civil Rights*, pp. 72–85.

88. Elijah Muhammad, *Message to the Blackman*, p. 26.

89. *The Recovery of Black Presence: An Interdisciplinary Exploration. Essays in Honor of Dr Charles B. Copher*, edited by Randal C. Bailey and Jacquelyn Grant, Abingdon Press, 1995, pp. 143–58.

90. Elijah Muhammad, *Message to the Blackman*, p. 9.

91. Grant, *Negro with a Hat*, p. 389.

92. For a more extensive discussion of art, theology and Black people see Robert Beckford, *Jesus is Dread: Black Theology and Black Culture in Britain*, Darton, Longman and Todd, 1998, chapter 4, pp. 71–95.

93. Tsoukalas, *The Nation of Islam*, p. 43.

94. Elijah Muhammad, *Message to the Blackman*, p. 17.

95. Ibid., p. 31.

96. According to Malcolm X, the name 'X' symbolized the true African family name that he could never know.

97. Malcolm X, with the assistance of Alex Haley, *The Autobiography of Malcolm X*, Penguin, 1965, p. 291.

98. Lincoln, *The Black Muslims in America*, p. 77.

99. Manning Marable, *Black Fundamentalism: Farrakhan and Conservative Black Nationalism*, Race and Class, volume 39, issue 4 (1998), p. 11.

100. Essien-Udom, *Black Nationalism*, p. 195.

101. Ibid., p. 53.

102. Elijah Muhammad, *Message to the Blackman*, p. xiii.

103. Tsoukalas, *The Nation of Islam*, p. 51.

104. Anthony B. Pinn, *Terror and Triumph: The Nature of Black Religion*, Fortress Press, 2003, p. 166.

105. Ibid., p. 166.

106. Lincoln, *The Black Muslims in America*, p. 87–88.

107. Malcolm X, *Autobiography*, p. 348.

108. Lincoln, *The Black Muslims in America*, p. 91.

109. The prevalence of imprisonment in 2001 was higher for Black males (16.6%) and Hispanic males (7.7%) than for White males (2.6%), and for Black females (1.7%) and Hispanic females (0.7%) than White females (0.3%). An estimated 40% of inmates in the USA were black: 19% Hispanic, 1% Native American, 1% Asian and 3% of more than one race/ethnicity. Blacks or African-Americans make up 13.5% of the US population. Taken from the US Department of Justice, Bureau of Justice statistics, Criminal Offenders Statistics. See http://www.ojp.usdoj.gov/bjs/crimoff.htm.

110. Eldridge Cleaver, *Soul on Fire*, Hodder & Stoughton, 1979, pp. 74–75.

111. Lincoln, *The Black Muslims in America*, p. 109.

112. Malcolm X, *Autobiography*, p. 325.

113. Daniel Wolff and others, *You Send Me: The Life and Times of Sam Cooke*, Virgin Books, 1995, p. 269.

114. Ibid., p. 1.

115. Essien-Udom, *Black Nationalism*, p. 76.

116. Knight, *The Five Percenters*, p. 32.

117. Louis E. Lomax, *To Kill a Black Man*, Holloway House, 1987, pp. 65–76.

118. Malcolm X, *Autobiography*, p. 362.

119. Gardell, *Countdown to Armageddon*, p. 224.

120. Lomax, *To Kill a Black Man*, p. 78.

121. 'Message to the Grassroots', in *Malcolm X Speaks: Selected Speeches and Statements*, edited with prefatory notes by George Breitman, Grove Press, 1966, pp. 4–17.

122. Essien-Udom, *Black Nationalism*, pp. 53–54.

123. Tsoukalas, *The Nation of Islam*, p. 55.

124. Cleaver, *Soul on Fire*, p. 76.

125. Stanley Crouch, *Notes of a Hanging Judge: Essays and Reviews, 1979–1989*, Oxford University Press, 1990, p. 169.

126. Michael Eric Dyson, *Making Malcolm: The Myth and Meaning of Malcolm X*, Oxford University Press, 1995, p. 11.

127. Marable, *Black Fundamentalism*, p. 13.

128. Tsoukalas, *The Nation of Islam*, p. 75.

129. Malcolm X, *Autobiography*, p. 403.

130. Dyson, *Making Malcolm*, p. 11.

131. Ibid., *Making Malcolm*, p. 3.

132. In his book *Soul Survivor*, the award-winning Christian author and journalist Philip Yancey explored the anger and hatred of many White American Christians toward the Revd Dr Martin Luther King. For some, he was 'Martin "Lucifer" King', a devil who was looking to destroy the very fabric of American society. See chapter 2 'Martin Luther King Jr: A Long Night's Journey into Day', Philip Yancey, *Soul*

Survivor: How My Faith Survived the Church, Hodder & Stoughton, 2001, pp. 11–41.

133. Lomax, *To Kill a Black Man,* pp. 84–90.

134. Malcolm X, *Autobiography,* p. 14.

135. Ibid., p. 31.

136. Lomax, *To Kill a Black Man,* p. 71.

137. Dyson, *Making Malcolm,* pp. 12–13.

138. Tsoukalas, *The Nation of Islam,* pp. 133–134. Ezekiel's Wheel refers to a vision recounted in the first chapter of the Book of Ezekiel which the Honourable Elijah Muhammad believed to have been a UFO sighting.

139. Lincoln, *The Black Muslims in America,* p. 223.

140. Dyson, *Making Malcolm,* pp. 64–65.

141. Tsoukalas, *The Nation of Islam,* p. 86.

142. Malcolm X, *Autobiography,* p. 339.

143. Lomax, *To Kill a Black Man,* pp. 133–34.

144. Malcolm X, *Autobiography,* p. 494.

145. Dyson, *Making Malcolm,* pp. 22–24.

146. Tsoukalas, *The Nation of Islam,* pp. 198–99.

147. Ibid., p. 91.

148. Gardell, *Countdown to Armageddon,* pp. 76–81.

149. Lincoln, *The Black Muslims in America,* p. 263.

150. Essien-Udom, *Black Nationalism,* p. 167.

151. Malcolm X, *Autobiography,* p. 352.

152. Dyson, *Making Malcolm,* p. 193.

153. Claude Andrew Clegg III, *An Original Man: The Life and Times of Elijah Muhammad,* St Martins Press, 1997.

154. Gardell, *Countdown to Armageddon,* p. 61.

155. Ibid., p. 63.

156. Ibid., p. 102.

157. Tsoukalas, *The Nation of Islam,* p. 98.

158. Cleaver, *Soul on Fire,* pp. 78–79.

159. Pinn, *Terror and Triumph,* p. 128.

160. William A. Henry and others, 'Louis Farrakhan: Pride and Prejudice', *Time* magazine (28 February 1994).

161. Crouch, *Notes of a Hanging Judge,* p. 165.

162. The Million Man March was dramatized in filmmaker Spike Lee's excellent 1996 movie *Get on the Bus.*

163. Marable, *Black Fundamentalism,* p. 2.

164. Henry, 'Louis Farrakhan'.

165. Pinn, *Terror and Triumph,* p. 129.

166. Daniel B. Wood, in *Christian Science Monitor* (14 February 2002), p. 3.

167. William A. Henry and others, 'Ministry of Rage: Pride and Prejudice' *Time* magazine (28 February 1994).

168. Pinn, *Terror and Triumph,* p. 129.

169. Marable, *Black Fundamentalism*, p. 15.

170. Ibid., pp. 3–4.

171. Ibid., pp. 16–17.

172. Ibid.

173. Ibid., p. 3, 16–17.

174. Gardell, *Countdown to Armageddon*, p. 63.

175. Wood, *Christian Science Monitor*, p. 3.

176. *The Times* (11 September 2008).

177. Rupert Cornwell, 'Warith Deen Mohammed: Imam Who Preached a Moderate Form of Islam to Black Americans', *The Independent* (15 September 2008).

178. Miyakawa, *Five Percenter Rap*, p. 150.

179. Eboo Patel, *Acts of Faith: The Story of an American Muslim and the Struggle for the Soul of a Generation*, Beacon Press, 2007, pp. 176–77.

Chapter 2

1. See Ray Costello, *Liverpool Black Pioneers*, The Bluecoat Press, 2007.

2. *Black British Culture and Society*, p. 2.

3. Mike Phillips and Trevor Phillips, *Windrush: The Irresistible Rise of Multiracial Britain*, HarperCollins, 1998, pp. 2–5.

4. *Race in Britain: Continuity and change*, 2nd edition, edited by Charles Husband, Hutchinson, 1987, p. 86.

5. Although there were rumours of the ship being turned around mid-Atlantic, its passengers disembarked on 22 June 1948 at Tilbury Docks in Essex.

6. Phillips and Phillips, *Windrush*, p. 70.

7. Peter Fryer, *The Politics of Windrush*, Index Books, 1999, p. 42.

8. Phillips and Phillips, *Windrush*, p. 96.

9. *Daily Mail* (22 June 1948).

10. Tony Sewell, *Keep on Moving. The Windrush Legacy: The Black experience in Britain from 1948*, Voice Enterprises, 1998, pp. 26–27.

11. Ekow Eshun, 'A Universal Colour', *The New Statesman* (11 October 2004), p. 34.

12. *20th Century Britain: Economic, Social and Cultural Change*, edited by Paul Johnson, Longman, 1994, p. 302.

13. Phillips and Phillips, *Windrush*, p. 57.

14. Peter Hennessy, *Never Again: Britain 1945–51*, Vintage Books, 1993, quoting Sir John Wheeler-Bennett, *King George VI: His Life and Reign*, diary entry for 21 January 1946, p. 274.

15. Dominic Sandbrook. 'Racist Nation?', *BBC History Magazine* (March 2008) volume 9, number 3, p. 29.

16. 'Many Winters On: Memories of Britain's Post War Caribbean Immigrants', *The Voice* (1988), p. 32.

17. Sewell, *Keep on Moving*, p. 21.

18. Fryer, *The Politics of Windrush*, p. 19.

19. Hennessy, *Never Again*, pp. 132–144.

20. Beverley Bryan, Stella Dadzie and Suzanne Scafe, *The Heart of the Race: Black Women's Lives in Britain*, Virago, 1985, pp. 89–90.

21. Martin Pugh, *State and Society: British Political and Social History 1870–1992*, Edward Arnold, 1994, p. 232.

22. Ibid., p. 232.

23. John Solomos, *Race and Racism in Britain*, 2nd edition, Macmillan, 1993, pp. 57–58.

24. Ibid., p. 59.

25. Harry Goulbourne, *Caribbean Transnational Experience*, Pluto Press, 2002, p. 27.

26. To mark the fiftieth anniversary of the SS *Empire Windrush* and its impact on Britain, a public open space in Brixton, opposite Lambeth Town Hall, was renamed Windrush Square.

27. Goulbourne, *Caribbean Transnational Experience*, p. 74.

28. One of the great ironies of Caribbean mass migration to post-war Britain was that many of these African-Caribbean men and women, descendants of the enslaved peoples who were brought to the Caribbean as part of the transatlantic slave trade, ended up living in towns and cities that were inextricably linked to that same miserable trade in human beings. Cities such as Liverpool, London and Bristol were slaving ports, while Manchester became known for the processing of slave-produced cotton and Birmingham produced firearms to police the trade and exchange for human beings. See Reddie, *Abolition!*

29. Lloyd Bradley, *Bass Culture: When Reggae was King*, Penguin Books, 2001, p. 117.

30. Sewell, *Keep on Moving*, pp. 28–29.

31. Dick Hebdige, *Cut 'n' Mix: Culture, Identity and Caribbean Music*, Routledge, 1987, pp. 38–40.

32. Stuart Hall, 'Calypso Kings', *The Guardian* (28 June 2002).

33. According to the writer Donald Hinds, 'some public houses still operated a colour bar, covertly or otherwise'. See *The West Indian Gazette: Claudia Jones and the Black Press in Britain*, Race and Class, 2008, p. 91.

34. Michael Manley, *A History of West Indies Cricket*, revised edition, Andre Deutsch, 1990, p. 93.

35. Quoted in Hall, 'Calypso Kings'. 'Mas' is akin to 'carnival' in Trinidad.

36. Ibid.

37. Sandbrook, 'Racist Nation?', p. 29.

38. Sewell, *Keep on Moving*, pp. 48–49.

39. *Oxford Companion to Black British History*, pp. 346–47.

40. *Race in Britain*, p. 92.

41. Solomos, *Race and Racism*, p. 62.

42. *Oxford Companion to Black British History*, p. 219.

43. Pugh, *State and Society*, p. 270.

44. Max Travers, *The British Immigration Courts: A Study of Law and Politics*, The Policy Press, 1999, pp. 157–58.

45. *20th Century Britain*, p. 419. Solomos, *Race and Racism*, p. 64.

46. *Race in Britain*, p. 117.

47. Ibid.

48. *The Autobiography of Martin Luther King*, edited by Clayborne Carson, Abacus, 2000, p. 258.

49. *Race in Britain*, p. 132.

50. Darcus Howe, *From Bobby to Babylon: Blacks and the British Police*, Race Today Publications, 1988, p. 16.

51. Hinds, *The West Indian Gazette*.

52. Ibid.

53. *Black British Culture and Society*, p. 9.

54. Dick Hebdige, *Subculture: The Meaning of Style*, Routledge, 1988, p. 6.

55. John Storey, *An Introductory Guide to Cultural Theory and Popular Culture*, Harvester Wheatsheaf, 1993, p. 2.

56. Storey, *An Introductory Guide*, p. 2.

57. Hebdige, *Subculture*, p. 49.

58. Sebastian Clarke, *Jah Music: The Evolution of the Popular Jamaican Song*, Heinemann, 1980, pp. 57–73.

59. Hebdige, *Cut 'n' Mix*, pp. 91–92.

60. 1961 census, Office for National Statistics.

61. Howe, *From Bobby to Babylon*, pp. 16–18.

62. Hebdige, *Subculture*.

63. Clarke, *Jah Music*, pp. 139–40.

64. Prince Buster, *On Tour* album sleeve.

65. Simon Jones, *Black Culture, White Youth: The Reggae Tradition from JA to UK*, Macmillan, 1988, p. 37.

66. Clarke, *Jah Music*, pp. 147–48.

67. Paul Doyle and others, *The Paint House: Words from an East End Gang*, Penguin Books, 1972, pp. 11–12.

68. Michael Thomas and Adrian Boot, *Jah Revenge: Babylon Revisited*, Eel Pie Publishing, 1992, pp. 62–66.

69. Barry Chevannes, *Rastafari: Roots and Ideology*, Syracuse University Press, 1994, pp. 222–56.

70. Thomas and Boot, *Jah Revenge*, pp. 62–66.

71. Chevannes, *Rastafari*, pp. 222–26.

72. Paul Gilroy, 'A New Crime, but the Same Old Culprits', *The Guardian* (8 January 2003), p. 35.

73. Dave Simpson, 'Roots Manoeuvre: What Happened When Reggae and Punk Went Head to Head in the UK', *The Guardian* (20 July 2007), p. 6.

74. Bradley, *Bass Culture*.

75. Paul Gilroy, *There Ain't no Black in the Union Jack*, Routledge, 1987, p. 148.

76. Hebdige, *Cut 'n' Mix*, pp. 106–114.

77. Dick Hebdige, 'Ska tissue: the rise and fall of 2 Tone', in *Reggae International*, edited by Stephen Davis and Peter Simon, Thames and Hudson, 1982, pp. 159–61.

78. Howe, *From Bobby to Babylon*, p. 51.

79. Jamie Doward, 'Yo, Blingland! Hip Hop Culture Rules for British Teens', *The Observer* (22 February 2004), p. 7.

80. Ibid.

81. Lola Adesioye, 'Invisible in Plain Sight', *The Guardian* (5 September 2008), features section, p. 5.

82. John Arlidge, 'Forget Black and White. EA is What's Hot', *The Observer* (4 January 2004), p. 19.

83. Jenny Booth, 'Blair Backs Ban on Hooded Sweatshirts', *The Times* (12 May 2005), p. 2.

84. Arifa Akbar, 'From Windrush to Ms Dynamite: 50 Years of Black British Style', *The Independent*, (5 October 2004), p. 10.

85. Eshun, 'A Universal Colour', p. 34.

86. In the article 'Young, Gifted and Black?', *Times* journalist Carol Midgley wrote: 'David Beckham is a black man. To be specific, David Beckham is "the most famous black man in Britain". Not my words, you understand, but those of a forthcoming Channel 4 documentary, *Black Like Beckham*. The thrust of the programme is that blond David is now the nation's premier black icon. He has adopted so much from black urban culture – the "bling, bling" taste in flash jewellery, the clothes, the beanie hats, the Bentley convertible, the penchant for garage music – that he must now be considered black in all but the trifling detail of skin colour. Still in doubt? Then here is a killer piece of evidence. His Rottweiler dogs are called Snoop (as in Dogg) and Puff (as in Daddy). His son, Romeo, is named after a singer from So Solid Crew. Case closed. How silly do you feel now?' Carol Midgley, 'Young, Gifted and Black?', *The Times* (27 March 2003).

87. *Black Like Beckham*, broadcast on Channel 4, 25 April 2003, 7.30 pm.

88. Arlidge, 'Forget Black and White', p. 19.

89. Ekow Eshun, 'Battle of the Brands', *The New Statesman* (17 January 2005), p. 34.

90. Paul Gilroy, *Small Acts: Thoughts on the Politics of Black Cultures*, Serpent's Tail, 1993, p. 228.

91. See Tony Sewell, *Black Masculinities and Schooling: How Black Boys Survive Modern Schooling*, Trentham Books, 2000.

92. Beckford, *Jesus is Dread*, p. 98.

93. Chevannes, *Rastafari*, pp. 222–66

94. Horrie and Chippendale, *What is Islam?*, p. 3.

95. Jones, *Black Culture*, back cover.

Chapter 3

1. Anthony G. Reddie, *Faith, Stories and the Experience of Black Elders: Singing the Lord's Song in a Strange Land*, Jessica Kingsley Publishers, 2001, p. 15.

2. Reddie, *Abolition!*, pp. 151–55.

3. See Stokely Carmichael, Charles V. Hamilton and others, *Black Power: The Politics of Liberation in America*, Penguin, 1967.

4. Eric A. Grant, *From Dawn to Dusk: A Biography of Bernie Grant MP*, Ituni Books, 2006, p. 103.

5. 2001 Census.

6. See Sophia Mwangi, in '15 Years of Building Bridges of Unity and Reconciliation', *Focus* (April–June 1999), p. 11.

7. Michael Nazir-Ali, 'Extremism Flourished as UK Lost Christianity', *The Daily*

Telegraph (11 January 2008), p. 1.

8. Sewell, *Keep on Moving*, p. 103.

9. Mark Sturge, *Look What the Lord Has Done: An Exploration of Black Christian Faith in Britain*, Scripture Union, 2005, p. 63.

10. Chigor Chike, *Voices from Slavery: The Life and Beliefs of African Slaves in Britain*, AuthorHouse, 2007, pp. 11–29.

11. Reddie, *Abolition!*, p. 196.

12. See David Killingray and Joel Edwards, *Black Voices: The Shaping of Our Christian Experience*, IVP, 2007.

13. Grant, *Negro with a Hat*, p. 46.

14. David Haslam, *Race for the Millennium: A Challenge to Church and Society*, Church House Publishing, 1996, p. 56.

15. *We Were There*, Ministry of Defence, 2006, p. 18.

16. Haslam, *Race for the Millennium*, p. 56.

17. Glynne Gordon-Carter, *An Amazing Journey: The Church of England's Response to Institutional Racism*, a report on the development of the Committee for Minority Ethnic Anglican Concerns (CMEAC), the former Committee on Black Anglican Concerns (CBAC), Church House Publishing, 2003.

18. Io Smith with Wendy Green, *An Ebony Cross*, Marshall Pickering, 1989, p. 40.

19. Steve Stephenson, *Cold Arrival: Life in a Second Homeland*, African and Caribbean Elders Society, 1998.

20. Joel Edwards, 'The British Afro-Caribbean Community', in *Britain on the Brink*, edited by Martyn Eden and others, Crossway Books, 1993, p. 104.

21. See Reddie, *Faith, Stories and the Experience of Black Elders*, also *Journal for Black Theology*.

22. J. D. Aldred, *Respect: Understanding Caribbean British Christianity*, Epworth, 2005, p. 87.

23. Morris Stuart, 'The Contemporary Church and Race', in *All One in Christ?*, edited by Patrick Sookhdeo, Marshall, Morgan and Scott, 1974, p. 26.

24. Wilfred Wood, *Keep the Faith Baby!*, Bible Reading Fellowship, 1994, pp. 11–13.

25. Haslam, *Race for the Millennium*, pp. 93–95.

26. Gordon-Carter, *An Amazing Journey*, p. 115.

27. Robinson A. Milwood, *Liberation and Mission: A Black Experience*, ACER, 1997, p. 98.

28. Sturge, *Look What the Lord Has Done*, p. 94.

29. Anthony G. Reddie, *Nobodies to Somebodies. A Practical Theology for Education and Liberation*, Epworth Press, 2003, p. 28.

30. Sewell, *Keep on Moving*, p. 78.

31. Aldred, *Respect*, pp. 75–78.

32. Sewell, *Keep on Moving*, pp. 70–75.

33. Jones, *Black Culture*, p. 82.

34. Chevannes, *Rastafari*, p. 1.

35. Nathaniel Samuel Murrell, William D. Spencer and Adrian Anthony McFarlane, *Chanting Down Babylon*, Temple University Press, 1998, p. 25.

36. Clarke, *Jah Music*, p. 43.

37. Ibid., pp. 43–44.

38. Grant, *Negro with a Hat*, p. 40.

39. Ibid., p. 439.

40. Thomas and Boot, *Jah Revenge*, p. 51.

41. William D. Spencer, *Dread Jesus*, SPCK, 1999, pp. 35–58.

42. Chevannes, *Rastafari*, p. 133.

43. Gad Heuman, *The Caribbean*, Hodder Arnold, 2006, pp. 146–47.

44. Grant, *Negro with a Hat*, p. 174.

45. Clarke, *Jah Music*, p. 47.

46. See M. G. Smith, Roy Augier and Rex Nettleford, *The Rastafari Movement in Kingston, Jamaica*, University of the West Indies, Kingston, 1960.

47. Stephen Davis, *Bob Marley: The Biography*, pp. 94–95.

48. Davis, *Bob Marley*, p. 94.

49. Herbert S. Lewis, 'Ethnicity in Ethiopia: The View from Below (and from the South, East and West)', in *The Rising Tide of Cultural Pluralism: The Nation-state at Bay?* edited by Crawford Young, University of Wisconsin Press, 1993, pp. 146–48.

50. Spencer, *Dread Jesus*, p. 75.

51. Walter Rodney, *Groundings with My Brothers*, Bogle-L'Ouverture, 1969, p. 51.

52. Horace Campbell, *Rasta and Resistance*, Hansib, 1997, p. 132.

53. Clarke, *Jah Music*, p. 93.

54. Michael Manley, *Jamaica: Struggle in the Periphery*, Third World Media Limited, 1982, p. 75.

55. Steve Barrow and Peter Dalton, *Reggae: The Rough Guide*, Rough Guides, 1997, p. 105.

56. Bradley, *Bass Culture*, pp. 396–97.

57. Chris Salewicz and Adrian Boot, *Reggae Explosion: The Story of Jamaican Music*, Virgin Books, 2001, p. 162.

58. Hebdige, *Cut 'n' Mix*, p. 100.

59. Sewell, *Keep on Moving*, pp. 78–79.

60. Beckford, *Jesus is Dread*, p. 1.

61. Ibid., p. 29.

62. Robert Beckford, *Dread and Pentecostal: A Political Theology for the Black Church in Britain*, SPCK, 2000, pp. 186–204.

63. Sturge, *Look What the Lord Has Done*, p. 101.

64. See *Ready for Business: The Contribution of Black Business to London's Economy*, Greater London Authority, 2004.

65. Wale Babatunde, *Great Britain Has Fallen! How to Restore Britain's Greatness as a Nation*, New Wine Press, 2002, pp. 91–93.

66. Sturge, *Look What the Lord Has Done*, p. 101.

67. Marcia Dixon, 'Prince Charles Visits Black Church', *The Voice* (22–29 November 2007), p. 33.

68. Sturge, *Look What the Lord Has Done*, pp. 22–23.

69. Ronald A. Nathan, 'Caribbean Youth Identity in the United Kingdom: A Call for a

Pan-African Theology', *Black Theology in Britain. A Journal of Contextual Praxis*, issue 1 (1998), p. 24.

Chapter 4

1. Polly Curtis, 'Education: Black Caribbean Children Held Back by Institutional Racism in Schools, Says Study', *The Guardian* (5 September 2008), p. 3.

2. See http://news.bbc.co.uk/1/hi/education/122618.stm.

3. See http://www.blackmentalhealth.org.uk/index.php?option=com_content&task =view&id=154&Itemid=139.

4. Annual Population Survey, January 2004 to December 2004, Office for National Statistics.

5. Patrick Wintour and Vikram Dodd, 'Blair Blames Spate of Murders on Black Culture', *The Guardian* (12 April 2007), p. 4.

6. Department for Children, Schools and Families, GCSE examination results for 2007.

7. Department for Education and Schools, *Priority Review: Exclusion of Black Pupils 'Getting It. Getting It Right'* (September 2006).

8. Keith Davidson, 'We Must Enter the Education Arena', *Focus* (February–April 2000), pp. 10–11.

9. John Carvel, 'Black Evangelicals Plan Their Own Schools to Combat Under-Achievement', Religion in the UK: Special Report, *The Guardian* (12 November 1999), p. 7.

10. David Gilbourn, 'Racism, Policy and the (Mis)education of Black Children', in *Educating Our Black Children: New Directions and Radical Approaches*, edited by Richard Majors, RoutledgeFalmer, 2001, pp. 20–21.

11. Robin Richardson and Angela Wood, *Inclusive Schools, Inclusive Society: Race and Identity on the Agenda*, Trentham Books, 2000.

12. See *Black Voices: An Anthology of Acer's Black Young Writers' Competition*, edited by Paul McGilchrist, ACER, 1987.

13. One of the first supplementary schools for Black pupils was established by Bishop Wilfred Wood, the former Bishop of Croydon, in Shepherd's Bush, west London in the 1960s. This was followed by others established by the Methodist minister the Revd Hewlette Andrews and the Oxford theology graduate Professor Gus John. See Wood, *Keep the Faith Baby!*, pp. 11–13.

14. The first Making the Grade conference took place on Monday 17 April 2000 and was facilitated by ACEA's Children and Youth (CandY) Commission. ACEA also established an Education Forum Network which hosted Teachers' Reception for the numerous Christian schoolteachers.

15. Richard Reddie, 'Don't Play Snakes and Ladders With Your Children!', *Focus* (September–February 2002), pp. 6–7.

16. See http://www.blackboyscan.co.uk/page-contents.php?pid=2.

17. Dominic Bascombe, 'Black Boys Begin to Believe in Themselves', *The Voice* (21–28 August 2006), pp. 9–10.

18. Rowena Mason, 'Street Pastors Making a Difference After Hours', *The Sunday Telegraph* (1 June 2008), p. 12.

19. Les Isaac, *Dreadlocks*, Marshall, Morgan and Scott, 1984.

20. Kate Burt, 'Praise to the Pastors Who Are Cutting Crime', *The Times* (27 July 2005), p. 9.

21. Mason, 'Street Pastors', p. 12.

22. See www.bringinghope.co.uk.

23. See www.themens-room.org.uk.

24. See www.eyla.org.uk.

25. See www.africandevelopmentforum.org.uk.

26. Doreen McCalla, 'Black Churches and Voluntary Action: Their Social Engagement With the Wider Society', *Black Theology: An International Journal*, volume 3, number 2 (July 2005), pp. 149–54.

27. Sturge, *Look What the Lord Has Done*, p. 109.

28. See *Black UK Christian Directory 2008*, Black UK Publication Limited, 2008.

29. See *Who is My Neighbour? A Church Response to Social Disorder Linked to Gangs, Drugs, Guns and Knives*, Churches Together in England and Churches Together in Britain and Ireland, 2008.

30. Robert Beckford, *God and the Gangs, an Urban Toolkit for Those Who Won't Be Sold Out, Bought Out or Scared Out*, Darton, Longman and Todd, 2004, pp. 2–3.

31. John Steele, 'Where Life Is Guns, Drugs and Violence', *Daily Telegraph* (16 February 2007), p. 11.

32. Some commentators have argued that Trident was a slow response to the violence that had been occurring in sections of the Black community in the 1990s.

33. Steele, 'Four Guilty of New Year Party Murders', Press Association, *The Independent* (18 March 2005).

34. Beckford, *God and the Gangs*, pp. 2–3.

35. Marcia Dixon, 'The gun and the Cross', *The Tablet* (11 January 2003), p. 9.

36. At a meeting organized to discuss gun and gang violence in Tottenham, north London, in the wake of these killings and others in London, several church members argued that the girls were careless to be out at such a late hour and that their parents must take some of the responsibility. Others suggested that because one of the girls had a sibling involved in gang activity her death was 'a logical consequence of this behaviour' and that 'if you sleep with dogs, you get fleas'.

37. See www.ligali.org/article.php?id=444.

38. *Legacy in the Dust: The Four Aces Story*, directed by Winstan Whitter, Beaquarr Productions, 2008, 93 minutes.

39. Many of the buildings in the area, including churches and the site where the nightclub was located, were compulsorily purchased by Transport For London several years ago for the development of Dalston Junction station.

40. Many of these nightclubs closed for business at 5 am. Only revellers with a super-human constitution could party all night then attend church in the morning.

41. These comments were made by a Pentecostal minister at a church service in Stamford Hill, north London.

42. Statistics produced by the Prison Reform Trust, 2006.

43. See *Black UK Christian Directory 2008*.

44. *The State of Race Equality in London*, The Greater London Authority, 2008, pp. 5–30.

45. Sturge, *Look What the Lord Has Done*, p. 109.

46. See *Black UK Christian Directory 2008*.

47. Doreen Morrison, 'Resisting Racism – by Celebrating "or" Blackness', *Black Theology: An International Journal*, volume 1, number 2 (May 2003), p. 221.

48. Derek Humphry and David Tindall, *False Messiah: The Story of Michael X*, Hart-Davis, MacGibbon, 1977, pp. vi–vii.

49. Nathan, 'Caribbean Youth Identity', p. 24.

50. *The Real McCoy* (BBC, 1991–96) was the first real showcase for young black comedy on primetime British television.

51. Mia Maugé, 'Leo X', *Touch*, issue 51 (September 1995).

52. 2007 was the bicentenary of the abolition of the slave trade in Britain, and a memorial service was held to mark the occasion at Westminster Abbey. Toyin Agbetu staged a protest that disrupted the service, demanding an apology for slavery.

53. See Reddie, *Abolition!*, pp. 128–30.

54. See www.setallfree.net.

55. The Set All Free project made personal visits to nearly all the major BMC leaders. It also hosted a number of public meetings, to which they were invited. Over the three years of the project's existence, only three senior BMC leaders attended meetings.

56. Reddie, *Abolition!*, pp. 17–18.

57. See http://www.ipsos-mori.com/content/marking-the-bicentenary-of-the-abolition-of-the-tr.ashx.

58. In January 2008 the British government agreed that the 23 August – UNESCO's day for the International Remembrance of the Slave Trade and its Abolition – would be adopted as the focal date for national commemorations in the years to come.

59. The Cross Community Forum for the 2007 bicentenary is an initiative led by Rendezvous of Victory in conjunction with the World Development Movement and Anti-Slavery International. The aim is to bring people of different races and religions together to gain a broader understanding of the transatlantic slave trade – the Maangamizi (African Holocaust) – chattel enslavement of African peoples and how its legacies impact on the world we live in today.

60. This is a grave insult popularized by the late Malcolm X. He regarded Black people who were acquiescent or compliant with their enslavement as 'House Negroes'. Conversely, the so-called 'Field Negroes' were keen to use any means necessary to free themselves from enslavement. For more information see Malcolm X, *By Any Means Necessary*, Malcolm X, Pathfinder, 2005.

61. A good example of this was the Greater London Authority's Faith Symposium. In God's Name? The Role of the Church in the Transatlantic Slave Trade was held in City Hall Chamber in London on Friday 3 August 2007.

Chapter 5

1. Beckford, *Dread and Pentecostal*, p. 118.

2. V. S. Naipaul, *The Return of Eva Peron with the Killings in Trinidad*, Penguin, 1981, p. 28.

3. John L. Williams, *Michael X: A Life in Black and White*, Century, 2008, p. 13.

4. Ibid., p. 29.

5. Humphry and Tindall, *False Messiah*, pp. 12–14.

6. Michael Abdul Malik, *From Michael de Freitas to Michael X*, Andre Deutsch, 1968, pp. 84–86.

7. Humphry and Tindall, *False Messiah*, p. 47.

8. Williams, *Michael X*, p. 54.

9. Malcolm X, *Autobiography*, pp. 31–32.

10. Malik, *From Michael de Freitas to Michael X*, pp. 126–27.

11. Dyson, *Making Malcolm*, p. 3.

12. Malik, *From Michael de Freitas to Michael X*, p. 146.

13. Ibid., p. 145.

14. Williams, *Michael X*, p. 117.

15. Humphry and Tindall, *False Messiah*, p. 50.

16. The term RAAS had many meanings. In Jamaican patois it was an expletive for something used to wipe the anus. See Malik, *From Michael de Freitas to Michael X*, p. 150.

17. Humphry and Tindall, *False Messiah*, p. 50.

18. Williams, *Michael X*, p. 116.

19. Thomas Hauser, with the cooperation of Muhammad Ali, *Muhammad Ali: His Life and Times*, Robson, 2004, p. 81.

20. Muhammad Ali with Richard Durham, *The Greatest: My Own Story*, Mayflower, 1976, pp. 94–97.

21. Hauser, *Muhammad Ali*, pp. 109–11.

22. Malik, *From Michael de Freitas to Michael X*, p. 193.

23. *The Oxford Companion to Black British History*, pp. 54–56.

24. Dyson, *Making Malcolm*, p. 12.

25. *The Black Power Movement*, edited by Peniel E. Joseph , Routledge, 2006, pp. 167–83.

26. Hollis R. Lynch, *Edward Wilmot Blyden: Pan-Negro Patriot, 1832–1912*, Oxford University Press, 1967, p. 55.

27. Herb Boyd, *African History for Beginners*, For Beginners Books, 1994, pp. 61–65.

28. Reader, *Africa*, p. 282.

29. Humphrey J. Fisher, *Slavery in the History of Muslim Black Africa*, New York University Press, 2001, pp. 14–17.

30. Ronald Segal, *Islam's Black Slaves: The History of Africa's Other Black Diaspora*, Atlantic Books, 2001, p. 52.

31. This meeting was organized by the Cross Community Forum 2007 which was established by Rendezvous of Victory, Anti-Slavery International and the World Development Movement. The meeting took place at South Bank University, Elephant and Castle, London, on Thursday 16 November 2006 and featured contributions from Adje Kouakou, Leo Muhammad and Richard Reddie. The Revd Paul Hackman chaired the event.

32. Lambeth and the Abolition – The Big Debate was organized by Lambeth Libraries to mark the slave trade bicentenary. It took place on Thursday 26 April 2007 in Lambeth Town Hall, Brixton, London. The chair was Colin Prescod of the Institute of Race Relations and the panellists were Lee Jasper (then advisor to the Mayor of London), Meg Munn MP (government minister for Woman and Equality), Richard Reddie (then

director of Set All Free), Aidan McQuade (director of Anti-Slavery International) and Naa Akofor Omaduro II – a Warrior Queen.

33. Comments made by Adje Kouakou at the Cross Community Forum 2007 meeting on Thursday 16 November 2006.

34. Chinua Achebe's classic novel *Things Fall Apart* speaks of the arrival of White men in the central character's African village, and how their religious practices and cultural customs bring about his downfall and lay waste to his tribe. See Chinua Achebe, *Things Fall Apart*, Heinemann, 1958.

35. See Olaudah Equiano, *The Interesting Narrative and Other Writings*, Penguin Classics, revised edition, 2003.

36. Williams, *Michael X*, pp. 185–92.

37. The father of the US Black Power movement, Stokely Carmichael, was born in Trinidad, like Michael X. By the early 1970s many Black Power supporters had converted to Islam from Christianity at a time of rising black nationalism in the Caribbean. They formed the group Jamaat al-Muslimeen, or Society of Muslims, drawing inspiration from the American Islamic movement in winning converts from Christian churches. They remained distant from the mainstream East Indian or Asian Muslim community who were the majority Islamic community in Trinidad. In 1990, the Jamaat al-Muslimeen group staged a coup attempt on the island, holding the then Prime Minister, Arthur N. R. Robinson, hostage.

38. Naipaul, *The Return of Eva Peron*, p. 75.

39. Humphry and Tindall, *False Messiah*, p. 45.

40. *The Bank Job*, Lions Gate Home Entertainment, directed by Roger Donaldson, 2008.

41. See Michelle Adabra, 'Tell Us the Truth about Michael X', *New Nation* (24 November 2008), pp. 1 and 4.

42. See Williams, *Michael X*.

43. Vanessa Walters, *Michael X*, directed by Dawn Walton (6–27 November 2008), The Tabernacle Centre, London.

44. Humphry and Tindall, *False Messiah*, p. 65.

45. Ibid., pp. 64–68.

46. Lee Glendinning, 'Muslim Cleric "Devoid of Remorse" Gets 4½ Years for Terrorism', *The Guardian* (19 April 2008), p. 4.

Chapter 6

1. Raymond Ibrahim, *The Al Qaeda Reader*, Broadway, 2007, pp. 2–11.

2. Goulbourne, *Caribbean Transnational Experience*, p. 50.

3. James Randerson, '9/11 Victims Identified From New DNA Finds', *The Guardian* (25 February 2008), p. 17.

4. Noam Chomsky, *Failed States: The Abuse of Power and the Assault on Democracy*, Penguin, 2007, pp. 166–84.

5. Sophie Goodchild, 'Four Bombing Suspects Still Being Questioned by Police', *Sunday Independent* (31 July 2005).

6. Danielle Weekes, in *New Nation* (16 June 2008), issue 592, pp. 1 and 6.

7. Matthew 27:5.

8. Damien Francis, 'London Bombing Victims Remembered', *The Guardian*

(8 July 2008), p. 11.

9. Steve Bird and Leslie Pierre, 'Bomber's Mother Prays for Victims', *The Times* (22 July 2005).

10. Tim Reiterman and John Jacobs, *Raven: The Untold Story of Rev. Jim Jones and His People*, Dutton, 1982, p. 533.

11. Darcus Howe, 'We All Could Have Been de Menezes', *The Voice* (22 December 2008–4 January 2009), p. 15.

12. Census, April 2001, Office for National Statistics.

13. Lester Holloway, 'I'll Beat the Ban', *New Nation*, (27 October 2008), issue 611, pp. 1 and 5.

14. Trudy Simpson, 'London Obama Style!', *The Voice* (28 July–3 August 2008), p. 7.

15. Danielle Weekes, 'Rise of the Black Suicide Bomber', *New Nation* (16 June 2008), issue 592, p. 6.

16. Philip Lewis, *Young, British and Muslim*, Continuum, 2007, pp. 44–47.

17. Paul Harris, 'Race Riots Ignite Bradford', *The Observer* (8 July 2001), p. 3.

18. Summary report on Islamophobia in the EU after 11 September 2001, European Monitoring Centre on Racism and Xenophobia.

19. Vikram Dodd and Alan Travis, 'Muslims Face Increased Stop and Search', *The Guardian* (2 March 2005).

20. Ibid.

21. Stephen Wright, 'More Stop-and-Search Can Beat Knife Crime, Says Top Black Police Officer', *Daily Mail* (22 October 2007).

22. Jason Bennetto, 'Crackdown by Police is "Driving Muslims to Extremists"', *The Independent* (2 February 2004).

23. *The Search for Common Ground*, p. 18.

24. Ibid.

25. The term Islamism is controversial, and has many definitions. Simply put, its adherents believe that Islam is not only a religion but also a political system and that Muslims should work toward the establishment of a caliphate – a worldwide Islamic political system or state. For this to take place, there needs to be an overthrow of the corrupt (Western) system, which is incompatible with Islamic values. See Graham E. Fuller, *The Future of Political Islam*, Palgrave Macmillan, 2003, pp. 13–47.

26. Ed Husain, *The Islamist: Why I Joined Radical Islam in Britain, What I Saw Inside and Why I Left*, Penguin, 2007, p. 93.

27. Kenneth R. Timmerman, *Preachers of Hate*, Crown Forum, 2003, p. 5.

28. See Melanie Phillips, *Londonistan: How Britain Is Creating a Terror State Within*, Gibson Square, new edition, 2007.

29. Husain, *The Islamist*, p. 141.

30. Ibid.

31. Hamida Ghafour, 'Radical Groups "Brainwashed Reid on Islam"', *Daily Telegraph* (26 December 2001).

32. Ghafour, 'Radical Groups'.

33. http://news.bbc.co.uk/1/hi/uk/7353136.stm.

34. Ibid.

35. Richard Ford, 'Racist Muslim Preacher Is Deported', *The Sunday Times*

(26 May 2007).

36. Ibid.

37. 'Top Terror Recruiter Guilty of Running Training Camps', *Independent* (26 February 2008).

38. Ghafour, 'Radical Groups'.

39. Tariq Ramadan, *To Be a European Muslim: A Study of Islamic Sources in the European Context*, The Islamic Foundation, 2005, p. 117.

40. Martin Bright, 'The Task Force Was a Sham', *The New Statesman* (3 July 2006).

41. Ruth Gledhill, 'Muslim Task Force Attacks Government Anti-Terror Plans', *The Times* (10 November 2005).

42. Patrick Wintour, 'Muslims Must Do More, Says Blair', *The Guardian* (5 July 2006), p. 10.

43. *Oxford Companion to Black British History*, pp. 69–70,

44. 'Whitelaw Expected to Announce Inquiry into Brixton Riots Today', *The Times* (13 April 1981), p. 1.

45. See Lord Scarman, *Scarman Report: The Brixton Disorders*, 10–12 April 1981, Penguin, 1986.

46. Martin Huckerby, 'Looters Moved in as the Flames Spread', *The Times* (13 April 1981), p. 4.

47. The 'sus' law was a much vilified piece of legislation which permitted a police officer to act on suspicion, or 'sus', alone to stop and search a member of the public.

48. In the late 1960s and early 1970s some within the Black Panther Party, a US organization committed to fighting for the rights of Black people, came to the decision that 'revolutionary struggle would end only in victory or revolutionary death', and coined the phrase 'revolutionary suicide'. However, these ideas never came to fruition in the USA or caught on in Britain.

Chapter 7

1. *Oxford Companion to Black British History*, p. 54.

2. Fryer, *Staying Power*, p. 10.

3. *Oxford Illustrated History of Christianity*, pp. 71–174.

4. *Muslims in London*, The Greater London Authority, 2006, p. 14.

5. Fryer, *Staying Power*, pp. 19–32.

6. *Oxford Companion to Black British History*, p. 54.

7. 'Somalis in Cardiff', p. 6.

8. Census, April 2001, Office for National Statistics.

9. Ibid.

10. *Muslims in London*, p. 3.

11. Laura Smith, 'More Switch to Faith', *The Guardian* (16 July 2005), p. 5.

12. *Oxford Companion to Black British History*, pp. 54–56.

13. Fryer, *Staying Power*, pp. 4–13.

14. I am not including other traditions here such as Wahhabism, which is a conservative form of Sunni Islam founded by Muhammad ibn Abd-al-Wahhab, an eighteenth-century Arab scholar who advocated a return to the practices of the first

three generations of Islamic history.

15. David Cook, *Understanding Jihad*, University of California Press, 2005, p. 136.

16. Danielle Weekes, 'Rise of the Black Suicide Bomber', *New Nation* (16 June 2008), issue 592, p. 6.

17. See www.communities.gov.uk/documents/communities/pdf/reach-report.pdf.

18. Andrew Alderson, 'Revealed: 170 Gangs on Streets of London', *Sunday Telegraph* (14 August 2007), p. 3.

19. Peter Oborne, 'The Enemy Within? Fear of Islam: Britain's new Disease', *The Independent* (4 July 2008).

20. Mark Tessler, *A History of the Arab-Israeli Conflict*, Indiana University Press, 1994, p. 53.

21. Cook, *Understanding Jihad*, p. 136.

22. Spike Lee, *By Any Means Necessary*, pp. 48–58.

23. Ibid., pp. 128–29 and 138.

24. By the early 1990s booksellers were reporting that Malcolm X's autobiography was outselling books by the Revd Dr Martin Luther King Jr by at least twenty to one.

25. Words from the eulogy delivered by Ossie Davis at Malcolm X's funeral on 27 February 1965 at the Faith Temple Church of God, Harlem, New York.

26. Dyson, *Making Malcolm*, p. 87.

27. Horrie and Chippendale, *What is Islam?*, p. 9.

28. Some Christians in Black Majority Churches regard Islam in the same way they do any other non-Christian faith – as heretical and something which draws people away from God's Word, which can only be found in the Bible. Christ's statement that he was 'the Way, the Truth and the Life' is interpreted by some to mean that any dealings with other faiths will draw a believer away from Christ.

29. Tsouklas, *The Nation of Islam*, pp. 135–36.

30. Vikram Dodd, 'Banned Farrakhan Reaches UK Audience via Satellite', *The Guardian* (23 December 2002), p. 7.

31. Hauser, *Muhammad Ali*, p. 81.

32. The boxers Mike Tyson and Hasim Rahman, both former heavyweight champions, were also Muslim converts.

33. Harry Mullan, *Ring Wars: A Pictorial History of Boxing*, Parragon, 1997, p. 9.

34. See 'To March or Not to March?', *Focus* (December 1998–February 1999), p. 7.

35. Ibid.

36. http://news.bbc.co.uk/hi/english/static/stephen_lawrence/timeline.htm.

37. Stephen Bates, 'In Memory of Stephen', *The Guardian* (23 April 2008), p. 7.

38. See 'UK Scuffles Suspend Lawrence Inquiry' (29 June 1998), http://news.bbc.co.uk/1/hi/uk/122402.stm.

39. See 'Nation of Islam – Who are they? Tuesday, 30 June, 1998, 17:34 GMT 18:34 UK. http://news.bbc.co.uk/1/hi/uk/123554.stm.

40. www.noi.org.uk/about_us.html.

41. www.newmindschool.org.

42. Chris Gray, 'Militants Prey on London Mosque for New Recruits', *The Independent* (27 December 2001), p. 7.

43. Ibid.

44. Smith, 'More Switch to Faith', p. 5.

45. Esposito, *Islam*, pp. 130–32.

46. 'Mosque Leader Warns Over Extremist Converts', *The Guardian* (26 December 2001), p. 6.

47. *Sociology of Religion: Selected Readings*, edited by Roland Robertson, Penguin, 1971, pp. 19–40.

48. *Women in the Nation of Islam*, Women's Hour, first broadcast on BBC Radio 4 (9 August 2001).

49. Ibid.

50. Michele Wallace, *Black Macho and the Myth of the Superwoman*, John Calder, 1979, pp. 166–225.

51. Lloyd Evering, Kofi Mawuli Klu and Richard Reddie, *The Transatlantic Slave Trade and its Legacies*, Set All Free, 2007, p. 28.

52. Angela Davis, *Women, Race and Class*, The Women's Press, 1982, p. 15.

53. Dyson, *Making Malcolm*, p. 97.

54. bell hooks, *Outlaw Culture: Resisting Representation*, Routledge, 1994, p. 184.

55. Ibid., p. 185.

56. Wallace, *Black Macho*, p. 81.

57. Marable, *Black Fundamentalism*, p. 3.

58. Davis, *Women, Race and Class*, pp. 3–14.

59. Single Muslim women are expected to marry once a suitable partner is found.

60. Evering, Klu and Reddie, *The Transatlantic Slave Trade*, pp. 20–21.

61. Within Islam, male headship of a family is the norm. See John Esposito, *Islam*, p. 94.

62. See Rita Marley and Hettie Jones, *No Woman No Cry*, Pan Books, 2005.

63. Qur'an 4:3.

64. Esposito, *Islam*, p. 95.

65. Awa Thiam, 'Black Sisters Speak Out', in *African Intellectual Heritage: A Book of Sources*, edited by Molefi K. Asante and Abu Shardow Abarry, Temple University Press, 1996, p. 778.

66. See Sturge, *Look What the Lord Has Done*.

67. See www.communities.gov.uk/communities/racecohesionfaith/raceandethnicity/raceequalityadvice/reach/.

Chapter 8

1. Simon Woolley, 'New Model Parents', *The Guardian* (16 July 2008).

2. Social Trends, no. 37, Office for National Statistics, Palgrave Macmillan 2007.

3. *Race and the Criminal Justice System: An Overview to the Complete Statistics 2003/2004*, Home Office, 2005, statistics from section 95 of the Criminal Justice Act 1991.

4. Navin Foolchand, *The Mental Health of the African Caribbean Community in Britain*, Mind factsheet, 2006.

5. See Sturge, *Look What the Lord Has Done*.

6. Esposito, *Islam*, pp. 94–97.

7. See *The Search for Common Ground*.

8. Chevannes, *Rastafari*, pp. 248–49.

9. Ibid.

10. Barrow and Dalton, *Reggae*, pp. 94–97.

11. Census, April 2001, Office for National Statistics.

12. Rosemary Radford Ruether, *Christianity, Family, and the Rise of the West*, Beacon Press, 2000, pp. 60–83.

13. Frances Cress Welsing, *The Isis (Yssis) Papers*, Third World Press, 1995, p. 9.

14. V. S. Naipaul, *Among the Believers: An Islamic Journey*, Penguin, 1981, p. 16.

15. Brian Whitaker, 'Kilroy-Silk Investigated for Anti-Arab Comments', *The Guardian* (8 January 2004).

16. See Seyyed Hossein Nasr, *Islamic Science: An Illustrated Study*, Kazi Publications, 2007.

Chapter 9

1. Lynch, *Edward Wilmot Blyden*, p. 55.

2. Tsoukalas, *The Nation of Islam*, p. 157.

3. Malcolm X, *Autobiography*, pp. 454–55.

4. Lee, *By Any Means Necessary*, p. 57.

5. Dal Farah, 'The Rise of the Black Muslim Converts', *New Nation*, issue 605 (15 September 2008), pp. 4–5.

6. Joy DeGruy Leary, *Post Traumatic Slave Syndrome: America's Legacy of Enduring Injury and Healing*, Uptone Press, 2005, pp. 12–13.

7. Welsing, *The Isis (Yssis) Papers*, p. 9.

8. Nathan Hare, *The Black Anglo-Saxons*, Third World Press, 1991, pp. 138–39.

9. R. J. Crampton, *Eastern Europe in the Twentieth Century – And After*, Routledge, 2nd edition, 1997, pp. 391–419.

10. Azizia Mosque, 117–119 Stoke Newington Road, north London and the Al-Huda Mosque and Cultural Centre in Mile End, east London.

11. See Qur'an 24:31.

12. Hélène Mulholland, 'Elections Minister Targets London's Muslim Voters', *The Guardian* (17 February 2006), p. 9.

13. Census, April 2001, Office for National Statistics, showed that Britain had around 1.5 million Muslims. At least 9 per cent of these are Black. By contrast the Nation of Islam membership is said to be less than 10,000.

14. Marable, *Black Fundamentalism*, pp. 3–4.

15. Michael Eric Dyson explores the reasons why Black people give their offspring certain first names. See chapter 3, 'What's in a Name?', in *Is Bill Cosby Right? Or Has the Black Middle Class Lost Its Mind?*, Basic Civitas Books, 2005.

16. Hare, *The Black Anglo-Saxons*.

17. Gardell, *Countdown to Armageddon*, p. 295.

18. Miyakawa, *Five Percenter Rap*, pp. 144–45.

19. Ibid.

20. See http://news.bbc.co.uk/1/hi/entertainment/7809769.stm.

21. Bakari Kitwana, *The Hip Hop Generation, Young Blacks and the Crisis in African-American Culture*, Basic Civitas Books, 2002, pp. 3–4, 11.

22. Chris Salewicz and Adrian Boot, *Reggae Explosion: The Story of Jamaican Music*, Virgin Publishing, 2001.

23. Clarke, *Jah Music*, pp. 3–4, 93.

24. Bradley, *Bass Culture*, pp. 106–107.

25. Hebdige, *Cut 'n' Mix*, p. 60.

26. Lloyd Bradley, 'The Crown Prince', in *Bob Marley and the Story of Reggae*, Q Classic, 2005, pp. 3–4, 14–15.

27. Bradley, *Bass Culture*, pp. 141–42.

28. Nelson George, *Buppies, B-Boys, Baps and Bohos: Notes on Post-Soul Black Culture*, Harper Perennial, 1992, p. 44.

29. Jeff Chang, *Can't Stop, Won't Stop: A History of Hip Hop*, Ebury Press, 2007, pp. 3–4, p. 90.

30. Ibid., pp. 172–73.

31. Ellis Cashmore, *The Black Culture Industry*, Routledge, 1997, pp. 155–56.

32. Miyakawa, *Five Percenter Rap*, p. 1.

33. George, *Buppies, B-Boys, Baps and Bohos*, p. 43.

34. *Soul: Black Power, Politics and Pleasure*, edited by Monique Guillory and Richard C. Green, New York University Press, 1998, pp. 106, 155–56.

35. George, *Buppies, B-Boys, Baps and Bohos*, pp. 50–51.

36. *Rock File*, edited by Charlie Gillet, Pictorial Presentations Limited in association with New English Library, 1972.

37. George, *Buppies, B-Boys, Baps and Bohos*, pp. 155–56.

38. Cashmore, *The Black Culture Industry*, p. 157.

39. Chang, *Can't Stop, Won't Stop*, p. 245.

40. Knight, *The Five Percenters*, pp. 32–33.

41. Miyakawa, *Five Percenter Rap*, p. 16.

42. Knight, *The Five Percenters*, p. 35.

43. Miyakawa, *Five Percenter Rap*, p. 23.

44. Pen Black, *Gods, Earths and 85ers*, Tru Life Publishing, 2006, pp. 1–2, 155–56.

45. Ibid., pp. 1–2.

46. Ibid. and Miyakawa, *Five Percenter Rap*, pp. 33–35.

47. Miyakawa, *Five Percenter Rap*, p. 35.

48. Knight, *The Five Percenters*, p. 77.

49. *Soul*, pp. 1–2, 95.

50. Miyakawa, *Five Percenter Rap*, p. 2.

51. Chang, *Can't Stop, Won't Stop*, p. 100.

52. Ibid., p. 263.

53. Cashmore, *The Black Culture Industry*, p. 161.

54. Stanley Crouch, *Always in Pursuit: Fresh American Perspectives, 1995–1997*, Pantheon Books,1998, p. 292.

55. *The Final Call*, volume 27, number 44 (5 August 2008), pp. 3, 36–38.

56. Vic Motune, 'From Hajj to Hip Hop', *The Voice* (28 July–3 August 2008), p. 26.

57. Eid in the Square was organized by the Muslim Council of Britain and the Mayor of London.

58. Jerome Taylor, 'Introducing Hip-Hop's Songs of Praise', *The Independent* (16 May 2008).

59. Ibid.

60. Ibid.

61. See Alveena Salim, 'Sound of Islam', *Revival Magazine*, issue 10 (29 November 2007).

62. Motune, *From Hajj to Hip Hop*, p. 26.

63. *Oxford Companion to Black British History*, pp. 192–93, 292.

64. Lilian Quamina, 'Reggae got Christ!', *Focus* (April–June 1999), p. 17.

65. Ziauddin Sardar, 'Can British Islam Change?', *New Statesman* (3 July 2006).

66. Antony Barnett, 'Islamic Rappers' Message of Terror', *The Observer* (8 February 2004), p. 4.

67. Sean O'Neill, 'Islamic Hip-Hop Artists Are Accused of Indoctrinating Young Against the West', *The Times* (11 November 2006).

68. Michael Eric Dyson, *Between God and Gangsta Rap: Bearing Witness to Black Culture*, Oxford University Press, 1996, pp. 176–86.

Chapter 10

1. 'Black Christian Civic Forum', *Focus* (December 1998–February 1999), p. 2.

2. Ibid.

3. Ibid.

4. See Bilquis Sheikh and Richard Schneider, *I Dared to Call Him Father*, Kingsway Publications, 1979.

5. Maqsood, *Need to Know? Islam*.

6. See www.csw.org.uk.

7. See www.barnabasfund.org.

8. Jonathan Langley, 'Undercover Believers', *Christianity* (September 2008), pp. 27–31.

9. Patrick Sookhdeo, *Islam the Challenge to the Church*, Isaac Publishing, 2006, pp. 58–71.

10. Riazat Butt, 'The Guardian Profile: Michael Nazir-Ali', *The Guardian* (30 May 2008), p. 19.

11. Ruth Gledhill, 'British Muslim "Bullied" for Converting to Christianity', *The Times* (28 April 2008).

12. Ziya Meral, *No Place to Call Home: Experiences of Apostates From Islam – Failures of the International Community*, Christian Solidarity Worldwide, 2008, p. 56.

13. See Maud Blair, *Why Pick on Me?: School Exclusion and Black Youth*, Trentham Books, 2001, pp. 123–25.

14. See www.blackboyscan.co.uk.

15. See *The Road Ahead: A Christian-Muslim Dialogue*, edited by Michael Ipgrave, Church House Publishing, 2002.

16. *Christian-Muslim Relations*, Churches Together in Britain and Ireland. See the website: www.ctbi.org.uk/CDLB/305.

17. bell hooks, *We Real Cool: Black Men and Masculinity*, Routledge, 2003, pp. 15–32.

18. *Sort Out Stress*, Camden & Islington NHS Foundation Trust, www.sortoutstress. co.uk.

19. Maqsood, *Need to Know? Islam*, pp. 182–83.

20. Ibid., p. 183.

21. Carl Beech, 'A Man's World?', *Christianity* (March 2008), pp. 12–15.

22. There are now a good number of UK groups and resources that work to redress the gender imbalance such as Christian Viewpoint for Men, Walk of 1000 Men, Christian Vision for Men, the London and Northern Men's Conventions and websites such as www.geezersforjesus.co.uk and www.deadmenwalking.net.

23. Marjorie Lewis, 'Diaspora Dialogue: Womanist Theology in Engagement with Aspects of the Black British and Jamaican Experience', *Black Theology: An International Journal*, volume 2, number 1 (January 2004).

24. The Third International Congress on Islamic Feminism took place in Barcelona, Spain, from 24 to 27 October 2008.

25. Lewis, *Diaspora Dialogue*, p. 89.

26. Nicole Martin, 'Islamic Converts Defend Their Faith against Terrorism', *Daily Telegraph* (9 December 2002).

27. William Edward Burghardt DuBois, *The Souls of Black Folk*, Longman, new edition, 2002, p. 89.

28. John O'Sullivan, 'Barack Obama: the Enigma Must Point the Way to the Future', *Daily Telegraph* (20 January 2009).

29. Eboo Patel, *Acts of Faith: The Story of an American Muslim, The Struggle for the Soul of a Generation*, Beacon Press, 2007, p. xv.

30. *Improving Opportunity: The Government's Strategy to Improve Race Equality and Community Cohesion*, Home Office, 2005.

31. See Chevannes, *Rastafari*.

32. Sturge, *Look What the Lord Has Done*, p. 138.

33. Enver Masud, *The War on Islam*, 2nd expanded edition, Wisdom Fund, 2002, pp. 1–15.

34. Kate Zebiri, *British Muslim Converts: Choosing Alternative Lives*, Oneworld Publications, 2007.

35. Lucy Bushill-Matthews, *Welcome to Islam: A Convert's Tale*, Continuum International Publishing Group Ltd, 2008.

Bibliography

Achebe, Chinua, *Things Fall Apart*, Heinemann, 1958.

Aldred, J. D., *Respect: Understanding Caribbean British Christianity*, Epworth, 2005.

Ali, Muhammad with Richard Durham, *The Greatest: My Own Story*, Mayflower, 1976.

Asante, Molefi Kete and Abu Shardow Abarry, *African Intellectual Heritage: A Book of Sources*, Temple University Press, 1996.

Asante, Molefi Kete, *The History of Africa: The Quest for Eternal Harmony*, Routledge, 2007.

Babatunde, Wale, *Great Britain has Fallen! How to Restore Britain's Greatness as a Nation*, New Wine Press, 2002.

Bailey, Randal C. and Grant, Jacquelyn (eds.), *The Recovery of Black Presence: An Interdisciplinary Exploration. Essays in Honor of Dr Charles B. Copher*, Abingdon Press, 1995.

Barrow, Steve and Peter Dalton, *Reggae: The Rough Guide*, Rough Guides, 1997.

Beckford, Robert, *Dread and Pentecostal: A Political Theology for the Black Church in Britain*, SPCK, 2000.

Beckford, Robert, *God and the Gangs: An Urban Toolkit for Those Who Won't Be Sold Out, Bought Out or Scared Out*. Darton, Longman and Todd, 2004.

Beckford, Robert, *Jesus is Dread: Black Theology and Black Culture in Britain*, Darton, Longman and Todd, 1998.

Black, Pen, *Gods, Earths and 85ers*, Tru Life Publishing, 2006.

The Black UK Christian Directory 2008, Black UK Publication Limited, 2008.

Blue Beat: The Best in Blues, TSI Publications, 1987.

Blair, Maud, *Why Pick on Me? School Exclusion and Black Youth*, Trentham Books, 2001.

Boyd, Herb, *African History for Beginners*, For Beginners, 1994.

Bradley, Lloyd, *Bass Culture: When Reggae Was King*, Penguin Books, 2001.

Bradley, Michael, *The Black Journey of America: The Amazing Evidence of Daring Voyages by Ancient West African Mariners*, Personal Library, 1981.

Breitman, George (ed. with prefatory notes), *Malcolm X Speaks: Selected Speeches and Statements*, Grove Press, 1966.

Bryan, Beverley, Dadzie, Stella and Scafe, Suzanne (eds.), *The Heart of the Race: Black Women's Lives in Britain*, Virago, 1985.

Bushill-Matthews, Lucy, *Welcome to Islam: A Convert's Story*, Continuum, 2008.

Campbell, Horace, *Rasta and Resistance*, Hansib, 1997.

Carmichael, Stokely and Charles V. Hamilton, *Black Power: The Politics of Liberation in America*, Penguin, 1967.

Gordon-Carter, Glynne, *An Amazing Journey: The Church of England's Response to Institutional Racism*, a report on the development of the

Committee for Minority Ethnic Anglican Concerns (CMEAC), the former Committee on Black Anglican Concerns (CBAC), Church House Publishing, 2003.

Carson, Clayborne (ed.), *The Autobiography of Martin Luther King*, Abacus, 2000.

Cashmore, Ellis, *The Black Culture Industry*, Routledge, 1997.

Chang, Jeff, *Can't Stop, Won't Stop. A History of the Hip-Hop Generation*, Ebury Press, 2007.

Chevannes, Barry, *Rastafari: Roots and Ideology*, Syracuse University Press, 1994.

Chike, Chigor, *Voices from Slavery: The Life and Beliefs of African Slaves in Britain*, AuthorHouse, 2007.

Chomsky, Noam, *Failed States: The Abuse of Power and the Assault on Democracy*, Penguin, 2007.

Clarke, Sebastian, *Jah Music: The Evolution of the Popular Jamaican Song*, Heinemann, 1980.

Cleaver, Eldridge, *Soul on Fire*, Hodder & Stoughton, 1979.

Clegg, Claude Andrew, *An Original Man: The Life and Times of Elijah Muhammad*, St Martins Press, 1997.

Collins, Robert O., *Africa: A Short History*, Markus Wiener Publishers, 2006.

Cook, David, *Understanding Jihad*, University of California Press, 2005.

Costello, Ray, *Liverpool Black Pioneers*, The Bluecoat Press, 2007.

Crampton, R. J., *Eastern Europe in the Twentieth Century – And After*, Routledge, 2nd ed., 1997.

Cress Welsing, Frances, *The Isis (Yssis) Papers*, Third World Press, 1995.

Crouch, Stanley, *Always in Pursuit: Fresh American Perspectives, 1995-1997*, Pantheon Books, 1998.

Crouch, Stanley, *Notes of a Hanging Judge: Essays and Reviews, 1979-1989*, OUP, 1990.

Dabydeen, David, Gilmore, John and Jones, Cecily (eds.), *Oxford Companion to Black British History*, OUP, 2007.

Davis, Angela, *Women, Race and Class*, The Women's Press, 1982.

Davis, Stephen, *Bob Marley: The Biography*, Panther, 1984.

Davis, Stephen and Peter Simon, *Reggae International*, Thames and Hudson, 1982.

DeGruy Leary, Joy, *Post-Traumatic Slave Syndrome: America's Legacy of Enduring Injury and Healing*, Uptone Press, 2005.

Diouf, Sylviane A., *Servants of Allah: African Muslims Enslaved in the Americas*, NYU Press, 1998.

Doyle, Paul and others, *The Paint House: Words from an East End Gang*, Penguin Books, 1972.

DuBois, William Edward Burghardt, *The Souls of Black Folk*, Longman, new ed., 2002.

Dyson, Michael Eric, *Between God and Gangsta Rap: Bearing Witness to Black Culture*, OUP, 1996.

Dyson, Michael Eric, *Is Bill Cosby Right? Or Has the Black Middle Class Lost Its Mind?* Basic Civitas Books, 2005.

Dyson, Michael Eric, *Making Malcolm: The Myth and Meaning of Malcolm X*, OUP, 1995.

Eden, Martyn and others (ed.), *Britain on the Brink*, Crossway Books, 1993.

Edwards, Joel (ed.), *Let's Praise Him Again: An African Caribbean Perspective on Worship*, Kingsway, 1992.

Elias, Jamal J., *Islam*, Prentice Hall, 1999.

Equiano, Olaudah, *The Interesting Narrative and Other Writings*, Penguin Classics, revised ed., 2003.

Esposito, John, *Islam: The Straight Path*, 3rd revised ed., OUP, 1998.

Essien-Udom, E.U., *Black Nationalism: The Rise of the Black Muslims in the USA*, Penguin, 1966.

Evering, Lloyd, Kofi Mawuli Klu and Richard Reddie, *The Transatlantic Slave Trade and its Legacies*, Set All Free, 2007.

Fisher, Humphrey J., *Slavery in the History of Muslim Black Africa*, New York University Press, 2001.

Fryer, Peter, *The Politics of Windrush*, Index Books, 1999.

Fryer, Peter, *Staying Power: The History of Black People in Britain since 1504*, Pluto Press, 1984.

Fuller, Graham E., *The Future of Political Islam*, Palgrave Macmillan, 2003.

Gardell, Mattias, *Countdown to Armageddon: Louis Farrakhan and the Nation of Islam*, Hurst and Company, 1996.

George, Nelson, *Buppies, B-Boys, Baps and Bohos: Notes on Post-Soul Black Culture*, Harper Perennial,1992.

Gillet, Charlie (ed.), *Rock File*, Pictorial Presentations Limited in association with New English Library, 1972.

Gilroy, Paul, *Small Acts: Thoughts on the Politics of Black Cultures*, Serpent's Tail, 1993.

Gilroy, Paul, *There Ain't no Black in the Union Jack*, Routledge, 1987.

Gordon, Matthew S., *Understanding Islam: Origins, Beliefs, Practices, Holy Texts, Sacred Places*, Duncan Baird Publishers, 2002.

Goulbourne, Harry, *Caribbean Transnational Experience*, Pluto Press, 2002.

Grant, Colin, *Negro with a Hat: The Rise and Fall of Marcus Garvey and His Dream of Mother Africa*, Jonathan Cape, 2008

Grant, Eric A., *From Dawn to Dusk: A Biography of Bernie Grant MP*, Ituni Books, 2006.

Guillory, Monique and Green, Richard C. (eds.), *Soul: Black Power, Politics and Pleasure*, New York University Press, 1998.

Haslam, David, *Race for the Millennium: A Challenge to Church and Society*, Church House Publishing, 1996.

Hare, Nathan, *The Black Anglo-Saxons*, Third World Press, 1991.

Hauser, Thomas, with the cooperation of Muhammad Ali, *Muhammad Ali: His Life and Times*, Robson, 2004.

Hebdige, Dick, *Cut 'n' Mix: Culture, Identity and Caribbean Music*, 1987.

Hebdige, Dick, *Subculture: The Meaning of Style*, Routledge, 1988.

Hennessy, Peter, *NeverAgain: Britain 1945–51*, Vintage Books, 1993.

Heuman, Gad, *The Caribbean*, Hodder Arnold, 2006.

hooks, bell, *Outlaw Culture: Resisting Representation*, Routledge, 1994.

hooks, bell, *We Real cool: Black Men and Masculinity*, Routledge, 2003.

Horrie, Chris and Peter Chippendale, *What is Islam? A Comprehensive Introduction*, revised and updated, Virgin Books, 2003.

Howe, Darcus, *From Bobby to Babylon: Blacks and the British Police*, Race Today Publications, 1988.

Humphry, Derek and David Tindall, *False Messiah: The Story of Michael X*, Hart-Davis, MacGibbon, 1977.

Husain, Ed, *The Islamist: Why I Joined Radical Islam in Britain, What I Saw Inside and Why I Left*, Penguin, 2007.

Husband, Charles (ed.), *Race in Britain: Continuity and Change*, 2nd ed., Hutchinson, 1987

Ibrahim, Raymond, *The Al Qaeda Reader*, Broadway, 2007.

Ipgrave, Michael (ed.), *The Road Ahead: A Christian-Muslim Dialogue*, Church House Publishing, 2002.

Irwin, Robert, *The Alhambra: Wonders of the World*, Profile Books, 2004.

Johnson, Paul (ed.), *20th Century Britain: Economic, Social and Cultural Change*, 1994.

Jones, Simon, *Black Culture, White Youth: The Reggae Tradition from JA to UK*, Macmillan.

Katz, David, *Solid Foundation: An Oral History of Reggae*, Bloomsbury, 2003.

Kennedy, Hugh, *The Great Arab Conquests: How the Spread of Islam Changed the World We Live In*, Da Capo Press, 2008.

Killingray, David and Joel Edwards, *Black Voices: The Shaping of Our Christian Experience*, IVP, 2007.

Kitwana, Bakari, *The Hip Hop Generation: Young Blacks and the Crisis in African-American Culture*, Basic Civitas Books, 2002.

Knight, Michael Muhammad, *The Five Percenters: Islam, Hip Hop and the Gods of New York*, Oneworld, 2007.

Lee, Martha F., *The Nation of Islam: An American Millenarian Movement*, Edwin Mellen Press, 1988.

Lee, Spike with Ralph Wiley, *By Any Means Necessary: The Trials and Tribulations of the Making of Malcolm X*, Vintage, 1993.

Levtzion, Nehemia, and others, *The History of Islam in Africa*, James Currey Publishers, 2000.

Lewis, Philip, *Young, British and Muslim*, Continuum, 2007.

Lewis, Rupert and Warner-Lewis, Maureen (eds.), *Garvey, Africa, Europe, the Americas*, Institute of Social and Economic Research, 1986.

Lincoln, Eric C., *The Black Muslims in America*, 3rd ed., Africa World Press, 1994.

Lomax, Louis E., *To Kill a Black Man*, Holloway House, 1987.

Lynch, Hollis R., *Edward Wilmot Blyden: Pan-Negro Patriot, 1832–1912*, OUP, 1967.

Majors, Richard (ed.), *Educating Our Black Children: New Directions and Radical Approaches*, RoutledgeFalmer, 2001.

Malik, Michael Abdul, *From Michael de Freitas to Michael X*, Andre Deutsch, 1968.

Manley, Michael, *A History of West Indies Cricket*, revised ed., Andre Deutsch, 1990.

——, *Jamaica: Struggle in the Periphery*, Third World Media Limited, 1982.

Manners, John (ed.), *The Oxford Illustrated History of Christianity*, OUP, 1996.

Maqsood, Ruqaiyyah Waris, *Need to Know Islam? Understand the Religion Behind the Headlines*, HarperCollins, 2008.

Marley, Rita and Hettie Jones, *No Woman, No Cry: My Life With Bob Marley*, Pan Books, 2005.

Masud, Enver, *The War on Islam*, Wisdom Fund, 2nd expanded ed., 2002.

Mazrui, Ali A., *The Africans: A Triple Heritage*, Little Brown & Co, 1986.

McGilchrist, Paul (ed.), *Black Voices: An Anthology of ACER's Black Young Writers' Competition*, ACER, 1987.

Meral, Ziya, *No Place to Call Home: Experiences of Apostates From Islam – Failures of the International Community*, Christian Solidarity Worldwide, 2008.

Meredith, Martin, *The State of Africa: A History of Fifty Years of Independence*, Free Press, 2005.

Miyakawa, Felicia M., *Five Percenter Rap: God's Hop Music, Message, and Black Muslim Mission*, Indiana University Press, 2005.

Milwood, Robinson A., *Liberation and Mission: A Black Experience*, ACER, 1997.

Muhammad, Elijah, *Message to the Blackman in America*, 1965,1973, Secretarius Memps Ministries.

Mullan, Harry, *Ring Wars: A Pictorial History of Boxing*, Parragon, 1997.

Murrell, Nathaniel Samuel, William D. Spencer and Adrian Anthony McFarlane, *Chanting Down Babylon*, Temple University Press.

Muslims in London, The Greater London Authority, October 2006.

Naipaul, V. S., *Among the Believers: An Islamic Journey*. Penguin. 1981.

Naipaul, V. S., *The Return of Eva Peron with the Killings in the Trinidad*, Penguin, 1981.

Nasr, Seyyed Hossein, *Islamic Science: An Illustrated Study*, Kazi Publications, 2007.

Kwesi Owusu, (ed.), *Black British Culture and Society: A Text Reader*, Routledge, 2000.

Patel, Eboo, *Acts of Faith: The Story of an American Muslim and the Struggle for the Soul of a Generation*, Beacon Press, 2007.

Paterson, David, Willoughby, Doug and Willoughby, Susan, *Civil Rights in the USA, 1863–1980*, Heinemann, 2001.

Peniel E., Joseph, (ed.), *The Black Power Movement*, Routledge, 2006.

Phillips, Melanie, *Londonistan: How Britain is Creating a Terror State Within*, Gibson Square, new ed., 2007.

Phillips, Mike and Trevor Phillips, *Windrush: The Irresistible Rise of Multiracial Britain*, HarperCollins, 1998.

Pinn, Anthony B., *Terror and Triumph: The Nature of Black Religion*, Fortress Press, 2003.

Pugh, Martin, *State and Society: British Political and Social History 1870-1992*, Edward Arnold, 1994.

Radford Ruether, Rosemary, *Christianity, Family, and the Rise of the West*, Beacon Press, 2000.

Ramadan, Tariq, *To be a European Muslim: A Study of Islamic Sources in the European Context*, The Islamic Foundation, 2005.

Rattansi, Ali, *Racism: A Very Short Introduction*, OUP, 2007.

Reader, John, *Africa: A Biography of the Continent*, Penguin, 1997.

Ready for Business: The Contribution of Black Business to London's Economy, The Greater London Authority, 2004.

Reddie, Richard, *Abolition! The Struggle to Abolish Slavery in the British Colonies*, Lion, 2007.

Reiterman, Tim and John Jacobs, *Raven: The Untold Story of Rev. Jim Jones and His People*, Dutton, 1982.

Reddie, Anthony G. *Faith, Stories and the Experience of Black Elders: Singing the Lord's Song in a Strange Land*, Jessica Kingsley, 2001.

Reddie, Anthony G., *Nobodies to Somebodies. A Practical Theology for Education and Liberation*, Epworth Press, 2003,

Richardson, Robin and Angela Wood, *Inclusive Schools, Inclusive Society: Race and Identity on the Agenda*, Race on the Agenda & Trentham Books, 2000.

Robertson, Roland (ed.), *Sociology of Religion: Selected Readings*, Penguin, 1971.

Rodney, Walter, *Groundings with my Brothers*, Bogle-L'Ouverture, 1969.

Salewicz, Chris and Adrian Boot, *Reggae Explosion: The Story of Jamaican Music*, Virgin Books, 2001.

Scarman, Lord, *Scarman Report: The Brixton Disorders, 10-12 April 1981*, Penguin, 2nd revised ed., 1986.

The Search for Common Ground: Muslims,

Non-Muslims and the UK Media, Greater London Authority, 2007.

Segal, Ronald, *Islam's Black Slaves: The History of Africa's Other Black Diaspora*, Atlantic Books, 2001.

Sewell, Tony, *Black Masculinities and Schooling: How Black Boys Survive Modern Schooling*, Trentham Books, 2000.

Sewell, Tony, *Keep on Moving: The Windrush Legacy. The Black Experience in Britain from 1948*, Voice Enterprises, 1998.

Sheikh, Bilquis and Richard Schneider, *I Dared to Call Him Father*, Kingsway Publications, 1979.

Smith, Io with Wendy Green, *An Ebony Cross*, Marshall Pickering, 1989.

Smith, M. G., Roy Augier and Rex Nettleford, *The Rastafari Movement in Kingston, Jamaica*, The University of the West Indies, Kingston, 1960.

Solomos, John, *Race and Racism in Britain*, 2nd ed., Macmillan, 1993.

Sookhdeo, Patrick (ed.), *All One in Christ*, Marshall, Morgan and Scott, 1974.

— —, *Islam the Challenge to the Church*, Isaac Publishing, 2006.

Spencer, William D., *Dread Jesus*, SPCK, 1999.

The State of Race Equality in London 2008, The Greater London Authority, 2008.

Storey, John, *An Introductory Guide to Cultural Theory and Popular Culture*, Harvester Wheatsheaf, 1993.

Sturge, Mark, *Look What the Lord Has Done: An Exploration of Black Christian Faith in Britain*, Scripture Union, 2005.

Summary Report on Islamophobia in the

EU After 11 September 2001, European Monitoring Centre on Racism and Xenophobia.

Tessler, Mark, *A History of the Arab-Israeli Conflict*, Indiana University Press, 1994.

Thomas, Michael and Adrian Boot, *Jah Revenge: Babylon Revisited*, Eel Pie Publishing, 1992.

Timmerman, Kenneth R., *Preachers of Hate*, Crown Forum, 2003.

Travers, Max, *The British Immigration Courts: A Study of Law and Politics*, The Policy Press, 1999.

Tsoukalas, Steven, *The Nation of Islam: Understanding the 'Black Muslims'*. P&R Publishing Company, 2001.

The Voice newspaper, *Many Winters On: Memories of Britain's Post-War Caribbean Immigrants*, 1988.

van Sertima, Ivan (ed.), *African Presence in Early America*, Transaction, 1992.

Walker, Robin, *When We Ruled: The Ancient and Mediaeval History of Black Civilisation*, Every Generation Media, 2006.

Wallace, Michele, *Black Macho and the Myth of the Superwoman*, John Calder, 1979.

Williams, John L., *Michael X: A Life in Black and White*, Century, 2008.

White, John, *Black Leadership in America: From Booker T. Washington to Jesse Jackson*, 2nd ed., Longman 1990.

Who is My Neighbour? A Church Response to Social Disorder Linked to Gangs, Drugs, Guns and Knives, Churches Together in England and Churches Together in Britain and Ireland, 2008.

Wolfe, Michael and others (eds.). *Taking Back Islam: American Muslims Reclaim Their Faith*, Rodale, 2002.

Wolff, Daniel and others, *You Send Me: the Life and Times of Sam Cooke*, Virgin Books, 1995.

Wood, Wilfred, *Keep the Faith Baby!*, The Bible Reading Fellowship, 1994.

X, Malcolm, with the assistance of Alex Haley, *The Autobiography of Malcolm X*, Penguin, 1965.

X, Malcolm, *By Any Means Necessary*, Pathfinder, 2005.

Yancey, Philip, *Soul Survivor: How My Faith Survived the Church*, Hodder and Stoughton, 2001.

Young, Crawford, *The Nation-State at Bay?*, University of Wisconsin Press, 1993.

Zebiri, Kate, *British Muslim Converts: Choosing Alternative Lives*, Oneworld Publications, 2007.

Journals and Miscellaneous

Bradley, Lloyd, 'The Crown Prince', in *Bob Marley and the Story of Reggae*, Q Classic, 2005.

Legacy in the Dust: The Four Aces' Story, directed by Winstan Whitter, Beaquarr Productions, 2008, 93 minutes.

Lewis, Marjorie, 'Diaspora Dialogue: Womanist Theology in Engagement With Aspects of the Black British and Jamaican Experience', *Black Theology: An International Journal*, vol. 2, no. 1 (January 2004).

McCalla, Doreen, 'Black Churches and Voluntary Action: Their Social Engagement with the Wider Society',

Black Theology: An International Journal, vol. 3, no. 2 (July 2005),

Morrison, Doreen, 'Resisting Racism – by Celebrating "Our" Blackness', *Black Theology: An International Journal*, vol. 1, no. 2 (May 2003).

Marable, Manning, *Black Fundamentalism: Farrakhan and Conservative Black Nationalism, Race and Class*, volume 39, issue 4, 1998.

Quamina, Lilian 'Reggae Got Christ!', *Focus* (April–June 1999).

Index